D0476719

On Being Jewish

Julia Neuberger is Chair of the Camden and Islington Community Health Services NHS Trust, and Chancellor of the University of Ulster. She was Rabbi of the South London Liberal Synagogue from 1977 to 1989, and is a lecturer at the Leo Baeck College, where she trained.

She was educated at South Hampstead High School for Girls and at Cambridge, and is married with two children. She lives in London and in West Cork, Ireland.

Also by Julia Neuberger

Whatever's Happening
to Women?

The Things That Matter:
An Anthology of
Women's Spiritual Poetry

Caring for Dying People
of Different Faiths

A Necessary End
(ed. with John White)

Julia Neuberger

On Being Jewish

ARROW

Reprinted in Arrow Books, 1997

3 5 7 9 10 8 6 4

Copyright © Julia Neuberger 1995

The right of Julia Neuberger to be identified as the author
of this work has been asserted by her in accordance
with the Copyright, Designs and Patents Act, 1988

This book is sold subject to the condition
that it shall not, by way of trade or otherwise,
be lent, resold, hired out, or otherwise circulated
without the publisher's prior consent in any form
of binding or cover other than that in which
it is published and without a similar condition
including this condition being imposed
on the subsequent purchaser

First published in the United Kingdom in 1995 by William Heinemann

This edition first published in 1996 by Mandarin Paperbacks,
reprinted once

Arrow Books Limited
Random House UK Ltd
20 Vauxhall Bridge Road, London SW1V 2SA

Random House Australia (Pty) Limited
20 Alfred Street, Milsons Point, Sydney,
New South Wales 2061, Australia

Random House New Zealand Limited
18 Poland Road, Glenfield
Auckland 10, New Zealand

Random House South Africa (Pty) Limited
Endulini, 5a Jubilee Road, Parktown 2193, South Africa

Random House UK Limited Reg. No. 954009

A CIP catalogue record for this book is available
from the British Library

Papers used by Random House UK Limited
are natural, recyclable products made from wood grown in
sustainable forests. The manufacturing processes conform to
the environmental regulations of the country of origin

Printed and bound in the United Kingdom by
Cox & Wyman Ltd, Reading, Berkshire

ISBN 0 7493 2019 2

For my children
Harriet and Matthew

Contents

Acknowledgements

To Anthony, Harriet and Matthew Neuberger, who had to live with this book, and saw me disappearing time and again to work on it.

To Paola Churchill for her battles with my lack of grammar and punctuation, and her valiant attempts to get the chapters printed out as computers played up and printers had indigestion.

To Canon Geoffrey C. Cates, honorary archivist, the Anglican Communion, for finding the transcript of the Bishop of Oxford's speech at the 1988 Lambeth Conference, and to the Bishop of Oxford, the Right Reverend Richard Harries, for allowing me to quote from it, as well as all his other support and help.

To Gerald Jacobs, literary editor of the *Jewish Chronicle*, for all his advice and help and patient tolerance of cancelled lunches as this volume came nearer to completion.

To Penelope Hoare, editor and friend, who argued through the text with me and was sublimely patient with late delivery as a result of my father's illness. And to Charlotte Mendelson who was so good at telling me what it was I was trying to say, partly because she wanted to say it, too. To Kate Goodhart, who wrestled with the text and turned it into English. To Carol Smith, who made me do it, and actually had faith that I could.

To Babs Lugar, who made me endless cups of tea as I worked, and never lost her good humour as I covered the floor, tables and chairs with yet more paper.

To Matthew Kalman, who unwittingly sparked off some of the ideas about diversity.

To Gideon Lester, who pointed out that only I would go on radio the weekend before my son's bar-mitzvah to encourage him not to 'marry out'.

To Rabbi Tony Bayfield, for friendship and being prepared to argue the toss. And to Rabbi David Freeman, for all his inspiration and friendship. He knows how important he has been, even if he will not agree with all this.

To Angela Levin and Bob Low, best of friends, who made me think about some of these issues again; to Michael Waterhouse, for all his comments and marvellous argument; to the Baronesses Blackstone and Jay, and Professor Michael Adler, who may recognise a debate we had in my Irish kitchen in January 1995.

To Rabbi Dr Nicholas de Lange, who made me interested in the first place; to Rabbi Hugo Gryn who nurtured that interest; to Rabbi John Rayner who taught me to value the texts and who pointed out so many inaccuracies in this one; and in memory of Rabbi David Goldstein, who instilled in me a life-long love of Hebrew poetry.

And to my parents, who encouraged me to explore my Judaism, and my German-Jewish heritage.

Grateful acknowledgement is also made to the following for permission to reproduce extracts: The Bishop of Oxford, the Right Reverend Richard Harries and the Secretary General of the Anglican Consultative Council for permission to quote from *The Truth Shall Make You Free: The Lambeth Conference 1988* © The Secretary General of the Anglican Consultative Council 1988; Judge Israel Finestein and Vallentine Mitchell Publishers for permission to quote from *Jewish Society in Victorian England*, 1993; Faber and Faber Ltd for permission to quote from W. H. Auden 'Musée des Beaux Arts' from *Collected Poems* by W. H. Auden, edited by Edward Mendelson; The *Jewish Chronicle* for permission to quote from an article by Gerald Jacobs, and other unsourced material; Souvenir Press for permission to quote from Herman Wouk *This is my God* 1992; Icon Books Ltd for permission to quote from Bresheeth, Hood and Jansz, *Holocaust for Beginners* 1994; Cambridge University Press for permission

Acknowledgements

to quote from Richard Bolchover *British Jewry and the Holocaust* 1993; Weidenfeld and Nicolson for permission to quote from Naomi Shepherd *A Price Above Rubies* 1993; New York University Press for permission to quote from David Feldman *Birth Control in Jewish Law* 1968; The estate of James Joyce for permission to quote from *Ulysses*; Yale University Press for permission to quote from David Feldman *Englishmen and Jews – Social Relations and Political Culture 1840–1914* 1994; The Union of Liberal and Progressive Synagogues for permission to quote from the ULPS Haggadah 1981; Blackwells Publishers and Tony Kushner for permission to quote from *The Holocaust and the Liberal Imagination* 1994; Judge Pollak and Lord Lester Q.C. for permission to quote from 'Fundamental Rights: The United Kingdom Isolated', *Public Law*, Spring 1984 (Sweet & Maxwell); HarperCollins Publishers Limited for permission to quote from Ronald Dworkin *Life's Dominion* 1993; Sidgwick & Jackson for permission to quote from Gordon Williamson *The SS: Hitler's Instrument of Terror* 1994; Chatto & Windus and Gillian Rose for permission to quote from *Love's Work* 1995; Colombia University Press for permission to quote from Salo Baron *A Social and Religious History of the Jews* 1958; *The New Yorker* and Calvin Trillin for the extract from 'Drawing the Line', reprinted by permission © 1994 Calvin Trillin, originally published in *The New Yorker*. All rights reserved. Times Newspapers Ltd for permission to quote from 'Jews Honour the British Schindler, Frank Foley' by Rajeev Syal and Tim Rayment which appeared in the *Sunday Times* on 26 February 1995 © Times Newspapers Ltd 1995; Vallentine Mitchell for permission to quote from Edward Kessler *An English Jew* 1989; Frank Cass & Co Ltd for permission to quote from A. J. Sherman *Island Refuge – Britain and Refugees from the Third Reich 1933–1939* 1994; The London Diocesan Council for Christian-Jewish Understanding for permission to quote from David Daube's lecture 'He that cometh' 1966; Chatto & Windus and the Peters, Fraser and Dunlop Group Ltd for permission to quote from John Gross *Shylock – Four Hundred Years in the Life of a Legend* 1992; Constable and Co Ltd for permission to quote from Hermann Langbein *Against All Hope: Resistance in the Nazi Concentration Camps 1938–1945* 1994; Peregrine Worsthorne and the *Sunday Telegraph* for permission to quote from an article published on 10 January

1988; Tom Lehrer for permission to quote lines from *Too Many Songs* © 1965; Deborah Lipstadt and Penguin books for permission to quote from *Denying the Holocaust – The growing assault on truth and memory*, 1995.

Every effort has been made to trace the copyright holders and clear permissions. We regret any inadvertent omissions, which can be rectified in future editions.

Author's Introduction

For many years I have put off writing about what, for me, is probably most important of all: being Jewish. This is what affects every aspect of my life. The excuses I can give for not writing about it before are many and varied: that I would find it boring because I already 'know' about it, for instance, which is precisely what I said to my publisher, Helen Fraser, when she suggested it. And that there are enough books already about Judaism, many of a very high quality. My reply is both arrogant and complex – first, that there is no book, other than one for children, by *me* on the subject, and secondly that I might have a distinct view because of my background and career.

I am writing from the perspective of being female, British, with strong Irish connections, the child of a refugee mother, with a strong sense of being German-Jewish, immensely pro-European – and, of course, a rabbi. The British in general, and Jews in particular, often ask themselves about their identity; and it is these complex questions which are central to my thinking on the subject of being Jewish. Woven within the text of this book are the beginnings of answers to the question: 'Who, and what, am I?'

That can only be the central core if the rest of the picture is filled in. This book is not an autobiography, but it is intensely personal. There will be many people who will disagree with my interpretations of Judaism. There will be more who write me off as 'not properly Jewish'. To them I can only say that traditional Judaism has not served women well. Nor has it served men well in an open society. I am simply trying to come to terms with some of the contradictions we all face. No one has to agree with me. But it is essential for readers to recognise that this is as honest as I can make it, and that my reluctance to write on this subject may be to do with the difficulty we all have in facing the complexity of what makes us tick.

Is it tribalism? Am I Jewish because my parents and grandparents and ancestors, as far back as any of us can tell, were Jewish? Or am I Jewish because I am a believer – in God, in Torah, in the Jewish way of life? If the latter, what do I mean by God, Torah and the Jewish way of life? Is it more difficult being British as well as Jewish in relation to the state of Israel? Am I a Zionist? If so, why do I go to Israel so rarely? How has my life been coloured by being of refugee origins on one side? The Holocaust coloured my childhood in a very definite way and is still one of the major forces in my Jewish identity – how has the memory of the holocaust affected me, born as I was in 1950? Am I a Jew by religion, by people, by tribe, by nationality, by race? What do those terms mean? What is my relationship with Britain, which took in my mother and many other refugees, more than any other country, yet behaved so badly when ships bringing refugees from Europe to Palestine were turned away, thereby sending people back to a certain death? What is my relationship to a Britain which refused to bomb the railway lines to Auschwitz, regarding it as not part of the war effort? Yet I am alive, I and many thousands of others like me, because the British did take in so many refugees. Do I have an obligation to care for the interests of refugees from all sorts of other regimes, as a result of my family's experience?

These are the beginnings of the questions. Some have no answers. We can only hazard a guess. There also has to be a sense of what it means to be part of a Jewish family, to observe Jewish rituals, to require of one's children that they do not go out on a Friday night, to wish passionately for them to marry Jews while accepting that many of them will not do so.

The Jewish community in Britain – and elsewhere – is diminishing more through intermarriage and lack of continuity of education and association than ever before. Is it possible to live in an open society and keep one's young attached to the faith and the tribe? Why should we want to? And, if they do not stay within the fold in marriage and partnerships (as more and more do not marry at all), what can we do to encourage them to bring up their children as Jews? What is the nature of this Jewish experience that is so intense, so strong, so rich, and in some ways so precious, that we want to pass it down through the generations?

As one of Britain's keenest enthusiasts of being Jewish, I want to tell you why it is important to remain Jewish. It has to be a positive sense of good that we want to convey, a sense of excitement, richness, closeness, family, community and support, rather than the negative argument of trying to stop complete assimilation in order to prevent Hitler having a posthumous victory. I believe that Jews have a distinct role in relation to non-Jews in all kinds of debates in our society, as well as a mission that dates from biblical times to convey messages to the world about freedom and the rule of law. That requires genuine education about other faiths, not only Christianity, in our schools. It requires an unbending respect for education and learning from my own people. What can we do to maintain our faith if we do not educate our young about their Judaism? How can we expect them to remain in the fold if they do not see the excitement – intellectual, emotional and spiritual? Yet Jews who have reached for the stars academically are loath to study their own faith intensively. Among those who are extremely orthodox, and especially among the 'born again', we might see an intensity of study that fits well with their strict background or their fresh 'conversion'. But the ordinary run-of-the-mill, work-a-day Jew becomes a great lawyer, accountant, or doctor. Few become rabbis, even fewer spend their time voluntarily acquiring a deep level of Jewish learning. Yet we are a people of the book, a learned people whose obsession has been with the text, with the law. We must work to enthuse our people once again, to make Judaism exciting, to convince them that there is much to learn, and that, by learning it, they will have much to contribute to other Jews and to society.

Education is one arm of the restatement of value. Charity, in the sense of social justice, is another. For me, Judaism as a way of life has always been about social justice. The tradition is so strong that it colours the way many Jews think. They do not see themselves as generous when they give large sums – it is just the natural order of things. They do not recognise themselves in the stereotype of mean cheese-paring skinflints either, because that has little basis in fact except when Jews were extremely poor. Charitable giving is a religious duty, not a sign of a noble soul. We give because we should. We receive no credit for doing so, unless we give so far above the recommended percentage of our incomes that it becomes a deed of loving kindness. This is a part of being Jewish I do not want to lose. But it is also a part of Judaism I would like others to understand, and maybe to emulate, so that as a society we might become a more generous community, with a sense in our minds that the better-off have a duty to help those less well-off, and that most of us can find someone worse-off than ourselves. We should understand that society functions better if we do not expect gratitude, and give because it is right.

So this book is for my children, and holds within it all that I regard as paramount about being Jewish. They already know what I am going to say, and would argue that they have heard it since they were born. This is an attempt to describe what being Jewish is about, what it could be in Britain, and what motivates me to remain within the Jewish fold and encourage others to do so. It is for anyone who is interested, Jews and non-Jews alike. It attempts to describe the experience and question the identity. For others who face the same questions, I hope it clarifies the issues.

As I write this in the wake of two bombings of Jewish–Israeli targets in London within the space of twelve hours, and a bomb at a Jewish community centre in Buenos Aires which killed more than a hundred people, I know that world events will always test our loyalty and sense of identity as Jews, while testing the non-Jewish world in its support. Thus far, I can only say that the sympathy extended to the London Jewish community from all sorts of people and sources has been heart-warming in the extreme. For those people who have been so supportive, and for those who simply want to know more, whatever community they come from, here is an attempt to provide just a few of the answers, and to ask many of the questions.

1

'A nice Jewish girl':

Growing up Jewish

In Hampstead, North London, in the 1950s, it was not unusual to be Jewish.

From the age of five to eighteen, I attended South Hampstead High School for Girls, part of the Girls' Public Day School Trust. About a third of the girls were Jewish – the only distinction was between the majority of the Jewish girls, who were not extremely orthodox and only took one day off for Jewish festivals, and the few who were brought up strictly orthodox and took two. The school had a few Muslims, Hindus and Sikhs, but by far the biggest minority group was us, the Jews.

We had separate prayers at the beginning of each day, in a school where morning worship, indeed religion in general, was taken seriously; the assumption was that people would want to have their prayers with others who prayed in the same way. After our Jewish prayers in the library were over, we would troop into the main hall to hear the notices. Nowadays, I might think that that made us noticeable, but then nobody cared and it was as normal as could be. Once a week, on Wednesday, we had what was fondly referred to as 'united prayers', where we all prayed and sang hymns together. I still remember Wednesday prayers with great affection. Christian hymn-singing is one of the pleasures of life. The Christians don't necessarily have all the best tunes, but they do have the best tradition of communal singing by far. It is hugely satisfying to belt out at the top of one's voice the verses of 'All people that on earth do dwell' or 'Praise to the Lord, the Almighty, the King of Creation'. When I became senior Jewish prefect at a time when there were no full-time Jewish staff at South Hampstead High, I was responsible for checking the theology of the hymns we might sing in united prayers. It still amuses me to be at a Christian service with Jewish friends or family and realise that we all expurgate differently, since what is theologically sound to one Jew may not be to the next. All I was clear about was that references to Jesus and the Trinity were out. I was less certain, aged sixteen, than I would be now about references to particular kinds of redemption or to pilgrims. As a result, I sang a lot of hymns I would not sing altogether happily now.

Growing up as a part of a minority, but a large minority, was not an unpleasant experience. There was, in the circles I moved in, no anti-semitism in those post-war years. My contemporaries did not know the full horror of what had happened in the holocaust until they were eleven or twelve years old, because their parents wanted to protect them. This attitude applied to both Jewish and non-Jewish families: the events of the holocaust were so shocking, hard to believe and horribly disturbing that a child of any faith would be appalled.

Indeed, the only difference us being Jewish made to our non-Jewish friends, or rather their mothers, was whether we would eat the food they normally prepared when we came to tea. It was natural that the parents of our non-Jewish friends might be confused, as Jewish families, who were in all other ways apparently similar in their degree of Jewish observance, apart from the few very orthodox ones amongst us, varied in their adherence to dietary laws.

Being accepted as normal was important to young girls growing up to take their places in what would turn out to be a less friendly society. The early recognition that the school would have to adapt to its Jewish pupils, rather than the Jewish pupils adapt to the school, was, I suspect, critical in shaping the way we thought, and in making us assume that we would be offered equality wherever we went. It also ensured that we would assume that other non-Jewish institutions, faced with a large number of Jews within them, would also choose to adapt. It has been a shock to me as a parent to find that other schools do not take the same view. I have also discovered that other institutions, including the army and the judiciary, while willingly opening their doors to Jews and other minorities, nevertheless expect and demand a degree of conformity to what they would describe as 'British norms'.

Some years ago, while on holiday in Ireland, a country well used to accommodating religious diversity, we invited a housemaster from one of Britain's most distinguished boys' schools over for a drink. The school has a large number of Jewish pupils – around fifteen per cent. It has compulsory Chapel attendance every day, and Saturday morning school. When I said how extraordinary it was to expect Jewish boys to go to a Christian service, the reply was that it was part of the school's tradition, that it was a Christian foundation, that no boy *had* to go to that particular school, and that in any case it did not matter because Chapel was somehow all about local colour and not to be taken seriously. I was horrified. By what right can one assume that a service is not to be taken seriously? Does that not devalue the whole religious experience? If the school happily takes Jewish boys, should it not be making provision for them? Should it not abolish Saturday morning school, or arrange an alternative for boys who would prefer to keep the Jewish Sabbath?

Since the school takes Jewish pupils in fair numbers, it has to be said to be discriminating against Jews who take their Judaism seriously. The argument that it is a Christian foundation will not do. Most institutions in Britain that predate 1800 are Christian foundations, or have a strong Church link. If other institutions have kept their Christian trappings, they take their faith seriously, and make allowances for those who do not share that Christianity. Thus Eton, which is also a Church foundation and also has a fair number of Jewish students, makes provision for those who do not wish to go to Chapel, and will also arrange for pupils to do lessons on Sundays if they wish to go to synagogue on Saturdays. It is the proper test of a tolerant Christian foundation, that it does not try to impose its views on others, but instead accommodates others whom it welcomes in its midst. A Christian foundation which makes provision for others is saying that it takes its Christianity seriously, and that it wants present for Christian services only those who can freely and happily participate – entirely in accordance with any tolerant religious point of view. That was the attitude with which I grew up in Hampstead and it is that attitude I wish to see in all institutions and all education systems.

The 1988 Education Act seems to be going exactly against what I grew up with. The assumption that all children must study Christianity at school, and that it should be the biggest component of the religious education syllabus even when Christian children are not in the majority, seems to me offensive and conversionist. Parents, of course, have the right to withdraw their children from religious education, but most would prefer them to stay in school to study the faiths of other people. I want my children to learn about Islam and Christianity. Many Christian parents I know want their children to learn about Islam and Judaism, but it is not the responsibility of a school to indoctrinate. It is the responsibility of a school to teach. Schools should teach children about different faiths, cultures and philosophies, and help them to form and encapsulate their own values. It is in religious education that children should learn about humanism, and pacifism. It is in religious education that they should learn about morality and the extent to which we have, or have not, a shared moral base in this country. It is in religious education that they should begin to work out the links between religion and morality, and question whether those without a faith in a personal god can nevertheless be 'good' people. An attitude that says Christianity *has* to be dominant precludes wider discussion of morality and goodness, and indeed makes a statement about Christianity being not only the main religion of Britain (which it certainly is) but somehow a more worthwhile faith than any of the others. The requirement that religious education should be mainly Christian sends out all sorts of alarm bells to those of other faiths. It is saying that this is a Christian country, and *your* faith does not belong here. It is not central to our culture. It is not embedded in it.

Jews have been in Britain from the time of William the Conqueror, indeed they probably came with the Romans. In 1290 they were expelled, but were readmitted under Cromwell in 1656, and have been here ever since. Muslims and Hindus are more recent arrivals, but the trading and Imperial interests of the British in the Indian sub-continent mean that the links with Hindus and Muslims go back more than 200 years.

India, Pakistan and Bangladesh have long been independent, and many people whose families originated from these countries live as British citizens here. How then can there be any justification for the British trying to dominate Hindus and Muslims religiously now? The British take to their hearts so much that is essentially drawn from the sub-continent of India. There is a romantic revival of the period of the Raj. Merchant Ivory films are hugely popular. Curry is now the favourite food of British people who have never been within 1,000 miles of Delhi or Karachi. Yet despite strong influences from the Indian sub-continent there is no recognition that its religions may have something different and special to bring to the religious life of Britain. We buy dresses from Monsoon and walk on carpets from Pakistan, yet we neither accept nor try to understand the religions of the sub-continent. All we hear are objections to Muslims which go far beyond the anger against the Ayatollah Khomeini's *fatwa* against Salman Rushdie, and a strong resentment of a particular kind of extremism among Muslims, which is undoubtedly deeply unattractive, but no more unacceptable than extremism among Orthodox Jews or fundamentalist Christians. Some of the anti-Muslim feeling amounts to racism. It was that racism, that sense of a desire for Christianity to dominate other faiths, that was missing from my childhood.

My first personal brush with anti-semitism was as an undergraduate at Cambridge. Until then, I had lived an admittedly sheltered life. I am not sure those who live in Hampstead today would say they had never experienced anti-semitism. Perhaps my experience was due more to being in the wake of the holocaust, at a time when there was still a sense of guilt that more had not been done to save the people who perished. Perhaps, too, it was because the political situation in relation to the State of Israel was different. Before 1967 it was 'brave little Israel' against the rest. After 1967, and even more after the Yom Kippur war in 1973, the mood changed: Israel was seen as the Jewish aggressor, which changed the way people thought of the Jews. Growing up in London in the 1950s and 1960s, in an area of relatively dense Jewish settlement, I was very fortunate.

That sense of good fortune did not make us feel that we had our roots in Britain, however. Many of us had refugee parents or cousins or aunts and uncles. My mother speaks with a strong German accent (which I cannot hear). I remember, aged about seven, discussing with some of my friends at school why it was their parents spoke with 'funny accents'. It was only when they told me that my mother also spoke with a 'funny accent' that I began to realise that maybe I could not hear it because I was so used to it. But my childhood was full of that German and Czech and Polish foreign-ness – full of a sense of being cosmopolitan.

Where we lived when I was a child was an area full of rented flats, and the rents were controlled, so a great mixture of people lived in the area. There were German refugees, like my mother, some of whom still had rooms in other people's apartments – quite against the rules. But no one minded, and most of the single people in those rooms were quiet, and often isolated. I got to know one of them quite well, a Miss Adler. She lived opposite, in a small room, with all sorts of things she had been able to bring from Germany – little bits of Meissen china that had

7

belonged to her mother. Max Ernst lithographs, drawings by Jankel Adler. There were screens covered in shawls and pictures, boxes full of papers, every inch of wall covered, and the two chairs were impossible to sit on, they were so deep in possessions. You had to move stuff along the bed to find a place to perch. I always wondered whether she managed to sleep by lying very still, without turning over.

Miss Adler's mother had died in May 1939, leaving no money. Things were very difficult for Jews in Germany by then, and her family had never been rich. They were eating simple meals, of soup and semolina as she recounted it, to save to pay the doctor for relieving old Mrs Adler's pain. When her mother died, she fled to England with nothing much beyond what she stood up in and a suitcase which contained not clothes but treasures. She had also posted what she could to a friend already in London. She found work as a domestic servant, but her eyesight was so poor she would not see the dust. She earned a living with a bit of private teaching, a bit of translation and a bit of dressmaking. Meanwhile, so grateful was she to this country that she spent her nights fire-watching – and ended up exhausted in hospital, in Kent. Her nerves never recovered, and by the time I knew her she was always grey-faced, a woman of little energy, just quietly pleased to be free and alive, to be coming and going as she pleased.

It was an area of London, then, where lots of German accents were heard. The middle-aged women who had come from Germany and Austria in their thirties and forties were by then wearing rather tatty Persian lamb coats, and drinking coffee with each other in the Dorice restaurant in Finchley Road. My mother was different. She had been younger when she came as a refugee. She worked as a domestic, a counter-hand and later a buyer at Marks &

Spencer's. By the time I was born, she was a social-worker, helping other older refugees who could no longer work.

I can still hear the accents in my head. There were several refugees who ran hand-made chocolate businesses in the area. Ackermann's still exists, producing the same elegant fine bitter chocolates they did then, while others, such as the two refugees who ran Blue and Red Chocolates in Belsize Park, and who gave us greedy schoolgirls chocolates on our way home, have disappeared. Eating continental chocolates still now recalls an elegance brought from Vienna, or Frankfurt, or Berlin.

The deli was a source of great joy. Its owners were called Mr and Mrs Schwartz, with no known first names. It was very old-fashioned, very formal. A wool merchant and a teacher, Mr and Mrs Schwartz had come to London as refugees. They set up a 'real' delicatessen. They had pickled cucumbers in barrels, and herrings in every shape and form. They had creamy heaps of sauerkraut, which Mrs Schwartz made, and piles of loose cream cheese. Childless themselves, they were the soul of kindness to the local children. Mrs Schwartz taught me to cook by giving me strict instructions and replacing for free ingredients I had ruined. When my father was ill, when I was about fifteen, she sent round delicacies to tempt his appetite – and told me to come and talk to her if I was feeling miserable. When my friend Mary emigrated to Canada, she sent her off with packets of biscuits for the journey. The lives of the Schwartzes had been totally disrupted by the Nazi period, but their experiences had made them kinder and warmer rather than suspicious – and they rejoiced in the new people they got to know.

Such were features of my childhood. Although most of these people were not relatives, their experiences were like those of my relatives. We were not very English, although my father had been born and bred in London, and educated at public school and Cambridge. His parents had come from Frankfurt in 1906, so that my grandfather could work with his uncle who had started a branch of the family bank in London. The story goes that my grandparents had come from the two opposing orthodox communities in Frankfurt, which were barely on speaking terms, and so the young couple had left for London to get away from the tensions – a Jewish Romeo and Juliet. They bought a house in Hampstead and lived there contentedly, in a moderately continental style. Around them were several cousins and friends who came from Germany – the Heinemanns, the Roans, and others I never knew. My father was one of three brothers, the first of whom was born in 1911, and the youngest, Harry, during the First World War. (It is an example of how non-British they still were that they apparently wanted Harry to be called Kurt Chaim, hardly the most English-sounding of names. Family legend has it that the registrar told my grandparents that as Britain was at war with Germany, it was not fair on the poor little mite to call him by a German name.)

We lived differently from many of my contemporaries, partly because of my mother, a German refugee who came to England in 1937 and who managed to get her brother and parents out before the war began, but also because of my paternal grandmother, a woman of considerable forcefulness. Until she died in 1963, she held the family together. We went to her house on Jewish festivals, so that all the members of family could celebrate together. The year was punctuated with those festivals, and it imposed a structure that was important to the way we thought. We would always have new clothes for Jewish New Year and for the three pilgrim festivals of Passover (Pesach), Pentecost (Shavuot) and Tabernacles (Sukkot) however badly-off my parents, aunts and uncles were at the time. We paraded our dresses in front of our grandmother, and there were occasions when she would buy us the clothes we really wanted, to our mothers' intense irritation, since our choice, as little girls of six, seven and eight within a group of very talkative cousins, was always something that would not wash.

At Pesach we would be allowed, from a very young age, to stay up for the Seder, the celebration around the table that told the story of the coming out of Egypt, out of slavery, to freedom in the promised land. We were made to have a rest in the afternoon, and I well remember the whispering and giggling that went on while we pretended to be asleep. My Aunt Anne was always the one who could hear us talking from two floors down, and I never did discover how she did it. There was always an air of great expectancy before Pesach. My grandmother's house bustled with activity. Masses of food was delivered, from Rabenstein the kosher butcher, whom my grandmother had managed to get out of Germany as a refugee, and who repaid her ever after with the most wonderful meat in the world.

In an orthodox house, as my grandmother's was, every-thing had to be changed for Pesach. Not only did she have separate crockery for meat and milk, in the normal way for those who keep the dietary laws and do not mix meat and milk at all, but she would also have a separate two sets of everything again for Pesach. All the Pesach crockery would have to be brought up from the cellar and washed, and all the other stuff taken down. The whole house had to be made Pesachdik, which meant that a hunt had to be staged for any sign of leaven, and any crumbs symbolically burned, while anything which was leaven had to be given to the neighbours. The ceremony was great fun, and included the children, who were usually excused the more mundane tasks like washing and drying all the Pesach crockery that had emerged filthy after fifty-one weeks of non-use.

The last meal before the Pesach Seder was always a peculiar one, at lunchtime on the day when the Seder was to be held in the evening. The house was by then Pesachdik, so there was no leaven left. We ate, often off paper plates, some wonderful concoction of fruit and cheese which had been kept entirely separate. My grandmother was orthodox, but not extremely so. Yet she would order all the normal groceries to be delivered kosher for Pesach, which meant that they had been checked to see that no leaven had somehow got into them. Lunch inside the house could be neither the kosher for Pesach, nor leaven – so if it was warm enough we would have a picnic in the garden and finish the remains of the leaven food.

Then came the evening, with us dressed in our finery. When we were very little, we did not last all evening, for we began at around seven or eight p.m. and went on until past midnight. It is one of my abiding memories of enormous pleasure sitting round, twenty or thirty of us, celebrating the Passover. The story would be told in great detail, from the Passover *haggadah*, the prayer book for the service. There were sections especially for the children, and the youngest who was able to do so asked the four questions: '*Mah nishtanah . . .*' 'Why is this night different from all other nights?' The questions go on to ask about the eating of unleavened bread, the dipping of herbs, the eating of bitter herbs, and leaning on cushions. We children, of course, already knew the answers, having heard them on previous years, and having studied them at religion school. We ate unleavened bread because the

Israelites, fleeing Egypt, did not have time to let their bread rise. We dipped herbs – usually parsley – into salt water to remind us of the tears shed by our ancestors as slaves in Egypt. We ate bitter herbs to remind us of the bitterness of their suffering. And we leaned as we ate to remind us that we were free people, and could eat as Roman free men had eaten, leaning to one side on a couch.

Tonight was different from all other nights. We were allowed to stay up for this big party and celebration. We could sing these fantastic songs with the adults at the end if we did not go to sleep first. We were there with our families, safe and secure, in freedom. Long before we were old enough to intellectualise that sense of freedom and safety, we children sensed that our Passover was additionally poignant, because also partaking were many refugees, as well as people who had been involved in getting other Jews out of Germany before the holocaust and helping them when they arrived in England. We were fortunate enough to be free and safe, but others had perished, cousins and aunts, family and, indeed, whole communities. We children, without knowing it or understanding it, could feel the emotion.

Passover was always a festival of great joy when celebrated in my grandmother's house, tinged with sadness, and without much discussion of the historical meanings of the symbols. For our group celebrated in the shadow of recent events. It was a heartfelt occasion, not an intellectual one.

It was not until I was much older, when my grandmother was dead and we had Passover regularly at home with my parents (the three brothers had decided not to combine families at Passover), that I learned a more intellectual approach. We revisited the four questions. I was often still the youngest present, though I was fourteen by this time. Why is this night different from all other nights? Well, we eat unleavened bread, unlike all other nights. Yet it was not really because the Israelites did not have time to let their dough rise, despite the legend. It was more likely, if Philo (in the section on the special laws of Passover, Loeb edition, vol. 7, 269–71) was to be believed, that there had been an ancient spring festival where the very first grains of corn were eaten, as a kind of fertility rite. No doubt they would have made those who ate them feel a little ill. Certainly bread made out of such corn would not have risen. The fertility symbolism of Passover is clear. On the main Seder dish there is always a roasted egg. It is not coincidence that Passover and Easter (following the same lunar calendar as the Jewish calendar) usually coincide. There are eggs at Easter, too, and it is likely that Jewish and Christian symbols have their origins in an ancient middle-eastern fertility festival in the spring. Jews also have the shank bone from a lamb on the Seder plate as a reminder of the lambs the Israelites sacrificed, the blood of which they smeared on the doorposts of their houses so that the angel of death would pass them by when he came to slay the first-born Egyptian sons, in the last and most horrific of the ten plagues designed to persuade Pharaoh to let the people go. So goes the story. In fact the sacrifice of a new-born lamb is much more likely to be a spring fertility rite, as was the eating of the tender young shoots of green herbs. This was the new beginning, the spring.

And so to the second question. Why do we dip herbs, not only once, but twice? The answer was probably that dipping herbs in vinegar rather than salt water was an ancient first course, or *hors d'oeuvre*, to whet the appetite. The interpretation of it reminding us of the tears shed by the Israelites in Egypt is a delightful one, but a story is all it is, for almost certainly that custom is more ancient than the Passover liturgy itself.

As for the bitter herbs, it may be that they were instituted in order to remind people of the bitterness of the suffering of the Israelites. It is much more likely they were the relishes customary with meat in Roman times, since we know that the Romans had a strong palate for sauces. When I was a child, my grandmother and parents never served the traditional horseradish neat; we had horseradish sauce which was rather mild. It was only when I began to give my own Seders with my husband that we instituted cutting up a horseradish root into thin slices and giving everyone a taste, to really get the effect of the strength of the herb. To see everyone with tears coursing down their faces, laughing and gasping at the same time, is fun and also makes the point – bitter herbs must be *really* bitter to experience the suffering at all. Traditionally, after the bitter herbs, according to the *haggadah*, one gets the chance to make what is known as the Hillel sandwich, by taking some herbs and some of the paste called *charoset*, which is similar to a spicy apple-pie filling, and wrapping them up between two pieces of matzah, our unleavened bread. The *charoset* is rather sweet and soothing, and I believe the sandwich used to be made and eaten quickly after the bitter herbs to take away the taste and to cool down the mouth.

At my grandmother's house, we would have a long stint of the service, as traditional, before the meal, and then the huge meal. Afterwards the whole thing would break up into a more informal gathering. We would sing the traditional songs, and, when we were very small, we still had with us a wonderful man, Paul Bachman, husband to the widow of my father's first cousin, Harold, who had died of polio. Paul had a sweet voice, and would lead us in the songs in a uniquely competent and unassertive way. After his death, the singing got more chaotic, because none of my grandmother's three sons could give a musical lead. But it was always great fun, and, though we could never have been described as a musical family, most of us enjoyed a good sing-song round the table.

Before the meal finished, we would enjoy the wonderful joke which is written into the *haggadah* and the whole Passover celebration – the hunt for the Afikoman. The Afikoman is a piece of matzah which is hidden and then retrieved. In some family traditions, the leader of the Seder hides it and the children have to hunt for it, and whoever finds it gets a prize. In others, the children escape with it and hide it, and the leader has either to find it or, more likely, pay a ransom for it, and give the children money or a present. The second half of the Seder cannot proceed without it, for everyone has to have a small piece of it before the grace at the end of the meal can be said and the service can be continued.

One explanation of this is that it was the original dessert. Afikoman is almost certainly originally a Greek word. Some have suggested that it comes from *epikomios*, the evening entertainment after dinner, which could link it to the sing-song at the end of the Seder. But in more recent years, David Daube, a distinguished lawyer, has suggested, in a lecture he gave under the auspices of the London Diocesan Council for Christian–Jewish understanding at St Botolph's Church in the City of London, that it comes from the Greek work *afikomenos*, 'he that cometh', the present participle of the Greek verb 'to arrive'. If that were the case, then the Afikoman is actually something rather serious and maybe Messianic. That would fit well, because there is early Messianism in the Passover celebrations. On the table there is the cup of Elijah, and in some traditions an extra place is laid for Elijah, the uninvited guest. In Jewish tradition, Elijah is the herald of the coming of the Messiah; in the Biblical story he never died but went up to heaven in a fiery chariot, casting his mantle down upon his successor, Elisha. It also ties in well with one of the other passages in the *haggadah*, about the four sons. In non-orthodox households we have equalised the sons into four children – the wise, the wicked, the simple, and the one who does not know how to ask. The wise one has the oddest passage. He asks what it all means. The reply is that the leader of the Seder must tell him all about it in detail, including the Afikoman. As this is the wise son, it suggests that there is some mystery with the Afikoman, which links up with David Daube's theory that it is Messianic. It also ties in with two other factors. One is that it is hidden and revealed in the game the children play with the leader of the Seder. The other is that it is shared – everyone eats a bit – which is reminiscent of communion in Christianity.

So, although as children we celebrated the Passover and carried out all the rituals, the significance of some of them was not clear to us – nor, indeed, I suspect, to our parents and relatives. Though people had a great deal of Jewish knowledge, their degree of investigation of the origins of the symbols was relatively limited. Rather, the atmosphere was emotional.

The emotion at Passover set the scene for the tone of much of our observance of Judaism in the larger family, gathered around my grandmother. There was a strong sense of being emotionally Jewish, with the festivals setting a pattern for the year. Passover, with the memories it evoked, gave us our strongest sense of not being wholly English – also brought about by having a refugee parent or two and eating different food. My family were largely German Jews in origin and did not eat much 'traditional' Jewish food, which is largely eastern European, and was as unfamiliar to German Jews as it was to non-Jews. Our food was much more continental. We ate rye bread when everyone else ate plain white. We ate pickled cucumbers before they became fashionable, and though my mother would see herself as a plain English cook, we had far more in the way of salads with fancy dressings than was usual in the 1950s.

Part of the family kept kosher, which was more complicated. The laws of *kashrut* are hard for any Jew, let alone any non-Jew, to understand. Kosher meals were always served at my grandmother's house, and at my orthodox aunt and uncle's home. The rest of us did not keep kosher, but would be careful not to offend the others when they came to eat with us, a relatively rare event. We usually went to my grandmother's, and would celebrate alternate Friday evenings at the beginning of the sabbath with her, not entirely dissimilar to the Passover celebration. There would be the *kiddush*, the blessings over wine and bread and the origins of communion for Christianity, before the meal began. Then a celebratory meal. After the meal was over, there would be a lengthy grace, led by whichever brother was there. We were all expected to join in, and it was often a puzzle because we were never given grace books from which to follow. I think the assumption was that we knew the text anyway, which as a very small child I certainly did not. The other, mistaken, assumption was that we would not be able to read Hebrew. (Two of my cousins, Susan and Aviva, went to a Jewish primary school, and I was taught to read Hebrew at the same time as I learned to read English.) Following a text would have been useful, but, more than that, I believe that you have greater concentration on prayers if you have a text to follow, rather than reciting by rote. It was not until I was about ten that I persuaded my grandmother that we should each have a copy of the prayer book to follow.

Part of her hesitation was the numbers of people who came on Friday nights for whom she would have to buy books. We were frequently twenty or more, sometimes even thirty, for dinner. Often we would have to wash up dishes in the middle to have enough for pudding. The assembled gathering could be any or all of my grand-mother's three sons and their wives and their children, six grandchildren in all. Then there was Grete, my father's cousin Harold's widow, with her husband Paul and two children and two step-children. There would be several elderly couples, distant cousins whom my grandmother had helped escape from Germany. There might be her old friend and cousin, Tully Roan, and Tully's husband Gustav. And there would always be a few people none of us really knew who just turned up. My grandmother was a woman of astonishing hospitality, which she learned as a young, and very badly-off woman in Frankfurt. She had seen in her family, which had little money, an instinct for hospi-tality which is very Jewish, and particularly a part of the sabbath and festivals.

To what extent it is part of a fear of the future, that you always extend the hand of hospitality in the present, is unclear. Certainly, the tradition stretches back to Biblical times. When three messengers, or angels, visited Abraham at Mamre, he set about preparing a great feast for the unknown guests. When Abraham and Sarah journeyed into Egypt, they were treated with royal hospitality. The tradition was to proffer the best of what you had to the uninvited stranger. Opening up one's doors has become distinctly less common. But elements of the tradition still survive – anyone without a place to go for Passover will usually be invited by a family, and many congregations make an effort to ensure that those on their own get invited to a family fairly regularly for the sabbath meal on Shabbat.

It does not always work, of course, and there are many people in the Jewish community who would say that they are all too lonely. But the symbolism is there, to the extent of laying the extra place at the Passover table and opening the door at one point in the Seder to let in Elijah or the unexpected guest. Indeed, the *kiddush*, the sanctification of wine and bread at the beginning of the sabbath and festival meals, is probably an old symbol of hospitality, particularly if the bread is salted, for bread and salt were the staff of life.

Growing up with these huge Friday evening meals at grandmother's house made me realise how very different I was from my non-Jewish friends who rarely had a large family gathering except at Christmas, and who certainly did not have a night during the week when everyone congregated and talked. As a teenager, I often complained about not being able to go out on the sabbath when my friends did. Yet the idea of meeting together as a small or extended family and talking over the events of the past week with a special meal and a veritable sense of occasion was so attractive even then, that, while resenting the ban on going out, I always still enjoyed my sabbath meal at home. Now, as my children become teenagers, I would never forbid them from going out, on the basis that they must choose for themselves how they will live their Jewish lives, but we usually have a good family sabbath with everyone around. We all like the sense of togetherness, and my children also comment how rare it is for their friends to have meals with their families on a regular basis.

Not all my Jewish friends observed the sabbath as strictly as we did, though many did something. But my hurrying to be back from school on a Friday, my desire to change into something more respectable than the disgustingly stained and proverbially rucked-up school uniform, was a sign of a weekly sense of the holy, a true sense of the importance of the sabbath, the day of rest, even though I could not have put it into words when I was a child. I knew only that that is what we did, that it made us different from others, that I liked it, and that there was something special, separate, about the Friday evening *en famille* that made me respond both to my close family and to the wider net. It is a sense I have never lost, a sense of wonder at the end of the week, at the day of rest, that is, I believe, quintessentially Jewish.

That tradition, that hospitality (which is only one part of it) seems to me one of the great contributions Judaism has made to family life. For to sit and eat together, to pray together without prayers being a separate and solemn event, makes the family a wonderful focus. It becomes the heart of the religious observance, and the home becomes the place of worship, suggesting that, while synagogue is important, that it is where you study and learn and go to pray in a congregation, it is not the heart of your Jewish being.

We went to synagogue every week, on Saturday morning. The Jewish sabbath begins at sundown on a Friday night and finishes at sundown on a Saturday, so there are two main services in the synagogue, on Friday night to welcome the sabbath, which we never went to as children, and on Saturday morning, the more important, because it was when the weekly portion of the law, the five books of Moses, was read as the central part of the service.

From a very young age, I was taken by my father to the children's service at the West London Synagogue, one of Britain's leading reform synagogues. The services there were largely in English. The interior is virtually unchanged since my childhood. The atmosphere was one of entering somewhere very solemn but not particularly Jewish-looking. It is, in fact, built in the Italianate Moorish style, similar to the main synagogue in Florence. It was intended to express great splendour and dignity, with its polished pews in dark wood, its strong smell of furniture polish, its dome and its marble and granite inlays. It is a beautiful building in many ways, but for children it was overwhelming, and rather on the dignified side for any desire to run around or to claim the place as one's own.

My father and I went there every Saturday morning. When I grew older, we went to the adult service, which I much preferred. It had more structure, and did not patronise. Somehow, the formality of the adult service was more fitting for that building. My father had become a member of West London during the war. Brought up orthodox by my grandparents, he abandoned his orthodoxy, as did his elder brother, during the war, because he could not see that it made sense. He felt he wanted to remain on the traditional side of reform, which is why West London, with its formality and its liturgy, in those days not very dissimilar to that at Bevis Marks, the oldest synagogue in London, in the city, traditional, Sephardic and formal, suited him. It suited me too. It was a kind of cathedral synagogue, with a large membership which came from all over London. Any sense of community it conveyed came as a result of its own efforts, for drawing on such distances made it hard for people to get to know each other well outside the synagogue. But it had a strong sense of commitment to religious education, as well as a sense of celebration, particularly at the festival of Sukkot (Tabernacles) when the temporary booth erected with displays of fruit and vegetables and greenery on the roof of the synagogue was one of the most splendid in London. It had, and still has, a commitment to communal service, and its ability to stay in touch with many of its elderly and frailer members all over London is impressive.

It was this formal congregation which was my entry into synagogal Judaism. At services, I would see the wardens (my father later became one) sitting in their box, wearing morning-dress and top hats. It was delightfully old-fashioned and eminently respectable. At the same time, its commitment to radical causes went back a long way. It was one of the first congregations to become involved in Amnesty International, and its tradition of helping people with alcohol and drug problems stretches back to the 1950s. It also did a considerable amount as a congregation during the war for refugees, and retained a strong social conscience.

Its religion school was, however, far from perfect, despite the commitment to education and despite the generally admirable nature of the values for which the congregation stood. Too much was taught by rote, and too many of the teachers lacked real dedication, though it must have been hard when faced with a gang of terrors such as we, who did not really want to learn, and who bitterly resented having to give up our Sunday mornings. The Jewish community has not solved this problem of how to make Jewish education attractive to children. Though I would not encourage sending children to specifically Jewish schools, because I do not wish to live in a separatist society, the problem of teaching children about their heritage is a considerable one. Sunday morning religion classes are deeply unpopular, and it is an inspired teacher who can make children want to be there at all. Holiday schools can be very successful, if the children themselves are keen on an intensive Jewish experience once or twice a year, but I am sure that I would not have been. So children, year on year, go complaining on Sunday mornings, and in some congregations on Wednesday afternoons as well, to learn Hebrew and about their faith. Once a week is optimum forgetting time, and learning a language this way is plainly absurd. There definitely needs to be a rethink.

Nevertheless, there were times at religion school when I learned a great deal. When we were taught by rabbinic students at Leo Baeck College (where I later studied), young men who had just made a personal commitment to devote their lives to Judaism, it all came alive. When we were taught the liturgy by an elderly German refugee of profound spirituality, so intense that it shone out of him, even the most hardened of the resentful boys became silent as we listened to him talking about how some of the prayers were said in the concentration camps by people going to their deaths. We began to understand. But that was rare. Mostly, we rebelled, and teachers grew impatient.

What I grasped in the way of Hebrew I learned largely not at religion school but from my father and from an Israeli who became my private teacher. By the time I was fifteen and decided to do Hebrew at O level I was quite a competent Hebraist. I had to go to classes at a local orthodox synagogue to learn the syllabus, because West London did not then aspire to its pupils taking public examinations in Hebrew or Jewish studies, something I still find depressing. Most young people would be keener to learn if what they were learning was going to be part of public examinations they would have to do anyway. Encouraging children to take Jewish studies and classical Hebrew for

GCSE may not be an answer to falling standards in Jewish knowledge, but it might help.

The only other motivating factor for many young people in studying Judaism, and specifically Hebrew, is preparation for their bar or bat mitzvah (literally, son or daughter of the commandment). Orthodox congregations do not have an absolute equivalent for girls, although increasingly, under pressure from feminist thinking, they have some kind of ceremony, such as a bat chayil (daughter of valour) ceremony in a group on a Sunday afternoon. But in non-orthodox congregations, the ceremony for boys and girls is identical. Both are called up to read the law from the Torah scroll, and have to learn considerable amounts of Hebrew to achieve the competence to be able to do it. The Torah scroll (the scroll of the law, the five books of Moses, Genesis through to Deuteronomy) is written in unpointed Hebrew, which means that the vowels are not there, and that the child either has to be reasonably competent at Hebrew grammar, to read without the vowels, or has to learn the passage at least in part by heart.

The preparation for bar and bat mitzvah can be very important for a young person. It is often the first chance to grapple with a text, and, if the children are well taught, they will discover something about how interpretations have taken place over the centuries. Most non-orthodox congregations require the bar or bat mitzvah to read and translate their passage and to give a commentary on it which they have written themselves. It is that task which for so many is the beginning of a fascination with Jewish texts. If the interest is there, the young person can begin to read the *midrash*, the rabbinic commentary which is a kind of theological interpretation of the text, giving a variety of possible explanations and wider interpretations.

They can also – if the passage they are preparing is a legal one – look at the codes of Jewish law for the first time and see how the text was developed by the rabbis in later centuries. Even if they cannot manage to read the texts in their original Hebrew or Aramaic, a glimpse of the rich heritage of Jewish learning that is available in English translation is enough to enthuse and encourage them, possibly at the very point when they had just decided to leave religion school. Many stay on and study further.

Many religion schools have a small number of young people who have stayed on voluntarily after bar and bat mitzvah to learn more about their heritage. For these people, doing a public examination in Jewish studies would be one way to take it further. For some, a real investigation of the text becomes enormously exciting. For others, Jewish history becomes the motiving force, and they read and read. For others, the horror of the holocaust begins to strike and perhaps to make some kind of sense, set against other world horrors such as events in Cambodia or East Timor, Rwanda, Chechenia or Bosnia. For still others, the question of being Jewish, and what that means, becomes key in the teenage years, when they are trying to establish who they are. Some become much more orthodox than their parents. Others drift away from Judaism, though they may return again in their twenties, when they have children of their own.

My own bat mitzvah was held, somewhat idiosyncratically, when I was fourteen. Neither my parents nor Rabbi Hugo Gryn, then very junior at West London, seem to know why. For most young people, both boys and girls, it is held at thirteen. In Jewish law, a boy becomes an adult, responsible for carrying out the *mitzvot* (religious commandments) at thirteen years and a day old. A girl reaches the same status, although she has far fewer positive commandments to carry out, traditionally speaking, at twelve years old. Most non-orthodox congregations equalise the bar and bat mitzvah age at thirteen. But I, and my good friend Victoria Neumark, with whom I shared the ceremony, waited until we were fourteen. We read the story of Pharoah's dreams in Genesis, interpreted by Joseph, still then in prison. First out of the river came the cattle – the fat, healthy-looking ones – followed by the thin starving-looking ones. Then came the ears of corn, first the fat ones and then the thin, wind-blasted ones. Joseph interpreted this as prophesying seven years of fat plenty, followed by seven bad harvests and starvation in the land. The rest of the story is well-known: Joseph was removed from prison and set in charge of food storage and planning. It was a wonderful passage to be given to read, and both Victoria and I as a result became fascinated by the interpretation of dreams.

More than that, we had classes for post-bar and -bat mitzvah students with Rabbi Hugo Gryn, then a new, very junior rabbi at the West London Synagogue. He began to tease out questions about our own identity, and how we could demonstrate to the wider world what mattered about being Jewish. He tried to argue through with us the justification for being non-orthodox Jews, a concept we found difficult in our teenage years, when extremes of all or nothing seem much more attractive. Briefly, at that age, I decided to be orthodox. The sense of being a second-class citizen because I was female very quickly turned me back to being a reform Jewess, but the intellectual justification for reinterpretation of the law was something which eluded me until I was in my twenties. I spent two years or so discussing with my colleagues and Hugo Gryn questions about such as the meaning of life, and trying to work out, from a Jewish point of view, where we stood on some of the great moral dilemmas of the day.

This post bat-mitzvah studying was an extremely enjoyable experience, from which I derived the conviction that it is possible to use Jewish thought to add to a wider moral debate about almost any issue. That does not mean that there is a 'Jewish' view, for there is usually more than one. The old joke of two Jews and three opinions is not a joke at all. There is often a different way of looking at things which derives from a knowledge of Jewish law, Jewish history, theology and experience, which one can add to a debate about a moral problem. It was those post-bar and -bat mitzvah classes which started us thinking that we could – and should – get more from our Judaism than merely sufficient fluency to be able to read from the Torah on one occasion. We learned that there was a rich library, a great tradition to be tapped, of which I still feel I am just beginning to scratch the surface.

2

'There but for the grace of God':

Reactions to the holocaust

It was fate that made me hand over my English credit card that day. I had been living in the United States of America, on a Harkness Fellowship at Harvard Medical School, for over a month, and had just been given an American credit card by the bank. But my English card seemed more familiar, somehow. I had a pile of maps in my hand, some newspapers, some cough sweets. I was wandering slightly aimlessly in the drugstore round the corner from where I was working. My cash supply was low. As I paid, talking as I did to the elderly man behind the counter, he looked at my card and asked me my maiden name. Somewhat perplexed, I told him.

He looked at the card again, and then at me. His eyes narrowed behind his thick rounded spectacles: 'Was your grandmother anything to do with the refugee committee?'

I might have asked, 'Which refugee committee?' There have been plenty, God knows, and the need for them is as acute now as the time he was referring to. Except, in my family, there was only the one, run at Bloomsbury House, for refugees from Nazi Germany and Austria. Among its many other activities it had a welfare committee, which my grandmother chaired. She was no easy character, receiving near-hatred and a kind of veneration in equal measures. She bullied officials to let in more refugees, she bullied her staff to guarantee more people (a system by which British citizens guaranteed around two hundred pounds for each refugee, to ensure that they would not become a charge upon the state), she bullied everyone to work harder. She set an indefatigable example, working all the hours of day and night, and never, so my father says, having been happier or more fulfilled.

Occasionally, she met the trains carrying refugee children, the *Kindertransporte* (children's transports) from Germany and Austria. Most of that work was handled by others, but her committee sometimes took responsibility for the older children, the sixteen- and seventeen-year-olds who had only just been squeezed into a transport along with the three- and four- and five-year-olds clutching their teddy bears, disoriented, tearful, frightened. These older children were frightened too, had more idea of what was happening, and were more realistic about their chances of ever seeing their parents again. Their suffering was often acute, and for many of them it was impossible ever to make a go of it in a foreign land. But not for all. Not for this man . . .

My grandmother had been at Liverpool Street Station when the boat-train from Harwich came in. She was meeting some teenage children. Among them was the man in the drugstore.

As he looked at me, he remembered my grandmother's face from fifty-two years earlier.

I am not like my grandmother. But I have a *look* of her, and he never forgot her face, as she came to greet him, gave him his first English money, and made efforts to take care of him.

That was not the end of the story, strange enough as the coincidence was. He told me he had gone to a hostel, and tried to find a job, without success. So he had decided to go to a camp to train for emigration to Palestine (as it then was). The camp was run by my father.

My father became an ardent Zionist in his early twenties. He had given up his degree at Cambridge to go and work on a kibbutz. His parents, good middle-class Jews, originally from Germany, had not spoken to him or written to him for three years. They had sent him to public school, to Cambridge University – he was throwing away his chances, and all for some ridiculous romantic notion. They wanted him to be an English gentleman, and he simply would not oblige. How the words of that headmaster of his school must have rung in his ears, and stung his pride, when he heard him say: 'It would be so nice to have a boy with an English name getting an award for once . . .' So often the Jews won the scholarships in those days – and he felt the slight prejudice.

My grandmother contacted him on his kibbutz early in 1938. 'You were right,' she wrote, 'I was wrong!' – an admission she made all too rarely. 'Come back and help us with the refugees.' He returned, ran training camps, and taught at schools set up for refugee children. He, who could speak the faultless unaccented English of the upper-classes, as well as the German of the old aristocracy, was able to negotiate with the Gestapo who never guessed he was a Jew. He gave the young people they rescued a welcome in German that they understood, and also greeted them in the English that they would soon learn. He gave refugees a sense of purpose.

My new friend in the drugstore in Boston spoke of his

own experience, in such glowing words about my grand-mother and father that I blushed with joy and pride. In Europe in the 1930s, his world had increasingly narrowed as the war had come closer. He described to me the loss of schooling, and the loss of language, the loss of parents. But he had survived, and come to Boston to be with other family members who had not perished. He was deeply grateful, religious, deeply devout. After this occasion, he never again spoke to me about his experiences, almost embarrassed by opening up to a strange woman whose family had once been so important to him.

I returned to my apartment, and at once rang my father. I told him the story. For the first time in my life, I heard him weep.

'It was something to be thankful for,' he eventually said. 'We never managed much. And the best, the most modest, the simple people such as my schoolteacher relations, they perished. But he survived. Thank God . . .' And he put the phone down.

It is now 1995. My father is eighty-two and I am forty-five. He never weeps. But he has told me of experiences of the holocaust, both in England and Germany. More recently, my mother has recounted what happened to her very large family, of whom few survived. From them both I have some idea of what those months and years before 1939 were like. 'We felt so inadequate,' my father said, 'we helped so few . . .'

My entire childhood was coloured by the experience of knowing and living with refugees, either immediately, as with my mother and her parents, or less closely, through my grandmother's work and contacts, or simply because of the area we lived in. Yet, despite my familiarity with the refugees, I have found it astonishingly difficult to get a grip on what had actually happened to them. That is not to suggest that I do not know the historical facts – obviously I do. How those facts are interpreted, however, is another matter. As a teenager I, and no doubt many others, found that the only way to come to terms with the holocaust was to listen to people's stories and to read their recollections. Yet, until recently, memories of victims were somehow regarded as not being *proper* history. They were too close to it, they weren't analytical, they couldn't see the whole picture, they were too emotional.

It seemed extraordinary to me that the memories of those who witnessed the horror should not be taken seriously. Could it be that they were so prone to exaggeration that they would invent mass-murder? Or were they, as many people had thought before the war when the persecution in Germany had begun, simply whingeing about minor problems?

In his important study of the holocaust and the liberal imagination, Tony Kushner addressed this issue:

> The first major historians of the Holocaust, Leon Poliakov in France and Gerald Reiglinger in England, were in close agreement that the voice of the Jews themselves would be used sparingly in their narratives. . . . Both . . . were aware of the incredulity of their audience . . . 'authenticity' was thus required and it was assumed that evidence from the victim was somehow less persuasive and objective; it was somehow softer than material emanating from the prosecutor.

Kushner explains that many testimonies from those who experienced or witnessed events in the camps were simply not considered firm historical evidence. He points out that: 'A form of machismo was at work, shown in the preference for perpetrator evidence and a concentration on the "hard" world of the male mass murderers.'

Nowadays, the history of the holocaust is viewed differently, but it took many years for the evidence of eye-witnesses to be given serious credence. For me, it is only through the eyes of the victims themselves that we, who came after them, can ever begin to understand what they went through. I remember, for example, a French Jewess describing how she was rounded up in the Hippodrome d'Hiver. The heat was blazing and the prisoners were without food or drink. People dropped at her feet. One man drank his own urine to survive. I could *feel* her suffering. Claude Lanzmann's film *Shoah* relies on eyewitness accounts, often spoken with heart-rending hesitation. Steven Spielberg's *Schindler's List* has many memorable images. Words often evoke more than pictures, and if we are to have any grasp of what this kind of suffering is about, we need to sit with those who experienced it, even when they cannot speak about it coherently, or, indeed, speak at all.

Despite all of this, it is very hard to come to terms with the suffering. For many years, I refused to review books on the holocaust, on the basis that I had no specialised or personal knowledge. The truth was that I found reading holocaust material over and over again profoundly depressing, and extraordinarily difficult. The sheer size of the operation of destroying the Jews of Europe – the efficiency, the viciousness, the lack of mercy – is revolting. It is also almost incomprehensible. Going to Yad Vashem, the holocaust memorial in Jerusalem, gives one something of the sense of scale, but for me it is too horrifying to be properly moving. Other monuments, such as the memorial to the Paris Jews at the point of their deportation on the banks of the Seine, leave one without a sense of scale, but give me a poignancy, a sharpness of emotion, without excess of horror. Ironically, in the face of the holocaust, I find myself with no words. And, as I get older, I am more aware that the reason I find the holocaust so difficult is that I have not yet come to terms with what happened to my family before my birth.

By an accident of time I was not there.

Reading and hearing of the victims, fifty years afterwards, affected me deeply. Yet it has been argued that the Jews of England, safe and snug where they were, did not care. Richard Bolchover, for instance, in his *British Jewry and the Holocaust*, examined the published statements of the leaders of Anglo-Jewry between 1939 and 1945, set them against later assertions that they did not know what was happening to their co-religionists, and makes a convincing *prima facie* case that the bulk of Anglo-Jewry was indifferent to the plight of the Jews of Europe.

In his memoirs, published in 1960, Professor Selig Brodetsky, then President of the Board of Deputies, the representative body of Anglo-Jewry, claimed that he had not known what was going on in Europe until the Nuremberg trials. Yet the *Jewish Chronicle* had carried reports throughout the war years, and it seems incredible that he had not read them. *The Times* had described German intentions, towards Jews and others, in December 1939, in an article entitled 'A Slow Road to Extermination'. And on 30 June, 1942, every newspaper reported that over a million Jews had been massacred since the beginning of the war. Furthermore, Arthur Liebehenschel replaced the notorious Rudolf Hoess as commandant of Auschwitz precisely because the mass murders of Auschwitz became known to the world in 1943, and the BBC broadcast material directly from Auschwitz carried via the Polish resistance movement. Yet there was no public protest about events in Europe until October 1942. My father tells me that although people knew something of the atrocities, they were simply unable to comprehend them.

As A.J. Sherman puts it most poignantly in his book on the response of Britain to the refugees from the Third Reich between 1933 and 1945, in which he does not castigate the Anglo-Jewish community, as Bolchover does:

> The refugee crisis brought painfully into consciousness the ambiguities of assimilation, especially in a country as relatively insular and monochromatic as Great Britain in the pre-war period; and their anxiety over the number and conspicuousness of the refugees, their sheer foreignness, the likelihood that they would stir not only anti-semitism but anti-German feeling still latent from the First World War, was shared by government officials as well as Jewish communal leaders.

The Anglo-Jewish community was inclined to keep its head down and to show almost obsequious gratitude when non-Jews showed concern, offered help, or expressed their shared outrage at events in Nazi Germany.

I can remember, however, my grandmother talking with bitterness of the indifference of some English Jews, and of their unwillingness to take Jewish refugees into their homes. Yet she had some understanding of that attitude, if little sympathy with it. For the Anglo-Jewish community, inasmuch as it held attitudes in common at all, believed in liberal democracy. It felt that it should make its life alongside, and not apart from, the rest of the population, and that living with the British in harmony was a goal much to be desired. It also believed that things would generally get better for humanity, and therefore the Jews, and it certainly did not want to accommodate the idea that the opposite might be the case. Those who had lived in Britain for more than the previous fifty years had seen the emancipation of the Jews alongside the removal of disadvantages for Catholics and non-conformists, bearing out their beliefs and hopes in tangible improvements in status, acceptance and treatment by their fellow subjects.

It is, perhaps, this fragile acceptance which made some English-born Jews so unwilling to help, or to protest. Perhaps they feared that public outcry, or the admission of a flood of conspicuously foreign refugees into insular, uncosmopolitan England, would create, or re-awaken, suspicion and hostility towards the Anglo-Jewish community. The fear of being noticed led to very little campaigning for fellow Jews in Europe. There was a war on. British Jews must be seen to be 'British', involved in the war effort, and not diverted by uniquely Jewish concerns. Yet, at the same time, the records of the Central British Fund suggest a huge effort on behalf of those trapped in Nazi Germany as the war started, and pressure on the Home Office to let more people in, which may, at the time, have seemed all that one could do. Indeed, the estimates of the numbers of refugees allowed in, as given to parliament, seem to have been consistently undercounted; the home secretary announced 49,500 in October 1939 but the total number was probably nearer 70,000. Perhaps the officials knew when to keep quiet and, more importantly, were more kindly disposed than later critics have suggested. Even if many British Jews were keeping their heads down, there were many non-Jews who behaved magnificently.

Among these is the redoubtable Eleanor Rathbone, MP, who tried to persuade the government to appoint a committee for refugees which could formulate an international refugee policy. Other MPs shouted her down, hostile to the last to giving money for refugees when there were so many unemployed at home, but she persisted. She wrote memorably in the *Manchester Guardian* in May 1938: 'If the

British government feels itself too weak to be courageous, at least it might show itself merciful.' As a result of her efforts, an all-party committee of MPs was established in the wake of the arrival of the first of the child refugees. Captain Victor Cazalet chaired it; Eleanor Rathbone was the secretary. Meanwhile Sir Wyndham Deedes, another non-Jew, had joined Viscount Samuel in chairing the Movement for the Care of Children from Germany, and they organised with immense dedication the emigration and allocation of the children, in co-operation with over a hundred local committees. Lord Baldwin, the former prime minister, appealed to the nation on behalf of child refugees in particular, and launched the Lord Baldwin Fund for Refugees in 1938. When *The Times* opened its list for the subscription for Lord Baldwin's appeal, it emphasised that 'private charity cannot take, and must not be asked to take, the responsibilities which belong to the government'.

More ordinary but no less appealing examples include people such as the British passport control officer in Berlin, Captain F.E. Foley, and the consul-general in Frankfurt, R.T. Smallbones, now rarely remembered by the Jewish community for their sympathy and acts of generosity in issuing passports to Jews and other non-Aryans to protect them from brutal Gestapo interrogation and the concentration camps.

On 26 February, 1995, tribute was paid to Frank Foley in an article in the *Sunday Times*, entitled 'Jews honour the British Schindler' by Rajeev Syal and Tim Rayment, following suggestions that Foley be elected one of the 'righteous gentiles', commemorated in an avenue of trees at Yad Vashem, in Jerusalem. Frank Foley died unrecognised in 1958. Why was his work not recognised until 1994? A.J. Sherman writes warmly of both Foley and Smallbones in his excellent history of the period, *Island*

Refuge. Their activities were by no means unknown. Hubert Pollack, a German Jew involved with Foley in helping British intelligence in Berlin before the war, said, 'There is no word of Jewish gratitude towards this man which could be exaggerated'. Also working with Foley and Pollack was Wilfrid Israel, a Jewish businessman who remained in Germany until a few days before the war, and who provided money for bribes to the Gestapo officers.

At the Eichmann trial in 1961 one of the witnesses called Foley 'one of the greatest among the nations of the world'. Yet he did not feel he had done enough. When the concentration camps were liberated he wrote to a friend:

> We are now reading about and seeing photographs of those places, the names of which were so well known to us in the years before the war. Now the people here finally believe that the stories of 1938–39 were not exaggerated. Looking back, I feel grateful that our little office in Tiergartenstrasse was able to assist some – far too few – to escape in time.

Foley and Smallbones, with colleagues elsewhere in Germany and Austria, issued over 50,000 passports. Their kindness and actions beyond the call of duty, against declared government policy, contrasts markedly with the deliberate bureaucratic delays put in the way of would-be emigrants by the United States authorities.

Accounts by Karen Gershon and others of the children's transports which arrived from Germany, Austria and Czechoslovakia have provided many other examples of acts of kindness by British non-Jews. Two of my rabbinic colleagues came on children's transports, and one was helped by his hosts, a Christian clergyman and his wife, to to keep up his Judaism. There are countless examples of similar tolerance of a religion very different from anything the hosts had seen before. These children were desperately worried about their parents in increasingly Nazi-occupied Europe, and many received, via the Red Cross, last letters simply saying 'Pray for us . . .'. In a foreign country, powerless, everything deeply unfamiliar, these children must have suffered enormously. Some of their hosts dealt with these emotions, these very real concerns and fears, with great tenderness. These are the people who were kind, who wanted to help, who felt they had a human duty towards other human beings.

Outside Britain, of course, there were many others who helped Jews fleeing from the Nazis. In Germany, Austria and Czechoslovakia, Quakers led much of the rescue work. Many Hungarian Jews were saved by Raoul Wallenberg, a Swedish diplomat, who was later captured by the Russians and disappeared. Almost all the Danish Jews were rescued – among others the Danish royal family wore yellow stars alongside the Jews, and cleverly moved them to safety in neutral Sweden when it became clear the Nazis meant to round up the Jews.

There are examples of real heroes, such as the German communist Willi Marker who was already imprisoned in a concentration camp at Sachsenhausen, and who in 1940 found himself on barrack duty in a Jewish block, where the inmates were:

> upon orders from the camp administration subjected to indescribable tortures. . . . Since he, despite warnings, did everything in his power to ease the sufferings of the doomed men, he was replaced with a professional criminal, transferred to a punitive outfit and hanged in the washroom a few nights later.

While some of these heroes have been almost forgotten, Oskar Schindler has been immortalised twice, in Thomas Keneally's Booker Prize-winning *Schindler's Ark*, and in Steven Spielberg's *Schindler's List*.

Schindler, for reasons which never became clear, rescued some twelve hundred Jews by getting them to work at his enamel plant at Plaszow, which saved them from death in the camps. That was true heroism; yet he probably did not feel like a hero. Perhaps he could not stand the destruction; maybe this way he could be the great man, revered by all the people who owed their lives to him, when in his previous (and indeed in later) life he was unsuccessful in business and in his personal relationships. He was not honoured in Germany until long after the war. It is as if the Germans in embarrassment and shame wanted to forget that there had been even a few who had resisted from within the Nazi machine. While compensation was being arranged for those who had lost education or property through having to leave as refugees, while support came for the widows and children of those who rebelled against Hitler in the July plot of 1944, Schindler received no recognition and no help from the state.

Other aspects of the aftermath of the holocaust are difficult to understand or accept. If Tom Bower's *Paperclip Conspiracy* is to be believed, and no one challenged it, there are those whom the Allies helped to escape trial for war crimes in exchange for their skills and knowledge. The classic example of that is Werner von Braun, the rocket scientist, who ended up in America and immortalised in Tom Lehrer's song:

... once the rockets are up, who cares where they come down?
That's not my department, says Wernher von Braun.

Nor, in his view, was the indescribable torture of those used in rocket experiments and in slave labour to make them. There have been endless questions about the disappearance, and occasional sightings of, Josef Mengele, the vicious experimenter on concentration camp inmates, and several other major players. I still find it shocking that any of these men escaped trial. Equally shocking is evidence which came out at the trials that so few of the guards, torturers and soldiers actually questioned the orders they were given. It is that, I think, more than anything which makes it hard for me to go to Germany. It is not that I believe that everyone there now had something to do with the horrors. Plainly they did not. It is the normalisation of the destruction of six million people that still makes me appalled, and wonder whether that kind of dehumanisation could happen a second time.

I find it difficult to come to grips with the reaction – in Germany, France, Israel and the world – to some of the perpetrators of the horrors. The show trial of Eichmann may have been necessary for the Israeli psyche and for the survivors of his barbarity, but one wonders whether it was genuinely a fair trial. Hannah Arendt wrote in disparaging terms about the need to have such a trial at all. Gitta Sereny who, as a young woman, had worked with children who had been in concentration camps, decided to interview one of the commandants of the extermination camps. She talked to Franz Stangl about what he thought about what he had done. Only by interviewing him could she begin to understand.

More recently there has been the trial of so-called 'Ivan the Terrible', John Demjanjuk, or 'Ivan the not-so-terrible', as the authors of *The Holocaust for Beginners* describe him. He was acquitted, but not before many questions were asked. What was the point of trying him? Can witnesses to events fifty years earlier be reliable? How can they forget? But faces do change ... Was the trial to do with Jewish vengefulness? Is it time, as it was said, for the Jews to 'forget' the holocaust?

In the debates in the House of Lords about whether to try Nazi war criminals now living in Britain in British courts (though their alleged crimes were committed elsewhere and they were not British at the time), one of the themes that has recurred is the Jewish desire for revenge. Many people think that it is now time to forgive and forget. Yet Jews as a *whole* cannot ever forgive anybody. Only the *victims* can forgive the perpetrators, and most of them are dead. Otherwise forgiveness is for God, and not for man – a Jewish view very different from that of Christianity.

Nor do I personally think we should ever forget, nor can we, for the memory of the people who died is still very much alive in our minds. Indeed, we must use the history of the holocaust to try to prevent such a thing ever happening again. The generation directly affected is now dying out, and the important question has to be *how* the holocaust is remembered, not whether we *should* remember, or whether we should continue to hold war crimes trials.

Forgiveness is not the issue. Those who wish can ask the forgiveness of God, for themselves or for the sins of their fathers. For most of us it is remembering that is important, but remembering so that we can use the memory constructively, and so that those of us who still find it so hard to come to terms with it, can somehow make the memory alive to our children. It must to be a lesson for all of us about what can happen when a dictatorship flourishes and human life is no longer important, whether it be in Cambodia, Bosnia, or in Nazi-occupied Europe.

A wider view of how the holocaust should be regarded may not always suit the Israeli government's position. Israel has traded on its defence of the Jews post-holocaust. It has sometimes been criticised for becoming 'Speaker for the Jewish Dead' and using 'the holocaust as a perfect ideological justification for its less than benign policies and actions in the Middle East' (*The Holocaust for Beginners*). While many people, both Jews and non-Jews, would challenge this analysis, it is in fact a legitimate, if simplistic, view of how the holocaust has been used. One wonders whether legislation allowing the trial of alleged Nazi war criminals in Britain was passed because of Israel's and America's belief in the possibility that some were living in Britain, as well as British concern.

Reactions to the trial of Klaus Barbie, 'the butcher of Lyon', in 1987, are difficult to encompass. I felt distanced from many of the French who had believed Barbie was too old and sick to stand trial. His age must be an irrelevance, for he had been vicious beyond belief, as had his henchman Paul Touvier, who has since stood trial (in 1992) and been acquitted by French judges, who decided that he should not face trial for crimes against humanity. I was sickened by Barbie and Touvier's delight in cruelty, which was unfamiliar and frightening. Annette Kahn is head of the political desk at the French weekly, *Le Point*, and wrote her book, *Why My Father Died*, as a combination of factual reporting of the Barbie trial and recording her realisation of what had happened to her father and his comrades. Robert Kahn was a Jew and a Resistance leader. He was killed in one of Barbie's last massacres on 17 August, 1944, just a few days before the French liberation, in one of the last frenzied outbreaks of Nazi violence before the retreat from Lyon. Accounts from Barbie's victims of what they suffered and saw – young girls raped with Gestapo truncheons, ten-year-old boys kicked to death, a girl's spine broken with a mallet – are terrifying. None of it is new. Certainly, by this stage in my life, I have read it and heard it all before. I have, nevertheless, been greatly influenced by *Why My Father Died*, which is without exaggeration and does not set out to shock. Sometimes I think that domestication of the horror is necessary for us to be able to comprehend it, yet this domestication is virtually impossible.

I am left, as are many of my contemporaries, with an ambivalence. A part of me wants to read everything, know everything, understand everything, apportion blame for everything. Another part of me knows that we must learn to live again and use the memory for good purposes. The Barbie trial is an example of this. It sits at odds with the French still unable to come to terms with their collaboration with the Nazis; their honouring of the Resistance but not the victims of Nazi horror; President Mitterrand's government professed that Petain's government was an aberration, yet it continued to send a wreath for his grave on the anniversary of his death.

Annette Kahn's account of Barbie's activities is one of hundreds published over the last few years. The field of holocaust studies is growing rapidly, particularly in Israel and the United States. There is almost an 'industry' of holocaust memorial, which tries to stop the world ever forgetting. There is something peculiar, I think, about people making a career of digging out details of so vile a history, when they were not even born when it happened. It is the nature of historical research, yet it has the capacity to become obsessional, an obsession I think I sometimes share. Yet, they are right that we must not forget, and should use any legitimate occasion, such as the recent fiftieth anniversary of the liberation of Auschwitz, to remember.

*

Germany was my family's home for centuries. My mother's family in particular was well-integrated into the wider community of Heilbronn-am-Neckar, and my paternal grandfather had many Christian friends with whom he had been a prisoner of war in France in the First World War. Of course, there was anti-semitism – it would be ludicrous to pretend otherwise. Germany was not alone, either – there had been horrific pogroms in Russia and Poland from the early 1880s, and German Jews were shocked by what happened to their co-religionists in the east, although they often despised them, too. They thought them peasants and uncivilised. The massacres in the Pale of Settlement (the area on the Russian–Polish border where Jews were allowed to live) were legendary. Jews fled Poland and Russia to America and Western Europe, and it is likely that the Aliens' Act was passed in Britain in 1905 to stop waves of downtrodden Eastern European Jews coming into the country after the Kishinev massacres of 1903 and 1905. Even my beloved Ireland, no friend to anti-semitism despite the powerful Catholic church (which is always blamed for Polish anti-semitism), had a pogrom in Limerick in 1904. Poland, Russia and Lithuania were no strangers to bursts of anti-semitic outrage, and the Cossacks were well-known for it. There is a considerable amount of photographic material recording injuries to and deaths of Jews in Polish and Russian pogroms between 1880 and 1910.

The holocaust, the Final Solution, was different. It was systematic. It was not religious – it was racial. To understand the intellectual and social changes which led to the rise of Nazism, psychologists are asking questions about the German psyche in the first years of this century and looking for earlier signs of a belief in German superiority. Sociologists are examining the social composition of

Germany in the aftermath of its abject defeat in the First World War and the effects of starvation and inflation in the 1920s. Anthropologists are studying eugenics theory. Although many leading thinkers of the Weimar republic were interested in eugenics and were prepared to advocate that poor families have fewer children in order to improve the state of the 'Volk', they never demanded that it be so. Some believed that reduction in family size would alleviate the worst of the problems of extreme poverty at the height of inflation. Others argued, along the lines of *rassenhygiene*, 'racial hygiene', that reduced families for the poor and the 'defective' would improve the nature of the population, and that in itself would be good for German military and industrial strength. The 1933 Nazi law making sterilisation of 'hereditarily diseased offspring' compulsory, may have been a natural progression from the 1932 Prussian Bill for voluntary eugenic sterilisation, but the distinction between compulsory and voluntary sterilisation is a critical one. Many German churchmen objected to the sterilisations, and to later euthanasia programmes for the 'unfit'. Few objected to the deporting of the Jews.

For historians of ideas, the answer may lie in German unification in the 1870s, Bismarckian thought, and the operas of Wagner. Wagner's anti-semitism was well-known throughout his life, through his conversations with friends and his political and philosophical writings. The virulence of his anti-semitic feeling has led to long rows in Israel over whether the Israel Philharmonic should play any of his works (it does!), whether Jews should go to and listen to his operas, and whether his reputation as a great artist should be diminished. Wagner's anti-semitism was an integral part of his revolutionary thinking. It was as much a part of his belief in the new Germany, in rescuing the German spirit from the bourgeois, commercial interests that controlled it in the 1840s, as was his belief in uniting against contemporary political powers. His thought moved from a romantic form of socialism, to monarchism and back again. His nationalism, and his faith that freedom would be engineered by the new art and literature, were passionately held.

Wagner's view that Judaism was a corrupting force is clear in his 'Judaism in Music', in which he slated 'the Judaisation of modern art'. He believed the public were subverted in their artistic tastes by 'the busy fingers of the Jew'. He developed a concept of the 'folk soul' of the German people, to which the 'folk soul' of the Jews was infinitely inferior. In his first anti-semitic salvo, however, he did not develop his racial theories of Jewish inferiority. That was to come, in line with the new anti-semitism of the 1870s, for part of which Wagner was arguably to blame. He attacked Mendelssohn as a paradigm of the Jew's incapacity to take part in the culture of his own environment in a truly creative way. In so doing, he characterised all Jews as incapable of rising to great heights of artistic accomplishment. He extended this to the great poet Heine, and to the journalist Ludwig Boerne. This suggests that Wagner did not think religion made them inferior, for two of the three had been baptised. It was rather their racial origin and Jewish culture – something that they were born with and carried despite baptism – a lack of appreciation for the finest, the highest, art, a tendency towards the second-rate.

One can find traces of Wagner's racial theorising in the plots and even in the music of his operas. We could, of course, laugh it off. All those Germanic figures, larger than life and blonder than blonde, those mythical characters who show the superiority of the German spirit over all others ... why on earth should we take them seriously?

Indeed, early critics of the *Ring*, none of them Jewish, thought the plots ridiculous, with all that misplaced honour and ill-fated love, and rubbished Wagner's work at the time. However, ridiculous or not, there is a sinister undertext in the *Ring* – a pan-German revival, old Germanic values, what it means to have a truly German spirit – that is decidedly uncomfortable when it comes from the man who wrote 'Judaism in Music'. In the caricaturing in the *Ring* of Alberich and Mime, and in *Meistersinger* the hapless Beckmesser, the fierce critic of German true art (and modelled on Wagner's own critic, Hanslick, whom Wagner believed to have Jewish blood), there are supposedly stereotypical 'Jewish' qualities. His heroes were the large, strong, hearty characters of German myth. His bad guys are small, mean, dirty ... and that was how he, and other anti-semites of his time, caricatured the Jews.

After a concert in 1863, Wagner complained: 'To my horror, I saw almost the whole place ... occupied by Jews.' Yet, he did have a few Jewish friends, and their unwillingness to attack his theories about Jewish inferiority, and their adulation of the man despite his revolting views, is extremely surprising. Did these newly assimilated Jews of the nineteenth century, many of whom were converts for convenience, and apparently also mildly anti-semitic, have no pride? Modern Jews may hate their feebleness, but their age was so different from ours that we cannot judge them according to our lights. Jew-baiting was not uncommon in the 1860s and 1870s, but in accepting and developing racial theories, Wagner is at least partly responsible for the vastly increased anti-semitism that ultimately bore its fruit in the Jewish annihilation in the 1940s. His views and music were the theme songs for a new anti-semitic movement based on false theories of 'race'.

Under the Third Reich, Wagner epitomised all things German and un-Jewish. His music was even played in the concentration camps – a horrifying and bizarre expression of Nazi ideology. It is small wonder, then, that some Jews, and I am among them, have difficulty with the *Ring*. We could refuse ever to listen to it. Yet all we would achieve is cutting ourselves off from a sublime musical experience. We could listen and pretend that the music has nothing to do with the man's thinking. Yet this is hard to swallow, given the intrinsic message of the *Ring* cycle.

I love the music. I respond to it in an almost animal way. Yet I can sense within it a rage against me – against my Jewishness – probably because of what I know of the man. I do not go to Wagner at Covent Garden or the Coliseum, though I am a keen opera buff. I have tapes of the *Ring*, but I listen only by myself, in the car. I am ambivalent. It would be ludicrous to suggest that Jews should not listen to Wagner, but I do think that they, and everyone else for that matter, should understand how much of his foul views have made it into his words and music.

If adults should be aware of Wagner's views when they listen to his music, how much should children, particularly German children, he told about his anti-semitism and influence on Nazi thought? As the casualties of tribalism and nationalism increase – in the former Yugoslavia, Northern Ireland and elsewhere – the way we teach our children about racial theories and their consequences is crucial. I remain, perhaps understandably, nervous of the way German children are taught about the holocaust. They are taken to the concentration camps, which Germany has maintained and treated with immense respect. Yet when the children arrive, they write graffiti on the walls. Many of them will have seen *Schindler's List*, all will have been told something about the holocaust, but somehow the horror has not sunk in.

I was appalled when taken by the BBC to record an introduction to the first act of *Siegfried* at the Valhalla, a monument to German greatness built by the mad Ludwig II near Regensburg, in south Germany. The monument is a Grecian temple, with an entrance made to resemble the approach to a shrine at the end of a pilgrimage. In the 'shrine' are busts of great Germans – of course of pure 'Aryan' blood. It is full of forgotten bishops, and, naturally enough, there is Wagner. The first bust of a Jew, Albert Einstein, was only included some ten years ago. There have been so many famous German Jews and half-Jews – scientists, musicians, writers, philosophers, yet none is represented. Young parents and children visit this shrine to German greatness. Do they make links with Wagnerian thought? Has the lesson of the holocaust really been learned? As I returned from filming. I travelled by train to the airport. I was on edge, as I always am when on my own in Germany, and particularly when I am on a train. Ludicrous though it is, irrational though I know it to be, I cannot help thinking of the trains to the concentration camps. These are the same lines, though not, as I sit in comfort, the same trains.

In Germany I always feel a certain discomfort with non-Jews if they are old enough to have been involved, though I count several young Germans among my good friends. I am uncomfortable because I want to ask what they were doing during the war, and because in some ways I feel it is my country, too, though I could not be less at home. I look like them. I am their shape and size, buxom and blonde and Aryan-looking. I am also uncomfortable because sometimes, as during the Jewish-Christian Bible Week in which I used to take part as a rabbinic student, in Bendorf, near Koblenz, I feel I am being used. So few Jews now live in Germany, and those that do have such mixed feelings about it that I couldn't help believing that I was being imported to let the Christians experience the dialogue. It is important, of course, that there should be dialogue, yet I am more and more aware that Germany lost my presence when it made my mother's life unbearable. She left, but many of my family perished.

When I go to Frankfurt, I stand in the Jewish Museum in the Rothschild Palais and gaze at the wall of names of the Frankfurt Jews who perished. Many, many of them are my relatives. My father's family were from Frankfurt, and although many left before the First World War and others escaped as refugees in the 1930s, the list still goes on and on: Schwabs, Ellerns, Japhets, Feuchtwangers ... The first time I went I could not bear to go with non-Jews, except for one close non-Jewish friend. We were at a conference. Five Jews and one gentile set out together. We looked. We felt sick. Later we went out. To a man and a woman, we chose to eat at an Italian restaurant. Not German.

The monuments at Frankfurt and around the world are powerful reminders of the holocaust. There were enormous queues in Germany and elsewhere to see *Schindler's List*, a film which is completely honest about the holocaust, the use of poison gas and the destruction of six million Jews. Yet the Germans are still ambivalent about how they approach the holocaust with their young people, and German textbooks often gloss over some of the worst features. They even suggest different interpretations from those we would commonly find elsewhere in Europe. For instance, intellectuals in Germany were divided in the mid-

1980s by the *Historikerstreit*, 'historical battle', which came to a head in 1986. Ernst Nolte, holding one of the most extreme positions, argued that the Nazi extermination of the Jews resulted from the Nazi fear of becoming victims of the extermination policies of the bolsheviks. The gulag was the original and Auschwitz a copy, which makes the Nazis less blameworthy. (The assumption is that more fuss has been made about Hitler's holocaust than about Stalin's gulag.) The holocaust only came about, so those who hold this view argue, because a whole variety of other events conspired to make it essential to destroy the Jews. If other countries had taken them in, it would not have been necessary. If other countries had cared about the Jews, they would have been given homes. There was no original intention to destroy the Jews.

The view promulgated in Israel at Yad Vashem and elsewhere is the opposite – the original intention of the Nazis was to destroy the Jews, it was central to their thinking and to their success in mustering people to their cause, and it was bred of age-old anti-semitism rooted in the Church with its cry of the Jews being the killers of Jesus Christ. Nazism gave it the modern twist of arguing on grounds of race rather than religion.

Until recently, most educational material on the holocaust came from the United States, and tended to bring out the horror and challenge children to make parallels with other forms of prejudice. In Europe, there are additional questions. Questions in Italy about renewed right-wing successes (Mussolini had collaborated in sending Jews to their destruction). Questions in France about collaboration (and also resistance). Questions in Britain about the British National Party.

No one doubts that teaching the holocaust is fraught with difficulties, but almost everyone agrees that it *should* be taught. One of the obvious reasons is the increasing sense, political debate notwithstanding, that Britain is part of Europe. The holocaust took place on European soil. Its perpetrators were German, the parents and grandparents of Germans today. Their great-grandchildren and British schoolchildren might meet on an exchange. 'What were you doing in the war, Opa?' is a question German grand-children might ask.

There are questions for British children to ask, too. Although Britain was at war with Germany, she did little to prevent the exterminations, despite the appeals of Jews in this country as the news of the Final Solution reached our shores.

The BBC omitted to mention a crucial part of foreign secretary Anthony Eden's report to the Commons in December, 1942: 'Germany is carrying into effect Hitler's often repeated intention to exterminate the Jewish people.' A curious logic led the BBC management to claim that mention of the plight of the Jews might inflame anti-Jewish feelings in Britain. The BBC was to limit itself to reporting 'the facts ... of Jewish persecution', but there was to be no 'propaganda'.

British children might also ask why it was that there was such official procrastination over the request to bomb the death factories at Auschwitz, and why, when it was finally bombed in August 1944, the synthetic rubber plant took the brunt of the attack, rather than the crematoria. Children also need to understand that not only Jews were killed. In addition to the six million Jewish men, women and children who were murdered, at least an equal number of non-Jews also perished – not in the heat of battle, by military siege, aerial bombardment, or the harsh conditions of modern war, but by deliberate, planned murder.

All this must be set in a context of the increasing extent

of holocaust denial, which has become almost academically acceptable. The arch-villain was Paul Rassinier, a French schoolteacher and socialist who had himself been an inmate of Buchenwald. He used contradictions in the accounts of witnesses to cast doubt on the veracity of the whole history of the holocaust, and argued that witnesses relying on memory (for they could not have written much down in the camps), could not be wholly accurate in every regard. He also invented a numbers game to prove that six million people could not have died. Although it was easy to counter his arguments, they were nevertheless taken up by all sorts of people and political groups, and have kept on reappearing ever since Rassinier's death in 1967. The arguments are regularly reiterated in Britain and in France, as well as America, where there is a strong revisionist school, and where one of the most outspoken of the revisionists also designs systems for death chambers in state prisons.

The gradual move of holocaust denial into academic respectability on campus after campus in America has no real parallel in Britain, thank God. This denial seems bizarre to us, but has horrifying implications. Deborah Lipstadt, in her excellent volume, *Denying the Holocaust*, tells the story. In 1991, a Californian called Bradley Smith attempted to place an advertisement denying the holocaust in college newspapers across America, gaining considerable publicity when many colleges rejected him. In the angry backlash which followed his claims, Smith suggested that the universities were being politically correct at the expense of the truth. Universities, rising to the bait, began to accept the advertisement. The University of Michigan went even further. The advertisement probably slipped through the net unread, but once it had appeared, while the business staff published a six-column apology, the editorial board tried to turn a mistake into an issue of principle. The editor-in-chief said he would have published it had it been his decision, and the university president, James Duderstadt, asserted that the newspaper had a long tradition of editorial freedom that had to be protected even when 'we disagree either with particular opinions, decisions, or actions'. He elevated holocaust denial to a matter of opinion, rather than fact, and the editorial board began to draw on the First Amendment, guaranteeing free speech. The First Amendment, however, is only a guarantee preventing *government* from interfering with an individual's or group's right to publish. It does not suggest that every journal has to print. Some universities – Harvard, Chicago and Tennessee among them – claimed that this had nothing to do with the First Amendment, but the damage had already been done. The lesson of deconstructionism in academic life, half-understood by so many, was that all opinions were valid. Nothing was more important than anything else. Facts were simply received opinions.

The results of the Roper Poll in April 1993, to determine the extent of Americans' knowledge of the holocaust, should not be wholly surprising. The question, clumsily phrased (which may partly explain the result), was: 'Do you think it is possible or impossible that the holocaust did not happen?' Twenty-two per cent of American adults and twenty per cent of American high-school students answered, 'Yes, it was possible'. A similar question posed in Britain and France evoked only seven per cent of yeses. Another poll, by Gallup, found eighty-three per cent of Americans saying it had happened, thirteen per cent that it had probably happened, and only four per cent doubting. The holocaust deniers' success in influencing mainstream thought is limited, but they have clearly made some headway in claiming it is a matter of opinion.

Few would deny the Second World War, or even the long ago Battle of Agincourt. Anti-semitic motives are clear. What is less clear, are the motives of those who give them house-room in magazines and colleges. The muddle and disregard for the truth are frightening. It is bizarre that holocaust denial should be a free speech issue in America. It is very dangerous. The fact that these arguments keep being used despite the evidence against them – the mass of Eastern European Jews transported to the east who never returned, films of the Nazi transports, human remains at some of the camps, reports of survivors and many photographs – means that the revisionists must have their own agenda.

In Britain, David Irving, arch-revisionist and holocaust denier, achieved a passing respectability in the *Sunday Times*. Respectable publishers, such as Sidgwick and Jackson of London, publish volumes which half apologise for the Nazis, such as Gordon Williamson's *The SS: Hitler's Instrument of Terror*, a tale which displays a fascination with Nazi uniforms and memorabilia. While Williamson condemns the Nazis' views, he almost admires their bravery, and includes sentences like 'maltreatment of the Jews was by no means a particularly German phenomenon'. That is true, but the Nazis brought it to new depths, and wanted to rid the world of Jews, a point Williamson does not make clear. And when he argues that 'some of the worst atrocities committed during this dark period in history were carried out by foreigners serving with the Germans', he forgets to mention that it was under German orders, however anti-semitic these 'foreigners' may have been.

Much of this revisionism reflects the increase in anti-semitism in Europe. It is particularly acute in the former Soviet bloc, but it is also noticeable in France, Italy, and

Britain. Though the holocaust looms large in my life for personal, family reasons, as well as because I am Jewish, its message beyond the Jewish community must be about the lengths to which unbridled racism can take people who are apparently nice, normal, kindly, civilised human beings. It is a message which needs to reach everyone, and which must be emphasised in teaching in schools and universities, in the texts of any memorials still to be erected, or commemorations still to come, so that everyone can see where hatred leads, and how the pain of it, the damage, is not only buried with the victims, but lives on with their grandchildren and great-grandchildren, who still cannot forget.

My maternal grandfather lived his last years convinced he was escaping his Nazi compatriots, who were chasing after him. That they never did is irrelevant. He was anguished, and fearful of his best friends and drinking companions. The memory of his terror does not evaporate – such memories must be used to better effect than remembering simply because one cannot forget.

The celebrations of the fiftieth anniversary of VE Day, and the marking of the opening and liberation of the camps, have had their effect on me. I am more able to talk about the holocaust, like those who are genuine survivors, many of whom are speaking about their experiences for the first time. I do not want my children to feel as muddled and angry and desperate as I did going to the Jewish museum in Frankfurt and as I do on trains in Germany, and when meeting elderly Germans. Such ambivalent emotions are not yet resolved, although I know that they do not make sense, and cut across everything important about the new Europe. I desperately hope my children will be clearer, and fairer, in their reactions to Germany and the Germans, but I do not believe they can be unless the holocaust is taught properly in schools in Britain, in Germany, in America, in Israel, and indeed all over the world. It must be taught alongside other genocides, particularly those taking place in our time. It is a lesson which matters.

3

My Yiddishe Mama:

Attitudes to women and family in Judaism

Many years ago, we were travelling up to see my parents in their cottage outside Cambridge. My father, then in his late sixties, had been unwell, and was just out of hospital. I made some chicken soup for him, the traditional remedy in Jewish folklore for all ills, put it in a plastic box with a tight-fitting lid, and packed the car. On the motorway we had to brake suddenly, and the soup slopped out of the 'secure' container, all over the back of the car. The smell never left the vehicle, and we ended up selling it because we could no longer stand the scent of rotting chicken soup, somehow more than a little symbolic of the incompetent Jewish mother.

The ideal of the Jewish mother who is always making chicken soup is long-established. Much has been written about this paragon of virtue. Jews are reported to have wonderful family lives, and jokes about Jewish mothers abound. Sophie Tucker used to sing of *My Yiddishe Mama*, as if she were a legendary figure – but in fact she exists. My yiddishe mama is a character of strong personality, who does not give in easily and has high expectations of her children, as well as protecting them fiercely and having them phenomenally well-organised. These women are the butts of jokes, including Philip Roth's devastating attack on Jewish mothers in *Portnoy's Complaint*: the final anti-mother insult is our hero's masturbation with a piece of liver, no doubt ready to make that well-known Eastern European Jewish dish, chopped liver. The Canadian-Jewish comedienne, Rita Rudner, jokes about her protective Jewish parents: when she went on the swing in the garden, she would merely sit in the seat while her parents ran backwards and forwards, in order to give her the sensation she was moving!

In the middle ages, when the men were obeying God's word and studying the Torah, the most important of the *mitzvot* (religious duties), it was the women who kept the home-fires burning, organised the family and earned a living sufficient to pay for all that they needed. The men sometimes worked too, but usually there was not time – study came first.

As far as we know, these women were relatively uneducated, until the modern age. Jewish law prevented them from learning Talmud, though they could study Torah and Mishnah, the first legal codification, completed probably around 200 CE. (Jews use the expression Common or Current Era instead of Anno Domini, the Year of Our Lord.) The women did not have great fluency in reading Hebrew or Aramaic; but, once they were living in Europe, they knew Yiddish. There were many Jewish story-books, sermons and prayers for Jewish women published in Yiddish, which was the language spoken by most Jewish communities throughout Eastern Europe until the last war, and in Germany until the nineteenth century. Yet the women were sufficiently educated to run businesses and to teach their daughters to read (the boys were educated by their fathers from a relatively early age, but the women encouraged literacy among their daughters).

These were formidable women, who usually bore the brunt of the difficulties of everyday life. The men would go to the synagogue and take part in study and public worship, while the women usually stayed at home. The separation of the sexes in the modern orthodox synagogue may go back to the courtyard of the women in Temple times in ancient Judea. The Second Temple was finally destroyed by the Romans in 70 CE, and was replaced by local synagogues, where exclusion of women from the main areas of the building came to be common. Women were increasingly discouraged from taking part in worship and study within synagogues, though not forbidden. Indeed, it may well be that the exclusion became established only gradually, for there is a discussion in the medieval period instigated by one of Rashi's disciples (Rabbi Solomon Isaac of Troyes in France, a famous eleventh century teacher and commentator) as to whether a woman might legitimately be called up to read from the Torah. The response, in the twelfth century, was that, according to the law, a woman might be called up, but that out of respect for the congregation, she should not be. The implication that she might show up some of the less educated men is not hard to draw. For the question to be asked, women must have been present in the synagogue.

Gradual change may have come about as a result of what was originally an exemption of women from carrying out the *mitzvot* for which there was a fixed time, which constituted the vast majority of the positive commandments. Most positive commandments suggest a particular time for the action concerned, such as morning prayers.

Women were presumably originally exempt in order to free them to carry out their domestic and family duties, taking care of small children and unweaned babies, whose demands were considerable. We must assume that what was meant as a liberation came to be a restriction, for single women, barren women and women whose children had all grown up were similarly exempt and later excluded from synagogue activity.

The domain of most women, gradually excluded from active synagogue life, was the family. Indeed, some of the apologists for the second-class status of women in rabbinic Judaism have argued that women were excluded from public synagogue activity because, when God had created them, he took one aspect of the human personality, a characteristic entitled *tseni'ut* in Hebrew, and wrote it large in woman. A famous verse from the prophet Micah (Micah 6:8) reads: 'And what does the Lord require of you, but to do justly, love mercy, and walk humbly with your God.' The verb for 'walking humbly' is precisely that which leads to the Hebrew word *tseni'ut*. But these apologists do not read it as 'humility'. Legitimately, they read it as 'privacy'. They argue that God created woman with a capacity and talent for privacy well in excess of anything men could achieve. Her privacy enabled her to have a rich spiritual life at home, alone. She did not need the hustle and bustle of congregational life; neither did she need to be part of the ten men required to have a full service. She could manage, because she was superior to men in her personal spirituality.

The response to this piece of apologetic has to be: 'Nice try!' It is good to read apologists allowing at least that women are superior to men in something, even if that assertion is made merely in order to justify the status quo. Were women even consulted about their personal spirituality? Was this arrangement, designed to allow them to carry out their domestic duties, really for their convenience, or did it just suit the men? What about those women who are no longer – or never were – embroiled in the sweet bliss of domesticity? Many questions have been left unanswered.

Being a religious, even if non-orthodox, Jewish woman, is fraught with difficulties. Religions the world over have not, on the whole, offered equal opportunities to women, and Judaism is no exception. In many religious systems, women are second-class citizens, their roles clearly defined and their lives seriously circumscribed. The nature of their religious longings and their spirituality has frequently been left to one side, whilst men debate theological issues such as whether angels can fit on to the head of a pin, or whether an inadvertent lump of butter, less than one sixtieth of the volume of the chicken, can be ignored when cooked with the chicken, or whether it renders the whole dish non-kosher. Of such issues, to lampoon only gently, can male theological discussion be made!

I exaggerate, but there is, without doubt, a conscious denigration of women in many religious faiths, to this very day. The debate about the ordination of women in the Church of England, which, to my great delight, resulted in women's ordination to the priesthood from 1994 onwards, illustrated all too clearly the low image of women. A past Bishop of London, Dr Graham Leonard, said that seeing a woman in the pulpit would make him wish to take her in his arms. An Anglican curate, interviewed in the *Independent* (23 February, 1987), said that 'you might as well ordain a pot of anchovy paste as a woman'. Meanwhile, some used theoretically theological arguments, arguing that Jesus had not had female disciples, and therefore a priest could not be female. Or, worse, quoted St Paul on the subject of Eve's sin:

> A woman must be a learner, listening quietly and with due submission. I do not permit a woman to be a teacher, nor must women dominate over man; she should be quiet. For Adam was created first and then Eve; and it was not Adam who was deceived; it was the woman, who yielding to deception, fell into sin.
>
> (1 Timothy 2:11–14)

Similarly, in a recent report on the position of women in Anglo-Jewry set up by Chief Rabbi Dr Jonathan Sacks, questions are left unanswered, and it emerges that Dr Sacks himself put the dampers on several conclusions, so that no immediate action to encourage women into religious observance would be allowed (*Jewish Chronicle*, 8 July, 1994). There is no active encouragement in orthodox Judaism of women-only services, using the Torah scroll, even though there is no theological objection. There is no will to look at the structure of services and establish a women's liturgy, particularly relating to childbirth and to a girl's maturation at twelve (the traditional age in Judaism), so that, with orthodoxy, the girl might be allowed to conduct the service and read from the scroll in the same way as the boys do at bar mitzvah. These are things which could fit within orthodox Judaism, and require none of the radical rethink which is an essential component of reform and liberal Judaism, with their abandonment of the traditional liturgy in the morning service when a man thanks God for not making him a woman and the woman simply thanks God for making her as she is. Though apologists argue that this is said because men have to perform all the religious duties for which there is a fixed time, and they are delighted to carry out God's will, while women are exempt, the reply to that has to be that women did not ask to be exempt and indeed are now largely excluded, which is clearly not for their benefit.

There are hundreds of examples of quotations from the religious texts of Judaism which are less than favourable to women, and often deliberately denigratory. One of the classics is this:

> Engage not in much gossip with women ... for he who engages in much gossip with women brings evil upon himself, neglects the Torah, and will in the end inherit Gehinnom.
>
> (Mishnah, Ethics of the Fathers: 1:5)

From the Mishnah, to the Babylonian Talmud (the development of the Mishnah with commentary and legal debate), to writings from about 500 CE, few women are mentioned and even fewer given credit. There are a few odd exceptions, such as Beruriah, wife of the famous Rabbi Meir, who was reputed to be wiser than he. Attention is given to sexual matters, all from the male point of view, and to matters of ritual impurity, particularly concerned with menstruation and childbirth. No woman, as far as we know, ever joined the debate to speak from personal experience.

Religion, self-proclaimed purveyor of all right and true thinking, never quite got to grips with women until this century. Why was it, in Judaism, that the position of women was allowed actually to diminish, from a period when women were exempt from performing religious duties, to one where the exemption became an exclusion? The lot of a woman who never married was a sorry one. Women who were childless could be divorced in favour of another wife, so that the man could fulfil the commandment of being fruitful and multiplying.

Women whose children had grown up, or indeed who never bore children, might have been relatively free agents. Why did nobody think that they should be included, rather than excluded? Were these questions never asked before the advent of feminism? Feminism is a brand of thinking which is not necessarily a belief pattern in itself, but has its roots in eighteenth century rationalism and in the right-based thinking of the late eighteenth and early nineteenth centuries. For it was then that there began to be talk about the education of girls, as *salons* were established by educated, witty and intelligent women in the great cities of Europe, women for whom intelligence was an art to be cultivated, rather than a disadvantage to be disguised. The nineteenth century brought the campaign for girls' education, the establishment of girls' schools and the gradual beginnings of the suffragist movement. Women had a new role – as social reformers. At last they had a role outside the family, in their own homes or in the homes of others as domestic servants (if poor) or governesses (if genteel). Religion, however, did not keep up. Women were still silent in the churches and the synagogues.

With the emancipation of the Jews in Germany, and the rise of the early reform movement in Judaism, there was at last a shift. There began to be talk about the education of girls. The Reverend D.W. Marks, in his consecration sermon at the West London Synagogue in 1842, poured scorn on the idea that one could possibly educate children without their mothers being educated in Judaism, too:

Woman, created by God as a 'help meet for man' and in every way his equal; woman, endowed by the same parental care, as man, with wondrous perceptions, that she might participate, (as it may be inferred from Holy Writ that she was intended to participate) in the full discharge of every moral and religious obligation, has been degraded below her proper station. The power of exercising those exalted virtues that appertain to her sex has been withheld from her; and since equality has been denied to her in other things, as a natural consequence it has not been permitted to her in the duties and delights of religion. It is true that education has done much to remedy this injustice in other respects; yet does memory live in the indifference manifested for the religious instruction of females.

In Germany, girls were confirmed (a reform version of bar mitzvah, held at a later age) in the early reform synagogue at Seesen. In the United States, where non-orthodox Judaism of one sort or another is numerically dominant over orthodoxy, women began to sit with the men rather than in the ladies' gallery. In mainstream orthodoxy, however, there remained an almost deliberate relishing of social conservatism.

Evidence has shown that young girls have stronger religious feelings than young boys, and in the Christian churches women usually outnumber men. The same is not true in Judaism and Islam. Many women often feel alienated. The rise of feminism has made many women, including the least radical, question the status quo. Feminism requires that women have equal opportunities, a position adopted in theory by non-orthodox Judaism in the last century but nowhere near true in practice. Feminism demands that the world be looked at through women's eyes. Why then does Judaism rate the patriarchs, a pretty appalling bunch if truth be told, over the matriarchs? Why are women ritually impure for seven plus thirty-three days after the birth of a boy, but for fourteen plus sixty-six days after the birth of a girl? Why does Christianity set an impossible standard for women in the shape of the Virgin Mary – a virgin, thus sex-denying, but a mother as well? How can women emulate the impossible? Why does Islam demand the hiding of women's faces behind the veil, so that they will not tempt other men, a view held as well by orthodox Judaism, in which married women have to cover their heads with a scarf or a wig to prevent anyone but their husbands seeing their crowning glory.

A feminist would ask why the liturgy is so male, and why God is mostly thought of as male. Why is the female element of God not more fully expressed? Why is the role of the Shechinah in Judaism, the female presence of God, almost denied except among the Hasidic ultra-orthodox sects? Why do Judaism and Islam have so few female figures as role models for our daughters? (At least Christianity has a fair number of female saints.) A feminist would ask why wife-beating has never been taken seriously by religious organisations.

The feminist critique of religion has pointed out the obvious. It is not religion itself, the faith, the hope, the spirituality, the attempt to carry out God's will, which discriminates against women. How can it, when it is all about human aspiration? It is the religious structures, carved out by men, which are so hostile to women, and which allow men the lion's share of the public roles in religious institutions, without caring that women are excluded. Religion itself bears no part of the blame. Community, a search for God's law, a desire to know God, do no damage to women or to men. Hierarchies of men are responsible for the institutions of religion, the laws of religious communities, the interpretation of texts, the marginalisation of women and their concerns, and the failure to listen to women's voices.

The men who function as religious leaders should ask themselves as honestly as they possibly can, how they would view the structures of religious organisations if they were female. Some have done this exercise. Some have campaigned long and hard for women's religious needs, feelings and status to be recognised. Those who fought recently for the ordination of women to the priesthood in the Church of England did so out of a sense of justice and fair play; they also recognised that huge talents were lost to their community if women continued to be sidelined, and they feared increasing weakness as a result.

Despite the way they have been treated throughout history, women have not allowed their religious sense to diminish. Women have always found, and will continue to find, ways of expressing their spirituality. With the advent of feminism, some women are content to be in women's groups, and others express their religious longings with other women. Some go out and seek participation in mainstream religious organisations as they become more accepting. What remains clear is that women will not have true religious equality with men until they are involved in the shaping of religious communities, and those communities accept that much of their law and tradition is written by men for men. Women, religious as well as secular, have no intention of staying in that male-defined place.

Feminism has done religious organisations nothing but good. It makes us question the moments when it seems we have things in our favour. For instance, on the eve of the sabbath, we say to our daughters: 'May God make you like Sarah, Rebecca, Rachel and Leah.' Some of us now add, under our breath: 'God forbid . . .' for we are not sure we want our daughters to be exactly like those matriarchs, formidable as some of them were.

It is encouraging to young Jewish girls to realise that at the beginning of the Torah, there were powerful women and good role models. Sarah, childless wife to Abraham, gave her handmaid Hagar to her husband so that he could have a child. They produced Ishmael, theoretically ancestor of the Muslims. A miracle happened. Three men, or angels, came to see Abraham at Mamre. They told him that Sarah, now in her nineties, would give birth. She was listening at the opening of the tent, and could not restrain her laughter. She did conceive and gave birth to Isaac. Some time later, Ishmael was teasing the toddler Isaac, to Sarah's great rage:

Cast out this bondwoman and her son: for the son of this bondman shall not be heir with my son, even with Isaac. And the thing was very grievous in Abraham's sight because of his son. And God said unto Abraham: Let it not be grievous in thy sight because of the lad, and because of thy bondwoman; in all that Sarah hath said unto thee, hearken unto her voice; for in Isaac shall thy seed be called. And also of the son of the bondwoman will I make a nation, because he is thy seed. And Abraham rose up early in the morning and took bread and a bottle of water and gave it unto Hagar, putting it on her shoulder, and the child, and sent her away; and she departed and wandered in the wilderness of Beer-Sheba.

(Genesis 21:10–14)

Eventually Hagar ran out of water, put Ishmael under one of the shrubs, and said: ' "Let me not see the death of the child", and she sat over against him and lifted up her voice and wept' (Genesis 21:16). And God heard her and comforted her and said: ' "Arise, lift up the lad, and hold him in thine hand, for I will make him a great nation".' (Genesis 21:18)

According to our modern thinking Sarah behaved badly by making Hagar and Ishmael go into the wilderness with inadequate supplies. Equally Abraham should not have allowed it. God tells Abraham to listen to Sarah. The medieval commentator, Rashi, says this passage teaches us that Sarah is superior to Abraham in prophecy. In other words, she knew that God would protect Hagar and Ishmael. The other explanation is less generous. It is that, despite Abraham being seen as the great patriarch, founder of monotheism, what we have here is actually the remnants of a matriarchy. Sarah was to be obeyed. Sarah, not Abraham, was the one in charge. It was she who gave Hagar to Abraham. It was she who laughed at the very idea of having a baby herself – and her laughter caused Isaac's name, since it means: 'He will laugh'. It was she who ordered Hagar and Ishmael's expulsion, because she had had enough of them. Within this apparently male-dominated story, here is a woman who gets her way. Here is a woman who believes that God will look after those who need it. It may have been a simple faith, but she got what she wanted, and indeed Ishmael himself became father of a great nation, so all was well in the best of all possible worlds.

The second matriarch in the group of four is Rebecca, probably the most powerful of them all. Isaac is portrayed in the Hebrew Bible as something of a wimp. When his father Abraham thought it was time for Isaac to marry, he sent his servant off to the land from which he had come, Haran, to the city of Nahor. As the servant drew near, he decided that the first woman who came out and greeted him in a friendly way when he asked for water to drink, and who offered to give water to his camels, was the woman for Isaac. Rebecca greeted him and offered water for his camels. She even went one better. She saw the gold bracelets Abraham's servant was holding out, and offered him a room to lodge in and stabling for the camels.

The servant negotiated with Rebecca's father, Bethuel,

and brother, Laban, who said that the proposal came from God and that they would not interfere. After Rebecca had agreed to go with him to the distant land where Isaac was living, her brother and her mother nevertheless decide to try to delay her. What is odd in this story is that her father is no longer one of the players. Some have argued that it is because Bethuel had suddenly died, but Genesis does not suggest that. Others say that this is a form of fratriarchy, where the brother and the mother make decisions. Certainly one feels that Rebecca herself is no minor player. She gets what she wants, by fair means or foul.

Married to Isaac, Rebecca gave birth to twins, Jacob and Esau. Esau was the first-born, and Jacob was the favourite. Jacob soon succeeded in making his brother Esau sell his birthright for a mess of pottage. Later, when Isaac was blind with age, Rebecca decided to cheat her husband. She dressed her favourite, Jacob, in animal skins to make him hairy like Esau:

> And Rebecca spoke to Jacob her son saying: Behold, I heard thy father speak unto Esau thy brother saying: Bring me venison and make me savoury meat that I may eat and bless thee before the Lord before my death. Now therefore, my son, obey my voice according to that which I command thee. Go now to the flock and fetch me from thence two good kids of the goats: and I will make them savoury meat for thy father, such as he loveth. And thou shalt bring it to thy father that he may eat and that he may bless thee before his death. And Jacob said to Rebecca his mother, Behold Esau my brother is a hairy man and I am a smooth man. My father peradventure will feel me and I shall seem to him as a deceiver, and I shall bring a curse upon me, and not a blessing. And his mother said to him: Upon me be thy curse, my son. Only obey my voice and go fetch me them.
>
> (Genesis 27:6–13)

Jacob did as he was told, and, sure enough, received the blessing intended for his brother Esau. Esau was furious and threatened to kill Jacob. Rebecca sent him away to her homeland, to take a wife from the daughters of her brother Laban.

Rebecca behaved with considerable unkindness towards her husband Isaac, whom she knew could no longer see. There appears to have been no doubt in her mind, no hesitation that her scheming might have been immoral. She was a moving force. Isaac is almost a cipher in these stories, sandwiched between two greater men, Abraham and Jacob, his father and his son. Rebecca's toughness and dètermination make us think.

The third and fourth matriarchs in the Jewish tradition are Rachel and Leah. After Jacob had stolen Isaac's final blessing, Esau fled to Laban's house. There he met Rachel, Laban's younger daughter, with the sheep. He got to know both Laban's daughters, Leah the elder, who was 'tender-eyed', and Rachel who was 'beautiful and well-favoured'. Jacob wanted to marry Rachel, and served Laban for seven years for her hand. After the wedding feast, he discovered that Laban had tricked him, and that he had married Leah instead. Laban's excuse was that it was not the custom in his part of the country for the younger sister to be married before the elder, but Jacob found himself labouring for Rachel's hand another seven years. The relationship between the two sisters cannot have been easy. Jacob loved Rachel, but it was Leah who bore children, six sons and a daughter, with the conviction that her fecundity would make Jacob love *her*. Eventually Rachel produced two children, Joseph and Benjamin, and the two women, and their handmaids, managed to co-exist in some way.

Jacob continued to work for Laban for no wages. The deal was that he would take all the cattle that were speckled – or, when there were too many of those, in Laban's view – striped or spotted. Laban kept changing his mind as Jacob's herd got larger. Jacob found a way of making it more likely that the strong cattle would bear spotted, speckled and striped young. Gradually Jacob became very wealthy and Laban very envious. Laban's sons complained that Jacob was taking all their inheritance. Jacob, Rachel and Leah left secretly, taking everything with them, back to his homeland.

Jacob did not know that Rachel had stolen her father's household gods, the figurines that he kept in the house and believed protected his household. We do not know exactly why she did it, except that she thought her father was behaving badly, and that the loss of the gods would give him ill-fortune. Laban found them missing, and chased after Jacob in a rage:

Now, whilst you wanted to be gone, because you longed for your father's house, why did you have to steal my gods? Jacob answered and said, I left at dead of night because I was afraid. For I said: Peradventure you would take by force your daughters from me. Whoever you find your gods with, let him not live. Before our brethren, you look for what is yours with me and take it back. For Jacob did not know that Rachel had stolen the gods. So Laban went into Jacob's tent and into Leah's tent and into the two maidservant's tents, and did not find them. Then he left Leah's tent and went into Rachel's tent. Now Rachel had taken the images and put them in the camels' furniture and was sitting on them. Laban searched the whole tent but could not find them. Rachel said to her father, Let it not displease my lord that I cannot rise up before them, for the custom of women [menstruation] is upon me. So he searched but did not find the images. And Jacob grew angry and chided Laban, and said: What is my trespass, that you have pursued after me so hotly? You have

searched all my stuff, but what have you found of yours –
put it here before thy brethren and mine that they may
judge between us. This twenty years have I been with you,
and your ewes and your female goats have not miscar-
ried, and I have not eaten the rams of your flock . . . I
served thee fourteen years for thy two daughters and six
years for thy cattle, and you have changed my wages ten
times . . .

(Genesis 31:33–38, 40)

Jacob had been badly treated by Laban, in this hotbed
of deceit and counter-deceit. Jacob had deceived Esau,
Laban had deceived Jacob, Rachel had deceived Laban,
and on and on. Is this what we want for our daughters
when we bless them on the sabbath and say: 'May God
make you like Sarah, Rebecca, Rachel and Leah'?

Although we may have our doubts about the tough,
scheming, deceitful, self-serving matriarchs as role models
for our daughters, I am not sure I want my daughter to
be like some of the other women in the Hebrew Bible,
either. I would not want her weeping so hard in the
Temple, as Hannah did, that Eli the priest thought she
was drunk. Nor would I want her to sleep at the feet (a
euphemism for crawling into bed with) of her kinsman the
wealthy landowner, Boaz, as Ruth does. The Talmud,
the code of Jewish law, features very few women – though
some are hugely admired, including the aforementioned
Beruriah. Women are gradually written out of history,
thought to be silly, or time-wasting, or unable to lead one
to heaven – even though it was men who had deprived
them of the education which would have enabled them to
keep up.

Perhaps we should tell our daughters that the precedents
are bad, and that we are only praying that they be like
Sarah, Rebecca, Rachel and Leah as an example of strong

women who left a mark on their societies. We could choose a new list – we could include the daughters of Zelophehad, for instance, who went to see Moses in order to be allowed to inherit their father's wealth since he had had no sons – and succeeded. We could include Ruth, who left her homeland for her mother-in-law and eventually, despite creeping into bed with him, or perhaps because of it, became wife to Boaz, and ancestress of King David, the greatest king in our tradition and, so we are told, founder of the Messianic line.

Whichever list of women we provide for our daughters, however much we analyse what has gone before, we must admit that we cannot re-write Jewish history. Women lived essentially domestic lives. Out of that scenario, the myth grew up of the Jewish mother. We can only point to the famous passage from the book of Proverbs in the Hebrew Bible (Proverbs 31:10–31) which, traditionally, a Jewish husband reads to his wife at the beginning of the sabbath, encompassing the nature of good Jewish motherhood in his words:

> A virtuous woman who can find, for her price is far above rubies? The heart of her husband shall safely trust her, so that he shall have no need of spoil. She will do him good and not evil all the days of her life. She seeketh wool and flax and worketh willingly with her hands. She is like the merchants' ships; she bringeth her food from afar. She riseth also whilst it is yet night, and giveth meat to her household and also a portion to her maidens. She considereth a field, and buyeth it: with the fruit of her hands she planteth a vineyard. She girdeth her loins with strength, and strengtheneth her arms. She perceiveth that her merchandise is good: her candle goeth not out at night. She layeth her hands to the spindle and her hands hold the

distaff. She stretcheth out her hand to the poor; yea, she reacheth forth her hand to the needy. She is not afraid of the snow for her household, for all her household are clothed with scarlet. She maketh herself coverings of tapestry; her clothing is silk and purple. Her husband is known in the gates, when he sitteth among the elders of the land. She maketh fine linen and selleth it: and delivereth girdles to the merchant. Strength and honour are her clothing; and she shall rejoice in time to come. She openeth her mouth with wisdom; and her tongue is the law of kindness. She looketh well to the ways of her household, and eateth not the bread of idleness. Her children rise up, and call her blessed; her husband also, and he praiseth her. Many daughters have done well, but thou excelleth them all. Favour is deceitful and beauty short-lived, but a woman that feareth the Lord, she shall be praised. Give her of the fruit of her hands; and let her own words praise her in the gates.

This, then, is the perfect woman. She does it all. She heads the family, while her husband sits among the elders of the land. The text is relatively early, and may have been written with a hint of irony, by an author whose other comments about women, for example, 'Endless dripping on a rainy day, that is what a nagging wife is like' (Proverbs 27:15), have a different tone. Nevertheless, Jewish tradition took this prototype seriously. This was true respect for a woman's role as head of the family. The Jewish mother colours the shape of the Jewish family.

Women have always played a significant role in creating strong family feeling. Part of the strength of that family feeling has its roots elsewhere in Jewish history, in the *shtetls*, the villages occupied largely by Jews in the Pale of Settlement, in the ghettos and Judengaessn of the sixteenth to nineteenth centuries. Previously, Jews had lived clustered together in special streets and areas in the medieval period, though not as far as we know under compulsion. (There are areas of London which are labelled 'Old Jewry' and 'Jews' Walk'.) The nature of that closeness, that intimacy, that persecution, made Jewish communities stick together, often with closely inter-related families, since they married only within the faith. In a small medieval community in England – in Lincoln, York or Cambridge, for example – the majority of the members of thirty or forty families would have arranged marriages with each other, while only the wealthiest would have made alliances with Jewish families in other cities or very occasionally abroad. That network would have made family ties close: children had a ready collection of aunts and cousins nearby, young apprentices stayed in the house of a family member who was also very likely their boss.

Later, from the sixteenth century onwards, when Jews were often forced to live in ghettos, that closeness became emphasised. (The first ghetto was in Venice in 1516, and was closely followed by ghettoes in Mantua, Ferrara, and other Italian cities.) Jews were crowded together in areas often too small for their population, and survival was made possible only by orderly lives and cooperative relationships between families. The women, organising the domestic details, played a major role in arranging marriages, and in looking after the poor and orphans, finding them work and protecting them in a hostile world.

In the eighteenth and nineteenth centuries, as travel became easier, the wealthy bankers of Germany would send their sons abroad to establish branches of their banks, and these young men might stay with a distant cousin already settled in Paris, Vienna or London. In a very different social stratum, the poverty- and persecution-stricken Jews of the Pale of Settlement began their emigration in 1881, and travelled to America, Canada, Britain, or South

Africa, often to join a cousin or uncle already there, with whom they would lodge while they found their feet. These are the family ties of minority groups. Though Jews still have relatively strong family ties, these are probably not as strong as one might today find in Britain among, for example, some Bangladeshi families who are newer immigrants.

Throughout history, Jewish women have found fulfilment in the role of pastoral carers. Organisations such as the League of Jewish Women and Jewish Care, with its two thousand or so volunteers, are still the backbone of Jewish communities. Women who have finished raising families give much of their time to helping others who are less fortunate than themselves. Today many men join them in this, particularly those who are retired or unemployed, but it is still the domain of women.

The role of the homemaker in the Jewish community has always expanded to that of organiser and volunteer. Women would be in charge of the marriage arrangements for orphaned girls (the community would make financial provisions for a dowry). Women looked after food for the needy and dealt with the distribution of poor relief. This ancient tradition, which appears to have been almost universal in Jewish communities, with the exception of some North African communities where the women had a lesser role, led to women heading up families with an eye on the outside world. They were not inward looking. They had experience of the outside world for business and charitable affairs, and their role of homemaker was tempered with that of adviser, counsellor, listener, nag and encourager. Decision-making about the future of the young of any family was shared in a worldly fashion by women in conjunction with men.

This is recognisable from the remarkable diary of a seventeenth century woman, Glueckel of Hameln, who wrote about events in her and her family's life with wit and self-awareness. She writes about the practical decisions she had to make to ensure the welfare of her children, and recounts the concerns she felt when her husband was away for a long time, and then she laspes into sadness, and a more traditional, weak or woman's role when she describes how she felt when he died:

> Unfortunately my pious husband was not a strong man. That was why he hastened to marry off all the children, and feared the day which was to fall on us ... My husband's time came and because of our sins God took from us my devout husband, the crown of my head. In the year 5449 [1689] God's wrath fell on us and He tore my dearest from me. I was left with eight orphaned children, and the four already married still had need of their faithful father. What can I say? I lost such a loveable husband and the children so exceptional a father. We were left like sheep without a shepherd ...

Beside my grandmother's chair there used to be a framed block of German stamps depicting the dignified, somewhat imperiously held, head of Bertha Pappenheim. The caption read: 'Helfer der Menschheit', 'Helper of Mankind'. Pappenheim, my grandmother's heroine, was an unpaid social worker, who worked among prostitutes, campaigning for an end to the white slave traffic. She was no ordinary middle class social reformer of the kind to be found among contemporary wealthy, young, Christian women. An unlikely character, traditional Jewess and feminist combined, she was enraged by prevailing Jewish attitudes to women and described the passage from the Book of Proverbs about the perfect woman whose price is far above rubies as: 'a lovesong with gefilte fish'. She was Freud's original Anna O, the deeply disturbed and extraordinarily talented young woman, whom Ernest Jones, in his biography of Freud, described as 'the real discoverer of the cathartic method'.

The Jewish authorities feared Pappenheim, believing that any publicity about Jewish involvement in prostitution would release even more anti-semitism, a fear which was proved correct in Hitler's Germany. The truth was that many Jews were caught up in prostitution and the white slave traffic, something Pappenheim saw as a stain upon the Jewish reputation. In retrospect, her desire to get the girls into domestic positions in families, with a respectability attached to what they did, seems curiously dated. After all, for many of the girls, life as a prostitute might have been preferable, with all its risks, to that of a poorly-paid and poorly-regarded domestic servant with very little free time or even freedom. Pappenheim could not abide the lurking anti-semitism of marvelling, on the one hand, at the life of orthodox and Hasidic Jews in their long kaftans, studious and other-worldly, and, on the other, refusing to admit that these same other-worldly figures, or their cousins and friends, were exploiting young women, importing them from Eastern European villages to Germany and Britain for prostitution. How could such hypocritical behaviour fit with the ideals of Judaism, whether the Judaism of the rabbis or the Judaism of the prophets? Despite opposition from many Jewish authorities who wanted to leave well alone, Pappenheim persisted. She regarded her work as a moral crusade. She founded the German Jewish women's organisation, the Jüdischer Frauenbund, which aimed to place women in senior positions in Jewish life. She despaired of the feebleness of the men, for German Jewry was still backward in promoting women.

It is no coincidence that Pappenheim was my grandmother's heroine, for my grandmother, too, had her feelings of impatience with men, her sense that change was too slow in coming, that men were too inclined to accept the status quo. She found enormous pleasure from the work she did with other Jewish women in the rooms at Bloomsbury House where the welfare committee of the Jewish Refugee Committee had its offices.

My favourite of all these unlikely formidable Jewesses is Ernestine Rose, born Ernestine Potowski, daughter of a Polish rabbi. She appealed to a secular court against her father's decision to marry her off in an arranged marriage (commonplace in Eastern European Jewish communities until 1939) and to confiscate the property she had inherited from her mother (to which she was entitled under rabbinic law). She won her case and later crossed Europe on the proceeds of the invention of a natural deodorant. She was one of the first supporters of Robert Owen in England and met and married one of his followers, William Rose. They emigrated to America, where Ernestine became one of the early American feminists and a signatory to the famous Seneca Falls Declaration of Sentiments, a statement of women's grievances modelled on the Declaration of Independence. She was quite a character and would have been a great role model for me and the girls among my Jewish contemporaries at the beginning of the women's movement in the 1960s – if only we had known about her!

There were other women, too, many from Russia and Poland, who were rebels against their background. Most saw persecution as an everyday occurrence and witnessed the gradual destitution of the Jewish community of the Pale of Settlement and the drift into the cities. Most also saw the 'enlightenment' affect their families, reducing religious involvement and allowing children a secular education. Some experienced a flight from persecution themselves, many were politically aware, as well as aware of their lives as women and Jews. Naomi Shepherd lists many of them in her volume about Jewish women radicals, *A Price Below Rubies*. Women such as Esther Frumkin, leader of the Bund – the Jewish socialists – and Rosa Luxemburg. Beta Kaminskaya, educated in Switzerland until the Tsarist government ordered foreign students home in 1873, infiltrated factories in the Moscow area, with her comrades disguised as peasants. She never faced trial. She went into a clinical depression in jail, was released into the care of her father, and eventually committed suicide. There was also Anna Kuliscioff, life-long companion of Filippo Turati, leader of the Italian socialists, whose funeral demonstrated her importance: large crowds followed her cortège to the cemetery and were attacked by Fascist thugs on the way.

The revolutionary zeal of these women was much stronger than that of their male counterparts. Was it a double rebellion – against the place of the Jewish woman, as much as against the conventions and oppression of their time – a combination which fired them up? Some of these women were privileged in being given an education, many outside the countries where they were born, which must be a contributory factor. So must the fact that the fabric of Jewish society in Eastern Europe was collapsing, with an even greater effect on women than on men, because they had hitherto been so relegated to the domestic sphere, divorced from decision-making, and powerless. I wish we had known about these women, since role models were few and far between.

*

Traditionally, women on their own have been expected to be under the protection of a husband, father or brother. Divorce, however, is not a major problem in Judaism, because though Jews often pick up the customs and thinking of those around them, Judaism, unlike Christianity, holds no shame attached to divorce. A divorced woman is not in disgrace. In traditional Jewish law a woman cannot sue for divorce, though there are rare circumstances when she can ask the *Beit Din* (Jewish court of law) to ask her husband to divorce her. A man who divorces does so because of the breakdown of the marriage or sometimes because the couple have been unable to have children. (Rabbinic law demands that a man divorce his wife of ten years' standing if she is barren, because of the religious duty to be fruitful and multiply). Similarly, after the death of a spouse, there is no belief that the surviving partner must wait a long time to remarry. Women of child-bearing age are expected to wait at least three months, presumably to see whether they are pregnant or not, and there is some sense of decency in not remarrying too fast. This is not the stuff of a romantic view of marriage or family – it is a view informed by a deep practicality, where the duty 'to build up a household in Israel' (as the marriage contract, given by the husband to the wife, states) is taken seriously.

Marriage in Judaism is a legally binding contract, and the negotiations before a marriage traditionally were legal ones, about, for example, the extent of the return of the woman's family's property should there be a divorce. Similarly, the woman had certain entitlements, including the right to sexual satisfaction. Two young people took upon themselves the obligation to build up a household in Israel, to have a family and continue the tradition, in a frame of reference which meant being turned in on a small community much of the time.

In the modern period, when there is not such a great necessity to stick to one's own community, Jews often choose to live in areas where there are many other Jews, to be near a synagogue, and to have that sense of closeness that the Jewish community brings, with its delights – as well as its downside of curiosity about one's private business. Even now, the Jews of western Europe and America, freed from the ghettoes, tend to live in Jewish communities, and many have remained committed, officially at least, to marrying within the faith. The very orthodox have achieved a lower intermarriage rate by creating their own self-imposed ghetto.

It is a harder task to throw open the ghetto walls, generation after generation, and say that you choose the Jewish path not because it is cosy and safe, but because it *matters* to you today. Oddly, I have found it easier in countries which are more religious than England. In Ireland, for example, religion is part of the way of life. Most people go to mass or the Protestant church. Religion is taken seriously, with its attendant bigotry certainly, but also with considerable understanding of the spiritual drive that some of us feel. The Jewish community in Ireland is very small, but in many ways it is simple to be Jewish there because there is a deep comprehension of what it means to have a faith and be part of a religious community.

In England there is a very low church attendance. Those who wish to be devout and to practise their religion may be seen as a bit odd, and even a little exotic. England is a Christian country on the surface – but many many people are non-believers or less than half-hearted in the practice of their beliefs. To be a member of a minority – not to be part of the mainstream in a country where the Christian church is established – may be difficult. In an irreligious country, the motivation to be religious is often hard to sustain. Jews are often syncretistic, and if the surrounding society is irreligious, Jews become irreligious too. In Britain, however, they cannot as easily replace religious Judaism with cultural Judaism, as the North American Jews have done so successfully.

Even in North America, Jews are trying to re-establish what it means to be Jewish. As divorce rates rocket and parents have more and more step-children between them, the traditional Jewish family is no longer the safe haven it once was. Jews may be confident in North America, but there is still a difficulty in establishing what it means to be Jewish. That was expressed by Mordecai Richler, the Canadian-Jewish novelist, in *This Year in Jerusalem*. Richler never visited Israel as an ardent young Zionist; he married out of the faith; he broke with his orthodox grandfather to the extent that his grandfather put in his will that Mordecai was not allowed to touch his body; he made his homes in Canada and Britain. He lived as a cultural Jew, not a religious Jew, and some of the time he lived in places where there isn't even much cultural Judaism. In the end, he went to Israel, to see what Zionism meant to him, to try to get a feeling of what he'd missed all those years ago. Though he enjoyed it, met old friends, and could see the point of it all, it was not for him. But he had not made sense of his Canadian/English Jewish life either. His identity was unclear, and a solution never quite emerged.

The Jewish family, and the Jewish community, need to look at what they have achieved.

For many of us, family life and a close community have given us our love of being Jewish. We have married within the faith, or, if we married out, we have continued to practise our Judaism. Yet we have not given our children a better Jewish education than we had ourselves. My children relish Friday nights, when we have *shabbat* dinner at home, usually but not always on our own, because it is specifically a family time, with a special dinner when we change our clothes and try to behave like civilised human beings. The rituals themselves apparently play a relatively small part in my children's thinking. Or do they? The children remember lighting the candles and making kiddush before they could speak. I wonder whether the symbolism of the sabbath, and the recognition of these symbols, carry a deeper meaning far more profound than the usual explanations suggest. As I get older, I believe that the rituals of Jewish family life may be more important, as part of the process of establishing identity, than all the education in the world. Ultra-orthodox Lubavitch Hasidic Jews go around in '*mitzvah* tanks', vans which they use to encourage Jews to perform religious duties. Maybe they have something there.

The associations with being Jewish may be established by seeing the rituals performed and by relishing the atmosphere. The actions which are required are not heavy, off-putting, alienating educational duty; they are simply to encourage young semi-rationalist Jews to carry out some of the traditional *mitzvot* with their young children because of the joy it will bring. Many Jews who are otherwise disaffected still celebrate Passover, with its meal and service and symbols all rolled into one. Perhaps they should also try to continue the ritual of the *shabbat* dinner. They do not need to justify their actions intellectually, but simply experiment with the feelings they arouse. Such an approach was used in the late 1960s and early 1970s to good effect by the then burgeoning *chavurah* (small group) movement among North American Jews, which allowed for Jewish experimentation on the basis that they should carry out rituals to see how they felt, and continue them if they felt right.

To my rationalist inclination, this was all a bit 'touchy-feely'. Nevertheless I have come around to the argument for encouraging young Jews who do little or nothing in the way of observance to try one thing at a time, and particularly to join in those rituals which might mean something to their children. The future of Jewry should perhaps combine an intellectual approach with a relaxed communal approach to inclusiveness in rituals.

These rituals take place in families, so that children see them as they grow up, from their youngest years. But many young Jews, like many other people, do not fit into families. The traditional Jewish family has to learn to open up to those who, for one reason or another, are not part of any recognised family – the gays and lesbians, unmarried aunts and uncles, widows and widowers, divorced people, drop-outs and cynics. These people need families too, be they expanded families or families very different from the norm. Our children need to understand that things have changed, that many of us will never again fit into the conventional family, but that families *can* adapt and become unconventional while being very traditional in the practice of rituals and encouraging the young in their midst.

The family needs to change to accommodate ever changing social mores, and to set a better agenda for being Jewish for its young. It also needs to come to terms with what it means to be living in an open society, and explain to its young what the implications of that are. I think it means choice. No person born Jewish in Britain today *has* to practise Judaism. He or she does it voluntarily. Families, in my view, need to make Judaism within the family circle so attractive, so exciting, so stimulating and so important, that it will be obvious to the young which way to go.

Nothing is given any more. Women have changed, and men have had to change. Whether the modern Jewish family can keep up with the changes, and make something of them, is as yet an unknown. I believe it is possible to encourage young people to stay within the fold because it matters.

4

Sex, contraception and pleasure

Sexual shame is foreign to Jews. In our tradition, a man is supposed to make love to his wife on the sabbath, because it is a form of joy and one should rejoice on the sabbath. When the sixteenth century mystics were proclaiming 'Come, my beloved, to greet the bride', that wonderful song by Solomon Alkabetz to welcome the sabbath bride, they were referring to the sabbath perceived as a female entity. The imagery of the sexual joy of the sabbath should not be lost on anyone. Sexual delight is part of what the sabbath is all about.

Jewish law regulates all things, and sexual matters are an area of life with which rabbinic law concerns itself. Unlike the negative feelings towards sexuality often expressed in Christianity, within Judaism a woman is entitled to sexual satisfaction from her husband. Women, who are not able in traditional law to sue for divorce, can ask the rabbinic court to press for divorce if their sexual needs are not satisfied. Judaism also lays down the frequency of the sexual act, according to a man's profession

or occupation. It ranges from once every six months for a
tanner (perhaps because the smell of his work made him
undesirable) to even less frequently for a sailor (for reasons
of being away), to weekly for a scholar. Clearly the scholars
wrote these rules! It is also clear they were written from a
man's point of view. These stipulations, however, were for
minimum frequency, and if a wife wanted more she should
have it; her sexual satisfaction was of paramount
importance.

It is a splendid irony that the story of Adam and Eve,
originally from the Book of Genesis in the Hebrew Bible,
is taken by Christian interpreters as the story of the fall
from grace and the loss of innocence predicated on sexual
knowledge and shame. In Judaism it is the story of how
we came to be in the world today. The curse of Eve in the
Jewish tradition – that her desire was to be 'unto thy
husband and he will rule over thee' (Genesis 3:16) – is said
to account for a woman's sexual modesty and inhibition
against her own overt initiation of sexual activity. Therefore it is a husband's duty to spare her this curse, and he
is obliged to initiate sexual activity, which she is presumed
to desire. This is a far cry from many Christians, who
regard sex without procreation as sinful. Jewish thinking
is a long way from the denial of the flesh, so ably docu-
mented by many Christian scholars, and perhaps most
impressively by Peter Brown in his studies of body and
flesh in early Christianity. Yet, early Christians were experi-
menting with men and women praying together, while
Jews of the same period promoted separation of the sexes.
Nor are the origins of sex denial in Christianity a bolt from
the blue – there are many who think that the Essenes, a
Jewish sect who were probably responsible for the Dead
Sea Scrolls, were sex-denying and had a system of purity
of extreme complexity which required ritual baths and

complicated arrangements about where people should sit at table. These attitudes were undoubtedly strong among many Jewish communities in the first centuries of Christianity.

Yet the Jewish tradition went on to be mostly sexuality-affirming, while Christianity retained its ambivalence. Jews are brought up, despite the extent to which we are influenced by the surrounding culture, to regard sex as positive and a delight, and one of the great things which God has created for human pleasure. This runs very deep in most Jews – though by no means all.

There are teachings throughout the rabbinic tradition which encourage a positive attitude towards sexuality. An example of which I am particularly fond is a letter called *Iggeret ha-Kodesh*, 'the letter of Holiness' in translation, though it is more about separation and difference than about holiness as most non-Jews would understand it. (The same verbal root is used for the expression for betrothal in Hebrew.) The man says to the woman: 'Behold, you are betrothed/separated/consecrated unto me according to the laws of Moses and of Israel.' The main sense is that of 'making separated', so that the woman is separated from others and becomes special for this man. Therefore, the *Iggeret ha-Kodesh* deals with the different, separate way a young Jew should behave. The author may have been one of the great rabbinic scholars, Rabbi Moses ben Nachman (1195–1270), Nachmanides as he is often called, who lived in Spain. In his *Iggeret*, here translated by David Feldman, Nachmanides writes about the quality for the sexual act:

> ... therefore engage her first in conversation that puts her heart and mind at ease and gladdens her, thus your mind and your intent will be in harmony with hers. Speak words which arouse her to passion, union, love, desire and eros,

and words which elicit attitudes of reverence for God, piety and modesty. Tell her of fine and good women who gave birth to fine and pure children. Speak with her words, some of love, some of erotic passion, some of piety and reverence. Never may you force her, for in such union the divine presence cannot abide. Your intent is then different from hers and her mood not in accord with yours. Quarrel not with her nor strike her in connection with this act, as our sages taught. Just as a lion tramples and devours and has no shame, so a boorish man strikes and copulates and has no shame; rather win her over with words of graciousness and seductiveness. Hurry not to arouse passion until her mood is ready. Begin in love that her semination [which some people think means orgasm] takes place first . . . know that sexual intercourse is holy and pure when carried on properly in the proper time and with the proper intention. No one should claim that this is ugly or unseemly, God forbid, for intercourse is called 'knowing' and not in vain is it called this. Understand that if marital intercourse did not partake of holiness, it would not be called knowing. The matter is not as our rabbi and guide of blessed memory supposed in his guide to the perplexed [a reference to Maimonides, one of Judaism's greatest teachers, who was less positive about sexuality than Nachmanides and wrote a renowned theological work, *Guide to the Perplexed*] where he endorses Aristotle's teaching that the sense of touch is unworthy. God forbid, that Greek scoundrel is wrong, and his error proceeds from his view of the universe. Had he believed that one God created the world, he would not have slipped into such error, but we who have Torah and believe that God created all in his wisdom do not believe that He created anything inherently ugly or unseemly. If we were to say that intercourse is repulsive, then we blaspheme God who made the genitals; hands can write a Sefer Torah [a scroll of the five books of Moses, the Pentateuch], and are then honourable and exalted. Hands too can perform evil deeds and then they are ugly. So it is with the genitals. Whatever ugliness there is comes from how a man uses them. All the organs of the body are neutral. The use made of them determines whether they are holy or unholy.

The argument is clear. The body is neither good nor bad, but it is God's creation, and we can use it as we will. Sexual intercourse in the proper time, with the proper person, the appropriate person, is holy. A thirteenth century author, Judah he-Chassid, of the *Sefer Chassidim*, the 'Book of the Pious', suggests even more:

> All these sexual matters must take her wishes and his into consideration. If a man finds a wife whose wishes happen to coincide with his own in these matters, then he has obtained favour of the Lord and God hath favoured thy deed.

In modern times, Herman Wouk, a successful novelist, wrote a book entitled *This is my God*, describing Judaism as it seemed to him. In it he wrote about sex:

> What in other cultures has been a deed of shame or of comedy or of orgy or of physical necessity or of high romance, has been in Judaism one of the main things God wants man to do. If it also turns out to be the keenest pleasure in life, that's no surprise to people eternally sure that God is good.

So much for the commentary. One could, however, say that the commentary is simply taking a favourable stance, the most lenient view possible of the legal material. But in fact that turns out not to be the case. Rabbi Jacob ben Asher (who lived in the late thirteenth century), author of a great legal work of codification commenting on Maimonides, affirms the unrivalled power of sex and adds:

> But a man's own wife is permitted to him, and, with her, he is allowed to do as he pleases. He may cohabit with her whenever he pleases, kiss her wherever he pleases, and cohabit naturally or unnaturally . . .
>
> (Even ha-Ezer 21, 9)

He adds that one should not indulge overmuch or find oneself always with one's wife for that is thought of as boorish and indecent. The point still remains that sex within marriage, and more or less any *kind* of sex (it is probable that the reference to kissing is to oral sex) is a delight, there by creation of God.

A woman's entitlement to sexual satisfaction dates back to the Biblical period. In Exodus (21:10) it states that a husband's obligations include: 'food, clothing and "onah"', always interpreted in rabbinic literature as 'sexual rights'. The linking of food, clothing and sexual rights suggests that all three were high on the agenda of the ancient Israelites who wrote the book of Exodus. There is a Christian parallel to this in the 'marital debt' or 'Pauline debt'. In the first letter to the Corinthians (1 Corinth. 7:3) Paul wrote: 'Let the husband render to his wife what is due to her and likewise the wife to her husband . . .' but it is made clear that this is by concession and not by commandment.

Most of the Jewish legislation in these matters applies to the man. This is partly because women had a second-class status in Jewish law, but it is also because the man is expected to initiate sexual activity, and non-compliance could lead to the rare circumstance of the woman asking the Beit Din to divorce her. If she, on the other hand, refuses him sexual relations, or housework for that matter, she is described as 'rebellious' and may have to forfeit part of her divorce settlement if he then divorces her. The basic

structure of the law on marital sexuality remains that
sexual relations are a man's duty and a woman's privilege.
He cannot waive his sexual duties temporarily but she can
– after he has fulfilled the commandments of being fruitful
and multiplying, which is normally interpreted as having
at least two children, one male and one female.

In the Biblical period, a newly married man could defer
his army service for a year while he rejoiced with the
wife whom he had betrothed but with whom he had not
previously had sexual intercourse (Deuteronomy 20:7). A
man is required to give his wife pleasure at times beyond
'onah', 'if she shows desire by her manner of dress or
action' (Babylonian Talmud Pesachin 72b). Sexual satisfaction for both partners is one way of ensuring *shelom bayit*,
'peace of the household' – strengthening the domestic
bond. Indeed, Rabbi Jacob Emden (who died in 1776) wrote
this in his introduction to the prayer-book:

> The wise men of other nations claim there is disgrace in
> the sense of touch. This is not the view of the Torah and our
> sages . . . To us, the sexual act is worthy, good and beneficial
> even to the soul. No other human activity compares with
> it; when performed with pure and clean intention it is
> certainly holy. There is nothing impure or defective about
> it, rather much exaltation . . . Because of its great sanctity, it
> requires privacy and much modesty . . . benefit and health
> accrue to the body, too, when the act is performed in proper
> measure as to frequency and quality.

Positive though it is, however, there are real problems
with the Jewish attitude. It certainly allows women
pleasure, and, indeed, insists on it; it allows oral sex,
though probably not anal sex. But it regards 'proper' sex as
penetration by a man of a women's vagina, and for that
reason, forms of sexuality which are non-penetrative, such

as lesbian sex, are of no interest; and forms of sexual union where penetration takes place but with the wrong person, such as male homosexuality, or sex with a close relative or an animal, is forbidden. This is the Biblical and rabbinic view, which can be applied to a relatively modern period and the theory of penis envy. Freudian thinking led to the belief that a woman needs to be penetrated by a man in order to have a 'proper' sexual experience. It is amazing that women appear not to have been consulted about this, but Freud is not wholly to blame. He was writing in his time and in his place, and he at least, unlike many of the Victorians, thought that women ought to have sexual experiences.

To understand just how important penetration was thought to be, one can look at world-wide legislation. Almost every kind of sexual relations that do not consist of 'normal' heterosexual sex are illegal in one or more states in America. These prohibitions include anal sex with people of either gender, oral sex, and various forms of sado-masochism. Lesbianism was excluded from legislation in Britain, not because Queen Victoria couldn't believe it happened and no one was brave enough to explain the details to her, but because 'it isn't real sex'. Sex between women is usually considered irrelevant – sex has been seen mostly from men's point of view, men have made most of the laws, whether religious or civil, ancient or comparatively modern. Those forms of sex which do not lead to pregnancy can all too easily be regarded as lascivious.

Much has been written about the Christian view of the body. Augustine argued that woman was the cause of evil, the source of temptation, the lure to man, based on the Christian interpretation of the story of paradise lost in the Hebrew Bible. The response of the Early Church was to make the body and sexuality sinful. Attitudes to the body in early Christianity make extraordinary reading. It was not only women's sexuality which was shameful, but men's as well. There are accounts of ardent young men who castrated themselves in order to be spared the temptation of sex, while some young women made themselves disgusting and wore fouled clothes to avoid the pitfalls of sensuality and to earn the respect of Christian men.

The Christian church developed the perfect role for women in the shape of the Virgin Mary, every man's ideal (and probably quite a few women's as well, given the subjection which many women suffer in their sexual relationships). Many generations of women humbly identified with her as a woman and a mother who would sympathise with their daily problems and understand their plight, but the Virgin Mary was no ordinary woman. She performed wonders: she gave birth to a child, in this case the Son of God, yet remained a virgin. No other woman could match her. She was impossible to emulate. Chastity became a major virtue in the Christian church. Yet throughout history the birth rate has needed to be maintained because of high infant mortality rates. Hence the insistence on sex, not as a source of pleasure for either gender, but because of the duty to people the earth for the greater glory of God.

These ideas may seem peculiar in the late twentieth century; but we are living in a time when religious belief, and specifically fundamentalist religious belief, is coming back into fashion. There is a danger that women will be denied sexual satisfaction, pushed back behind the veil, back into the home and even into the background of churches and synagogues. Attitudes to sex and sexuality are not perceived only in bed; they have a powerful effect on the way we are permitted to behave in other areas of life. The belief that women are a temptation seeped into Judaism, and probably accounts for women being banished to the galleries of synagogues. Is it thought that men can't keep their minds on their prayers in the presence of women? There is an element in Judaism which argues for the powerful nature of the male sex drive. The *yetzer ha-ra*, 'the evil inclination', is often taken to be the sexual inclination if not properly controlled. It is a mixture of the energy that drives us and of the inclination to have sexual relations with whomsoever we fancy, as opposed to with those with whom we are supposed to have them.

Nevertheless, Judaism has a much more permissive attitude to sexuality than Christianity and understands that it is a joy rather than a sin. This is something for which I will always be grateful. From my teenage years I was aware that my non-Jewish friends' attitudes to sexuality were far more complicated than mine. However much they tried to disguise it in the swinging Sixties, they laboured under a sense that what they were doing was sinful, which I never felt at all. It seemed to me that something which felt so good, and which did not harm anybody, could be nothing but wonderful, as long as there was no deceit and the person with whom the relationship was taking place was free to have that relationship. The theme tune of the period was 'let it all hang out', but my attitude of positively rejoicing in sexuality was uncommon among young women unless they had grown up in households similar to mine.

Jewish attitudes to contraception were generally easy. My non-Jewish friends, especially those who were Catholic, often went through agonies of guilt at even the thought of going on the Pill, let alone being fitted for a cap. They dreaded divine punishment, even though several of

them were not serious believers at all. The damage had
been done by being taught early on that contraception is
a sin; the fact that they did not intellectually believe it did
not mean that they did not suffer when they made the
choice to use contraception. In my late-teenage years, I
found myself accompanying Catholic friends to the Brook
Advisory Service for their contraceptives: though intellectually absolutely certain, emotionally they were terrified.
Jews do not find these matters hard to talk about. There
are very early rabbinic discussions about contraception,
spilling seed in vain and the sin of Onan (Genesis 38:4–10).
There is a sense of amusement among women rabbis at
the thought of young male rabbis, and their older male
teachers, sitting there solemnly debating details of female
anatomy. Did any of them get a salacious thrill? Such
issues are thought of as part of everyday life, part of God's
creation – sex for pleasure, contraception to enhance that
pleasure.

There is much discussion centred around a particular
Talmudic passage, which appears more than once, and
runs:

> Three categories of women must [or may – it is disputed
> as to what it means] use a *mokh* [some kind of barrier] in
> marital intercourse: a minor, a pregnant woman and a nurs-
> ing mother. The minor, because otherwise she might
> become pregnant and die. A pregnant woman because
> otherwise she might cause her foetus to become a *sandal* [a
> squashed foetus]. A nursing woman because otherwise she
> might have to wean her child prematurely and he would
> die . . .
>
> (Babylonian Talmud Yevamot 12b and 100b)

It is worth pausing a moment on the issue of child-
brides. Extreme anti-semites have alleged (in anonymous

material sent to leading members of the British Jewish community as recently as 1994) that Jews make a custom of sexual unions with girls as young as three years old. This is simply untrue. Child betrothal and marriage were common at various periods of Jewish history, for a variety of reasons. A Jewish man was obliged to fulfil the religious duty of being fruitful and multiplying, which he could not do by sexual union with a child-bride who had not yet reached puberty. So, one of the restrictions on men who wished to marry child-brides was that they had to have another, fecund, wife already. This goes back to an ancient period when men could marry more than one woman, if they could support more than one in a proper manner. Polygamy died out around 1000 CE and is now forbidden by ruling, and by custom and practice, among the Jews of Europe. It is not so among Sephardi Jews, particularly those from North Africa and the Yemen, where polygamy is also still common among other religious and cultural groupings. Polygamy was not at all uncommon in the ancient world, although later rabbinic codes, particularly those of the European Ashkenazi tradition, expressly forbade it. But a marriage between two minors, of the same generation, was a common practice. A father could arrange the marriage of his daughter who was still a minor (the mother and other siblings could do so if the father was dead), but the girl could refuse the union when she reached majority without going through a formal divorce. The rabbis tried to stop child-betrothal, by writing instructions such as: 'A man is forbidden to betroth his daughter while she is still a minor until she is grown up and says, "I wish to marry so and so" ' (Babylonian Talmud Kiddushin 41a), but it clearly continued and was defended somewhat querulously by several authorities listed by David Feldman in his magnificent work *Birth Control in Jewish Law*. It was argued that persecution was commonplace, and no man knew whether he would be able to give his daughter a dowry in the future. The Crusades had had a very destructive effect on Jewish communities in the Middle Ages. Life had become uncertain. Better to give your daughter in marriage when the cash was at hand than wait and perhaps see her never married. A married minor daughter would probably stay living at home with her parents until the age of majority, particularly if she was betrothed to a young boy who was also a minor. Feldman suggests that there may be something of a fear of invaders and rape here, for oppressors of several religious groups would not rape a betrothed woman. That cannot have been the only reason, because the custom, particularly among Jews in Sephardic communities, appears to have been widespread even in peaceful times.

The young bride was permitted to use the *mokh*, a contraceptive device, to prevent injury, as was the pregnant wife, in case her unborn child became a *sandal*. Jews had sex during pregnancy without any discussion of whether it was moral or not – it was assumed that it was fine. Many Christians, however, were convinced that sex with a pregnant woman was dangerous to the foetus. Sex during pregnancy was also condemned because it was purposeless, as the woman was already with child. In Catholicism, it came to be thought that there was danger of mortal sin if the embryo was damaged by sexual intercourse. With these attitudes around them, it is hardly surprising that within the Jewish tradition there was a nervousness about danger to the foetus from sex during pregnancy. Medieval commentators, especially the twelfth century Rabbi Abraham min-ha-Har of Montpelier, in southern France, argued that the *mokh* could be used by a pregnant woman to stop her husband from penetrating too far up the vagina, which might have squashed the foetus causing it to become a *sandal*.

The third group who could use the *mokh* were nursing mothers. This must be seen in the context of twenty-four months being the normal period for breast-feeding, when infant mortality was commonplace, and when lengthy breast-feeding probably helped babies survive because of the immunities they would gain from their mothers. A new pregnancy, during the period of breast-feeding, which would have meant premature weaning, was regarded as injurious to the baby.

There are volumes of rabbinic commentary on the subject of contraception, and many differences between one Jewish community and another in different parts of the world. The debate eventually fell into two camps, the 'permissivists', who allowed the use of a contraceptive device of some kind for a variety of reasons, and the others, who forbade it unless there was considerable physical risk to the woman concerned. The debate is written very much from a man's point of view; which is why, no doubt, the condom was never accepted by Judaism, since it 'interfered' with the proper sex act. It is cautiously allowed by a very few authorities, who permit unnatural coitus within the marital relationship in order to preserve the peace of the household. The majority still forbid the use of condoms, quite an issue in these days of AIDS and other sexually transmitted diseases. There is the beginning of a rethink among some less orthodox authorities on the matter.

Despite the diverse views about particular methods, this whole debate still suggests that it should be possible, within the confines of Jewish law, to move thinking on to allow many forms of contraception. For non-orthodox Jews, the significance of this debate is that it allows the discussion of contraception in polite society, it recognises the sexual urge as paramount among human beings, and suggests that sex should take place for love and desire without the necessity of procreation in every circumstance. Those of us who do not regard ourselves as bound by what rabbinic authorities tell us about what contraception we may or may not use, and who make our own decisions in the light of our informed consciences, are liberated by two millennia or more of a positive attitude about sexuality. For women, this is exceptionally liberating.

Almost all Jewish authorities, however, regard male homosexuality with a desperate horror. It is generally regarded as a great sin, listed in what are called the *Arayot*, the forbidden sexual unions of Leviticus, chapter 18. Only very modern authorities have come out defending male homosexuality, with a moral argument to do with the nature of human sexuality, saying that for homosexuals sex is as natural and normal and to be conducted in as proper and holy a way as heterosexual sex is for heterosexuals. It is rare, and a relatively modern phenomenon, to find male homosexual rabbis who are prepared to admit their homosexuality. Homosexuality must have existed in the enclosed male environments of the *yeshiva*, the rabbinical academies in which young men studied and no doubt often had to share a bed. Part of the reason for early marriage may have been to do with the fear of homosexuality.

I think that it is of enormous importance that some rabbis have courageously 'come out' as homosexuals, including Rabbi Lionel Blue, well-loved nationally for his broadcasts on *Thought for the Day*. There are also declared lesbian rabbis.

The previous Chief Rabbi, Lord Jakobovits, has written

in favour of gene therapy for homosexuality, since it has been suggested that a certain gene predisposes a person to homosexuality. He would like to see us breed homosexuality out of the human experience. Many homosexuals understandably find this deeply offensive, but Lord Jakobovits believes it is entirely in keeping with orthodox Jewish thinking. Many Jews no longer accept it is. The present Chief Rabbi, Rabbi Dr Jonathan Sacks, became enormously unpopular with many younger Jews, both gay and straight, when he refused the Jewish Gay Group the right to join in a Jewish walk in Hyde Park, in 1992.

In the eyes of many Jewish authorities, homosexuality really is an abomination. AIDS is often, therefore, interpreted as a punishment for unnatural practices – rabbinic thought likewise linked leprosy with sin. If homosexuals are more liable to contract AIDS, or, in some people's mistaken argument, to be responsible for bringing AIDS upon the western world (ignoring the spread of heterosexual AIDS across the continent of Africa), then AIDS must be the fault of those who contract it. It is this view that has led to calls for homosexuality to be made illegal – as if that would have any effect – and has allowed Jews and non-Jews alike to blame those suffering from AIDS.

In America, there is at least one gay congregation with a gay rabbi. Unions between gay couples are blessed, something which I believe to be right, but which is not permitted by any rabbinic body in this country. It is important to come to terms with the way our communities have regarded homosexuality. If we, in the modern world, are going to say that our ancestors were wrong to regard male homosexuality as an abomination, and that as sex is not only for procreation of children, but for peace and love and strengthening bonds between a couple, this should apply equally to a couple of the same gender, male or female (though lesbianism was not an issue for the rabbis of old). If we are also going to emphasise that we wish to take sex seriously and discourage promiscuity, and that we condemn the use of another human being purely for short-term gratification, we have to recognise the importance of permanence in homosexual relationships. I think it is essential that we develop a form of blessing for gay couples, male or female, and that we recognise those who wish to make a public commitment to one another, just as we celebrate a heterosexual couple who come for a marriage service. Rabbis who are involved in such blessings in America are often seen as being rather 'fringe'. I believe that this is neither a fringe issue, nor a particularly non-orthodox one. It is an issue for other communities as much as for the Jewish community. Jews start with an advantage – a positive attitude towards human sexuality. Should this not enable us to be more generous to those who are not sexually conformist to the heterosexual model?

Unfortunately, the Jewish community has for centuries treated badly those who have not conformed to its ideal models. A man who happened to be childless could divorce his disappointing partner and try again with a second wife. Gay unions were anathema if male, and unmentioned if female. Single women were an embarrassment, and lived under the protection of their fathers and brothers. In some cases, single women were not allowed to be full synagogue members, having to be part of a family without a full adult status, even when they were fully grown women with independent bank accounts. Although barriers have been broken down during this century, a rise in ultra-orthodoxy now threatens a return to denial of freedoms.

Deep in the debate about sexuality, there is the concept of what is 'proper' and 'fit' which underlies much Jewish thought. Those who do not conform are somehow behav-

ing in an improper way. This applies to many activities of
ordinary life, including what and how Jews eat and how
they keep their festivals. The idea that non-conformists are
such by nature, rather than due to rebelliousness, is foreign
to Jewish traditional thought. We, in modern Judaism,
must take the thinking further. We should extend Jewish
ideas about joyful human sexuality to embrace those
whom Jewish thinking does not at present include. We
should think again about the recognition and acceptance
of homosexual unions. I don't wish to encourage a specifically gay community, because I think that the community
as a whole must become more accepting of gay Jews. We
might have to recognise that official Jewish attitudes will
be very slow to change – after all, it took generations for
women to be given their proper due – and in the meantime
gays may be most comfortable among like-minded friends.
Either way, gay couples are going to form a significant
part of the Jewish community, and have a serious role to
fulfil within it. The debate about human sexuality will be
brought into a new dimension – sex will be seen to
be important although the possibility of children is not
there, other than by adoption. Such developments can only
be enriching for a Jewish community which has often
turned its back on what is happening in the world. It will
no longer be possible to turn one's back on homosexual
love.

The Jewish community has to come to grips with marital
violence, child abuse, sexual abuse and all the disagreeable
things we used to be told did not happen among Jews.
They do happen, and we should not shrink from talking
about them properly. We should be prepared to protect
minors from sexual abuse, which might well be at an older
age than the traditional rabbinic view of thirteen and a
day for a boy and twelve years and a day for a girl. We

have to look at attitudes to paedophilia, and be prepared to take a tough line about power and abuse.

Jews still regard sexuality as the greatest gift given by God to humanity, giving us a healthy start in life. Let us continue to seek and to celebrate human joys and be more generous to and less condemnatory of sexual minorities.

5

'A time to be born and a time to die':

Life and death in Judaism

On the streets of Boston, on Saturday mornings, demonstrators gather to prevent young women gaining entry to an abortion clinic on Beacon Street. Cohorts of campaigners link arms with the young women and escort them into the clinic.

It is an unlikely frontline. Its members are not obvious warriors. They are middle-class, middle-aged women, not necessarily wholly in favour of abortion. They are women who might never themselves have contemplated having an abortion, but who feel strongly that individuals should have the right to make their own decisions, particularly as the law allows them to do so.

Among the bravest women I have ever met were a few Jewish women who, having worked for years for planned parenthood or other contraceptive-promoting charities, decided that the time had come to be on the front line and faced abuse and even physical violence. Instead of synagogue, they went one Saturday morning a month to Beacon Street, to help young girls get into the clinic.

Why does abortion raise such passionate feelings? What is it that evokes such rage among its opponents and makes them react with such violence? Is it religious belief that motivates the anti-abortionists? Is it belief in fundamental rights and freedoms that fuels its supporters? Is abortion a feminist issue, or is it a human rights issue – for the mother, the child, or the foetus? How does abortion tie in with the debate about assisted reproduction? Is the abortion debate violent because life is sacred? If so, what does 'sacred' mean to those many people who, in the liberal west, have no real sense of the 'sacred' as conventional religions have understood it?

I was brought up with the view that human life was sacred, and that one did everything to preserve it, but no one ever suggested that 'sacred' applied to an unborn child, for such a being was not a human life. What does sacred mean to Jews?

In Hebrew, the word for 'holy', which is translated into Latin as 'sanctus' and means 'sacred' when translated into English, is *kadosh*. The root (Hebrew like other Semitic languages operates by a system of three-letter roots for all its words) is 'K-d-sh', for which the nearest accurate translation is 'to be separate, special, or consecrated'. When a man betroths a woman in the Jewish marriage service, he says to her, *'Harei at mekuddeshet li ke-dat Moshe ve-Yisrael'*. 'Behold, you are made special, separated out for, consecrated to me according to the laws of Moses and Israel'. When God says to the children of Israel in Leviticus 19, the so-called Holiness Code, 'You shall be kedoshim [holy] because I the Lord your God am kadosh [holy]', the meaning is separate, different. Christians have a strong sense of sacrament, but modern Judaism has no sacrament. Without a Temple, without animal sacrifice, we simply have rituals to order our lives and give thanks. There is no magic, no action, which is equivalent to communion.

When Christians talk about the sanctity of human life, Jews do not quite understand what they mean. We know that human beings are different from animals – Genesis makes that clear: 'And you shall rule over them . . .' (Genesis 1:28). We describe the cemetery as a House of Life, the *Beit Chayyim*. But the idea that a foetus is possessed of a sacred life before birth is foreign to us. The theory of the sanctity of the foetus stems from the ideas of ensoulment in Christianity. The Pythagorean Greeks' view that the soul enters the body at the moment of conception initially held sway among Christians. In the fifth century, Augustine, perhaps the most influential of all the church fathers on the subjects of sex, sin and the soul, introduced the view that homicide applied only to killing a formed foetus, one of forty (or eighty) days gestation (there is a variance). Only formed foetuses can be said to have souls. This comes from the Septuagint reading of Exodus 21:22. The standard translation of the Hebrew passage runs: 'If a man strive and wound a pregnant woman so that her fruit be expelled, but no harm befall her, then shall he be fined as her husband shall assess, and the matter placed before the judges. But if harm befall her, then you shall give life for life.' Human life is sacred, but the unborn child does not count as a life. The Septuagint translation reads one word differently. Where the Hebrew word *'ason'* was translated as 'harm', the Septuagint reads it as 'form'. The translation goes: '. . . if there be no form [yet to the foetus], he shall be fined . . . But if there be form, then you shall give life for life' – applying the life for life principle to the foetus instead of the mother.

In the Jewish tradition, it has always been clear that abortion is not murder. A woman whose life is threatened by the foetus within her can have it dismembered limb from limb while it is still inside her womb, but once the birth has begun and its head (or part of it) has emerged, the child becomes a separate person. Most rabbinic authorities do not permit abortion unless the mother's life is in danger, but a few permit it in cases of extreme mental anguish, and one, Rabbi Jacob Emden, who lived in the eighteeth century, allowed it for reasons of extreme shame, for example when a young woman has become pregnant by someone adulterously and is now contrite.

This is very different from modern Christianity. The Justinian code of the sixth century confirmed that foetuses under forty days did not have souls (temporarily ending an earlier forty/eighty debate). But in 1588 Pope Sixtus V rejected this view and sent forth a papal bull, *Effraenatum*, which declared that abortion was murder whatever stage of development had been reached by the foetus. That bull was rescinded three years later by his successor Pope Gregory XIV, but, in 1869, Pius IX reinstituted Sixtus V's bull. From that point on, the 'modern' view prevailed; foetuses under forty days are no different from any others. Almost everyone in the Catholic church believes the soul is infused at the moment of conception, which accounts for the absolutely negative view of abortion among most Catholics in modern times. The doctrine of original sin is relevant to the debate. Fulgentius argued (*De Fide*, 27, sixth century) that:

It is to be believed beyond doubt that not only men who are come to the use of reason, but infants whether they die in their mother's womb, or after they are born, without baptism, in the name of the Father, Son and Holy Ghost, are punished with everlasting punishment in the eternal fire, because though they have no actual sin of their own,

yet they carry along with them the condemnation of original sin from their first conception and birth.

Augustine had taken the same view; only Aquinas suggested that there might be a possibility of salvation for an
infant which did not survive until birth. Despite Aquinas's
liberal view, the theory of original sin continued to hold
sway – the unborn child which died or was aborted was
condemned to perdition, so that abortion came to be worse
than murder. Hence the practice of baptism of aborted
foetuses, and the invention of a variety of techniques for
ensuring baptism *in utero*.

By contrast, the unborn Jewish child and the Jewish baby
that dies under thirty days old have no proper burial at
all, and are not considered proper persons. Although there
is some discussion in Judaism about the stage at which the
soul enters the foetus, these discussions have no bearing
on the legal status of the embryo. Rabbi Judah the Prince,
editor of the *Mishnah*, the legal code compiled around the
end of the second century CE, and commonly referred
to simply as Rabbi, had two contradictory views. One is
discussed in a story about an encounter between him and
the emperor Antoninus, during which the emperor asked
him at what stage ensoulment took place. Judah replied
that it was from the time of formation. Antoninus replied:
'Can meat remain without salt for three days and not
putrefy? [i.e., either the initial form cannot exist without
the soul or, as some suggest, that three days is the
maximum time between coitus and impregnation and that
the sperm needs the soul to animate it] You must concede
that the soul enters at conception.' Judah concedes.
(Sanhedrin 91b.) Elsewhere, in an account of a conversation
which is impossible to date, when someone asks Judah '. . .
from when is the soul endowed in man; from the time he

leaves his mother's womb or before that time?', he replied, 'From the time he leaves his mother's womb.' (Genesis Rabba 34:10.) There are also numerous occasions where children are supposed to have taken some action in the womb: Jacob and Esau struggle against each other in the womb, and there is a Talmudic instruction to the child to be righteous before leaving the mother's womb. This all suggests that Judaism has had a variety of views on the subject. What is indisputable is that at the moment of birth, the child born at term has a life which is the equal of any other human life.

It is worth considering one more issue. The nearest parallel in Judaism to the Christian question of inheriting perdition rather than heaven comes with the discussion of when a child can enter the world to come. The answers are varied. It is possible from the time of conception, at birth, at the time of circumcision (eight days old), when the child can speak or respond Amen. Clearly, no one was certain. Nor does it seem that anyone was very concerned. The soul does not appear to be linked with immortal life.

The abortion debate in the United States of America is so violent that it even affects assessments of people's fitness to govern, or to hold academic positions. In Britain, although we are reluctant to be quite so judgemental over abortion, we have become very divided in the debate over research on, and using, human embryos, which was particularly obvious while the Warnock Committee, which examined the whole area of assisted conception, was sitting. A recent example of this was when Dame Jill Knight added a clause to the Criminal Justice Bill in 1994 to make it a criminal offence to use the eggs from an aborted foetus for treatment for infertile women, which became statute even though the technology is not yet in place to carry out such treatment. I imagine that anti-abortion campaigners felt that no good should ever be allowed to come of abortion – the view of a 'tainted source' for the eggs held sway. At the same time, an Early Day Motion was laid before the House of Commons, signed by nine Members of Parliament, which criticised the members of the Human Fertilisation and Embryology Authority (of whom I am one), saying that its membership was too easy on the scientists, too liberal, and that it did not represent a wide enough cross-section of views – presumably because it did not contain any out-and-out anti-abortionists.

The Warnock Committee discussed the vexed area of research in association with *in vitro* fertilisation, confronting the problem that some embryos would be 'wasted'. It was thought to be unwise to transplant an embryo on which research had been conducted into a human uterus, until it was known that the techniques used in that research were safe. The pro-research lobby argued that research would lead to safer assisted conception techniques and to reduced congenital disorders, such as cystic fibrosis. The Warnock Committee, holding the embryo in considerable respect and recognising that many people hold deep-seated feelings about human life, came up with a cut-off point for research on human embryos – the point when the primitive streak appeared, between twelve and seventeen days after fertilisation. Opponents of all research on human embryos then argued that this limit was meaningless. The early Voluntary Licensing Authority (on which I served) then made a mistake. We called very young embryos 'pre-embryos', without realising how that would appear a cop-out, politically and scientifically. Politically, the pro-research lobby were made to look as if they thought pre-embryos weren't yet really embryos at all, but some pre-existing form. Scientifically, it is an absolute truth that a pre-embryo, like an embryo, is a fertilised egg but it has not formed into an embryonic shape.

The oldest tale of assisted reproduction was when Sarah 'gave' her handmaid, Hagar, to her husband, Abraham, as a concubine, so that Sarah might have children by her. This was a form of surrogacy, but despite its roots in Torah, many Jewish authorities are extremely negative about surrogacy, arguing that it exploits women (an argument rarely used in Jewish debate), and that it complicates inheritance.

Surrogacy is just one form of 'treatment' for people who are infertile which is causing great disquiet among Jews. In the original Genesis story, it was regarded as a divine miracle that the same Sarah who used surrogacy later gave birth when she was ninety. Today, women in their late-fifties have been giving birth – not miraculously, but as a result of new technologies and stimulatory drugs. Black women can choose to have white babies – to match their husband's colour, perhaps, where there is a mixed marriage, given the technology, though that would be regarded unfavourably by most clinics in Britain. Before the ruling against it in 1994, it was thought it might be possible to use aborted foetuses to gain eggs for fertility treatment. Those who specialise in moral outrage may be all too ready to condemn previously undreamed of advances in science. Even those who consider themselves broad-minded may be challenged as new technologies ask moral questions we are poorly-equipped to deal with, however liberal we are. Jews have traditionally regarded a child as a gift of God, requiring three players – mother, father and God. Dabbling in assisted conception and surrogacy might be seen as interfering with God's will and God's design.

However, Jews have been among the greatest advocates of the wonders of medicine. With our strong life-affirming tradition, we do everything to keep alive, to invent new and better ways of healing and of alleviating disease. We never ask ourselves whether we are interfering with God's design. Instead, we regard ourselves as human beings with free will and God-given intelligence, to be used for the preservation of that most precious of gifts, human life. Modern science and modern medicine, however terrifying the speed of their discoveries, are simply using human intelligence, which is divinely given. We have every right to expect that intelligence to be exercised by morally responsible people for the good of others. If it is not, then it is up to other humans to ensure that abuse does not take place.

Childlessness was a source of terrible misery in Jewish history. Sarah supplied Abraham with Hagar. Rachel said pathetically: 'Give me children, lest I die.' (Genesis 30:1.) Hannah wept in the Temple so piteously that Eli the priest thought she was drunk. (1 Sam. 1:13.) Jewish law allows a man to divorce a wife who is barren after ten years of childlessness. The commandment to be fruitful and multiply is taken very seriously.

Within our background, we should understand women – and men – being desperate to have children by whatever means they can. Assisted conception *per se* should not be anathema to the Jewish community. Yet, stricter rabbinic authorities have spoken out against donor insemination, arguing that unless the donor is the husband, it is tantamount to adultery. They are also highly ambivalent about the use of tissue from aborted foetuses. Some authorities insist that egg donation has to be from another Jewess to ensure the child's Jewish status; others believe it is possible for a child of a donated egg to be Jewish by upbringing and intention like adopted children in non-orthodox Judaism. Some believe the use of more than one embryo for replacement in a woman's womb, in the knowledge that not all embryos would implant, as willingly engineering the waste of life, similar to spilling seed in vain. Similarly, there are different views on the scientific uses of aborted foetuses.

The broader questions still need to be examined. Is it right to make moral decisions on the basis of the aptly named 'yuk factor', because we do not like what we see? Or should we argue that moral debate rests on principles, and the question here must be whether we are providing a benefit or doing harm by allowing these treatments? Is it better for women to have children in their fifties than never have a child at all? Are elderly mothers necessarily worse mothers? There are rare women who have a child naturally in their fifties – we surely cannot legislate against them. Once the technology has been established, should we not all have the right to choose whether or not to use it?

How could one tell a child that its mother never lived because the egg from which it came was derived from an aborted foetus? To some, pregnancies from unborn foetuses would push the boundaries of science too far. To some others, it seems that at last we have a use for those unwanted creatures. To still others, there is something unethical about using the foetuses of women who did not want their children, to create children for women who desperately desire them. Would it not be simpler for the mother to go to full term and give the child to someone who wants it? Or is this failing to realise how important it is that the child has the genes of at least one half of the couple that will become its parents?

We do not know the answers to these questions. Our Jewish tradition just gives us some clues – about the value of human life, about the value of the gift of children, about the feeling that God is a participant in the creation of children. Jews must share in the debate, precisely because we feel differently about the unborn child. We respect children, we desire to have them, and we share sympathy, ages old, for women unable to conceive.

We live in an age when hardly a day goes by without another news story about some great advance in scientific knowledge. When the former Chief Rabbi, Lord Jakobovits, heard that it may be possible genetically to engineer the 'homosexual gene' out of future children, he suggested that parents might choose to do so. The furore caused by his view was considerable. The reaction from the gay community was understandably hostile, and cries of 'Eugenics!' were heard everywhere.

Eugenics has a bad name with good reason – its history is appalling. In the 1920s, discussion of racial hygiene was commonplace. Compulsory sterilisation of mentally ill and handicapped people seemed perfectly acceptable in America, and even Marie Stopes was concerned to limit the breeding of the very poor. There was undoubtedly a sense that it was right to create 'perfect' human beings – in one's own image – and equally right to limit or even eliminate others. When the Nazis came to power they held what had already become a respectable view of mercy killing, as propounded by the scientist and philosopher Ernst Haeckel (1834–1919). In the 1930s they set up the General Foundation for Welfare and Institutional Care, or T-4 as it came to be known, made up of doctors and psychiatrists, and killed 70,000 men, women and children in institutions before the programme was stopped because of protest, largely from clergymen. Eventually, the Nazis attempted, of course, to eliminate groups of people –

notably Jews, gypsies, and homosexuals. The resonance of eugenics is appalling.

Genetic engineering implies eugenics of a very sophisticated kind. If we can remove or repair one gene, we might, for instance, be able to prevent cystic fibrosis, a heart-rending condition leading to early death for many people. We might be able to deal with Tay-Sachs disease, a fatal disease for the children of some Jews from eastern Europe. It may also provide an answer to other common diseases. For instance, there is growing evidence that women are considerably more likely to develop some forms of breast cancer if their mothers or sisters have it – there is a genetic component, though its extent is unclear. A British woman recently had a double mastectomy for preventive reasons, as she was considered to be at a high risk genetically. If we were able to pinpoint those women at very high risk of breast cancer, we might be able to treat them preventively. We could watch them very closely, too, since early diagnosis leads to a better prognosis. We could work more directly on the women concerned to develop a form of genetic treatment to counter their increased risk. We might even be able to alter the gene so it did not carry the risk of breast cancer at all. These investigations and experiments rely on assisted conception techniques. Embryos will have to be treated and defective genes removed, altered or replaced.

Should we be trying to create 'perfect' human beings? Some of our talents may well be genetically transmitted – our degree of musicality, for instance, or our mathematical ability – as well as some of our defects. A world a century hence when genetically transmitted diseases may have been eliminated might see the genetic engineers' attention turning to creating geniuses. There have even been sperm banks in America which sell the seed of Nobel prizewinners to ambitious would-be parents. The technique is in place to select a 'designer' baby. Although the use of genetic engineering to provide healing is acceptable, even that requires strict legal and ethical governance, with full consent and the maintenance of confidentiality. But the creation of 'super-children' begs many questions, including what value is put on those of us who are less than 'perfect'.

William Rees-Mogg wrote in *The Times* (13 December 1993) that he would not have cared to have been part of an experiment to produce 'a pool of exceptional general talent, from which some pre-eminent talent will come'. His reasons are mixed, but he hopes it will not happen in his lifetime. If it is not to appear in his lifetime or ours, we must take care to debate these issues very widely, and to regulate assisted conception, genetic engineering and gene therapy in humans. Gene therapy is now vetted in Britain after the Polkinghorne Committee, set up to examine it under the chairmanship of scientist and clergyman the Reverend Dr John Polkinghorne, considered it in depth. Even if regulation via the Human Fertilisation and Embryology Authority is strict here, other countries may not be so demanding. The combination of assisted conception and gene therapy is where abuse could take place, and also where public understanding has not yet caught up with the speed of scientific advance.

The eugenicists may be in the ascendant in some countries where the birthrate is too high, where families are only allowed to produce one child, and where the prospect of one 'perfect' child seems remarkably attractive. One does not have to be a science-fiction addict to fear the rogue gene, or simply the gradual breakdown of genetic material as one moves further away from Mother Nature. Strict controls are necessary, with some international force, as is a public debate about what is acceptable, nationally and internationally.

We have the beginning of a genuine public debate about genetic screening, as the result of work conducted by the Nuffield Commission on Bioethics, which published its report in December 1993. Should insurance companies be able to require genetic screening, when it would materially affect policies? How should society deal with confidentiality? Should screening ever be required by employers? There is an urgent need for the debate to move on from genetic screening to genetic engineering, so that we can decide what kinds of interventions are acceptable, what we should try to prevent, and who, ultimately, should take control of this fascinating and extremely important series of scientific advances.

As Judaism has such a strong emphasis on life and healing, it should have much to contribute to this debate, which cannot be waged on traditional lines of orthodox versus reform. It will no longer be relevant to talk about the use of donor insemination, other than by husband, as adultery, for the donor *could* be the husband, with gametes considerably changed by genetic manipulation. It may be right to argue against placing more than one fertilised egg in *in vitro* treatment of women, but when those eggs have been genetically treated to remove or alter a defective gene which would lead to appalling suffering for a child, is it still right to say only one at a time, when chances of implantation may be very low? What is the right balance between the desires of parents to have healthy children to fulfil the *mitzvah* of being fruitful and multiplying, and the necessary research work that would have to be carried out to achieve this, necessitating the destruction of many human fertilised eggs? As Jews we must add our voices to views held outside our community. We have an underlying value system and a life-affirming tradition and can contribute by taking a different angle.

Thus far we have played a relatively minor role. Lord Jakobovits, contributed to discussions around the time of the Warnock Committee. I have served on the old Voluntary and then Interim Licensing Authority and now serve on the Human Fertilisation and Embryology Authority. Our views have not necessarily been the same, but the Jewish contribution to the debate has been relatively muted at a time when disagreements have been so violent that people became almost speechless with rage and reason vanished out of the window.

The Human Fertilisation and Embryology Act, which established the Human Fertilisation and Embryology Authority to inspect and monitor centres offering *in vitro* fertilisation and donor insemination went through as legislation some five years after it was originally planned, and gave rise indirectly to a new abortion debate. There was an attempt to reduce the legal limit of gestation for an abortion from twenty-eight to twenty-four weeks, which in practice would mean twenty weeks. There were good arguments in favour of the reduction. Medical technology had advanced so far that it was possible to sustain premature babies born at twenty-seven and twenty-eight weeks in a more or less routine way. Babies born at twenty-three weeks had survived, too, though the difficulties they would face in later life were fearsome to contemplate. There was more-or-less universal agreement that the limit should come down to below likely viability. This has now become the case. Some argue on to reduce the time to eighteen weeks, meaning fourteen weeks in practice, in the hope that legal abortion would be abolished in Britain.

Some might argue that we should think entirely differently about all this. The distinguished legal philosopher

Ronald Dworkin suggested that if it were indeed possible to encourage people to think differently, by hearing out the issues in a less emotional way, moral fundamentalism, on both sides, might be short-lived. Dworkin assumes it is unrealistic to believe that the abortion controversy will be solved by compromise, an assumption most people would have no hesitation in accepting:

> Is a foetus a helpless unborn child with rights and interests of its own from the moment of conception? If so, then permitting abortion is murder, and having an abortion is worse than abandoning an inconvenient infant to die. If not, then people who claim to be 'pro-life' are either acting in deep error or are sadistic, puritanical bigots, eager not to save lives but to punish women for what they regard as sexual sin.

No compromise. Suppose, however, that this kind of thinking is based on an intellectual confusion, which could be identified, analysed and dispelled? Then a responsible legal settlement, 'one that will not insult or demean any group', would be possible. Dworkin then adduces a 'derivative' objection to abortion, an objection based on the theory that foetuses, like grown human beings, have rights, including the right not to be killed. Anyone who accepts that argument believes that a government must protect those rights, as it does for other citizens. The second objection is what he calls the 'detached' objection. Not based on rights or interests, the theory states that abortion is wrong in principle because it 'disregards and insults the intrinsic value, the sacred character, of any stage or form of human life'. Anyone who holds that view believes that government has a 'detached' responsibility for protecting the intrinsic value of human life.

Dworkin argues convincingly that most people actually

hold the latter view, which is borne out by the religious views discussed above, and that most people, including those who are Catholics, Muslims or Jews, regard it as 'a bad thing, a kind of cosmic shame', when human life at any stage is extinguished. That view does not necessarily lead to the same kind of desire to force government to legislate against abortion. Indeed, he suggests that because most people hold that 'detached' view, it is perfectly possible for them to believe that abortion is morally wrong, yet also believe that the decision must be left to the pregnant woman, as the person with the greatest involvement. I am absolutely convinced by that argument. Though I would *never* have an abortion myself, I believe it not a decision that I should make for others.

That is an approach which has particular attraction for a country like America which, riven by abortion strife, with views on abortion being the acid test of respectability on a variety of other sorts of issues. Dworkin's book also includes the fascinating piece of information that in the United States, Catholic women are as likely as any other women in the population to have abortions, and Protestants and Jews are less likely. Catholic women are thirty per cent more likely than Protestants to have abortions. This is not merely a piece of fascinating but useful data; it actually displays to fine effect Dworkin's thesis that people really do feel differently about abortion, that it is not a question of the rights of the unborn child, but something to do with the sanctity of life, irrespective of people's religious attachments or upbringing.

Sanctity is a curious word, and indeed concept, to find in a book by a distinguished legal philosopher such as Dworkin. He does not define what he means by the sanctity, or inviolability, of human life. In that, he is very little different from the rest of us – most of us cannot articulate what we mean by the sanctity of human life. A complicated series of views make up the conviction in many of us that life *is* sacred – although we do not rate an unborn child as having value comparable with a born child, we do think it has a form of life, not to be treated frivolously. We derive these ideas largely from religious teaching, whether or not we are convinced by the teaching we were brought up with.

The concern is about the value of *human* life, which tells us something about the nature of religious thought in most of the world's great religions, and a disregard, in many ways, for the sanctity of animal life. Although there are rituals surrounding animal sacrifice, they do not suggest that the animal itself has a life which is sacred. It is regarded as legitimate, indeed praiseworthy, to sacrifice to God the best of the flock and the unblemished stock. The words surrounding the sacrificial rituals make it plain that regular sacrifices were made to feed God, and the priests and Levites could take some of the choicest meat for themselves. Sacrifices of the whole of the burned offerings, where human beings had none of the meat, were to appease God. God's anger meant that his nose grew hot – for the Hebrew words for anger and nose are the same – and the smell of the burning sacrifice soothed Him.

Animals always had to be treated properly under Jewish law. One had to feed one's animals before oneself and animals were entitled to a day of rest in the same way as human beings, although that did not make the lives of animals sacred. There is, however, a very curious facet of attitudes to animal blood. In the legislation surrounding ritual slaughter (*shechitah*) it is made very clear that the blood must be poured away on to the ground. 'For the blood is the life . . .' (Deuteronomy 12:23) and therefore goes back to the earth or God, from which it came. This suggests that the animal has something special about it – if not a soul, then certainly a life which is derived from God and returned to Him.

In Judaism, the attitudes towards ensoulment and to human rather than animal life do not present a wholly consistent picture, any more than in any other religion. In Judaism, a new-born baby which dies does not receive a full burial unless it has lived for thirty days or more. That must be a law made by men. No woman who has carried a baby to term, or has given birth to a still-born child, would feel less love and loss for a baby less than a month old than for a child more than a month old. Similarly, few women enter the abortion process lightly, and even fewer feel light-hearted about it afterwards. That is why taking what many women feel to be right – a belief that abortion is wrong – and removing from that principle the idea of the derivative rights of the foetus, is so helpful. A position can be espoused with which many women, and men, religious and secularist, will feel profoundly comfortable.

Despite a history of leaving babies on hillsides, killing female children, drowning babies and encouraging the deaths of children at the hand of their wet-nurses, some accounts of children's history seem truly terrible. The sophisticated John Boswell's *The Kindness of Strangers* is about foundlings and the tiny percentage of them who survived; Philip Bean's and Joy Melville's *Lost Children of the Empire* is a book about children sent abroad to Australia and Canada as child migrants, and the appalling treatment many of them received. Wartime and the period shortly after created conditions which allowed the authorities to send children abroad without telling their parents where they were. Their lives were important to the country, but not their emotions. Human life is sacred, but emotional needs come low in the pecking order.

We humans are different from animals, superior to them, and our lives are sacred, but in an ill-defined way. Deeply religious Catholics will rage against abortion and yet turn their backs on thousands of unwanted children who are dumped, raped, exploited and murdered in the towns of Latin America. Jews will allow abortion in most cases, but argue it on therapeutic grounds, rather than worrying whether the foetus has a soul. Catholics invented ways of baptising unborn infants in their dying or dead mother's wombs to prevent them from going into limbo or perdition for eternity. Jews did not give a still-born child or a child under thirty days old a full burial. Yet both believe that life is sacred and both are ambivalent (at best) about assisting women to have babies when they are infertile.

So much for the beginning of life. What happens at the end? When God said to King Hezekiah: 'Set your house in order for you shall die . . .' (II Kings 20:1–2), Hezekiah turned his face to the wall and prayed, reminding God of the good things he had done and the things for which he deserved a rethink of the sentence of death. On that occasion he recovered, and God added fifteen years to his life.

On the whole, in the Jewish tradition, we don't die well. We rage and we storm. None of us needs that verse, 'Do not go gentle into that good night' (Dylan Thomas). For us, life, *chayyim*, is the great blessing. *L'chayyim* is the toast to which we raise our glasses. Integral to our value system is the rabbinic teaching that to save a single human life one may, indeed must, break all but three of the commandments of our legal system. The exceptions are the prohibitions on murder, incest and idolatry. Within the Mishnah, we read:

> One single man was created in the world, to teach that, if
> any man has caused a single soul to perish, it is as if he
> had caused a whole world to perish. If any man saves alive
> a single person, it is as if he has saved a whole world.
>
> (Mishnah. Sanhedrin 4:5)

Add to that the belief, in traditional Judaism, that God has
decreed the time of each individual's death, and that at
the beginning of the ten days of penitence, on Jewish New
Year, the Book of Life is opened, in which, if God feels we
have done well, our names are inscribed for another year,
and the importance of life becomes entirely clear. The New
Year greeting is not only 'Happy New Year', but also, 'May
you be inscribed in the Book of Life.' Indeed, one can avert
a decree of death by charity, repentance and prayer – if
they are all sincerely meant – traditionally that is what
King Hezekiah did. In some Jewish folk-traditions you can
avert a sentence of death by changing the name of the sick
person – after all, the names are written in the book –
which is why in most *Ashkenazi* (European) Jewish traditions, children are never named after a living grandparent, because to do that would be tantamount to writing
the grandparents out of history.

Life is God's gift, and it is clear that we had better value
it, and do anything we possibly can to preserve it. Surgeons
and physicians are held in the highest regard because they
are thought to have been given the power to heal by God.
In the Talmud we read: 'The school of Rabbi Ishmael
taught: "And he shall cause him to be thoroughly healed
..." (Ex. 22:19) are the words from which it can be derived
that authority was given by God to the medical man to
heal.' (Berachot 60a.) In Ecclesiasticus (Ben Sira 38:1–2) we
read: 'Honour a physician according to thy need of him,

with the honours due unto him. For verily the Lord hath created him.'

In the Jewish tradition, we try everything to save life, including amazingly unlikely interventions which have little chance of success. When someone is dying and cannot be healed, the Jewish tradition comes unstuck. We are not, on the whole, kind. We read in a rabbinic collection (Ecclesiasticus Rabba v. 6): 'Even when the physician realises that the end is nigh, he should order his patient to eat this and drink that, not eat this and not drink that. On no account should he tell him that the end is nigh.' In the commentary to our legal code, the Shulchan Aruch, we read: 'It is forbidden to cause the dying to pass away quickly; for instance, if a person is dying over a long time and cannot depart, it is forbidden to remove the pillow or cushion from underneath him.' We don't, traditionally, make the going easy. The eighteenth century tradition of the good death is utterly foreign to the Jewish view.

We might reflect on why that should be. If human life is valued so highly, there is an obvious reason to cherish every last moment of it, even if the patient is deeply uncomfortable, or in intense pain. Perhaps even more importantly, Jews are what Christians might call 'a bit shaky' on the afterlife – since we know what we have in this life, we tend to stick with it as long as possible, rather than abandoning ourselves to the uncertainties of the next.

Despite orthodox Jews' assertion in their daily morning prayers that they believe in an afterlife, the nature of that afterlife is unspecified. Rabbinic statements about this life being a prelude, or an anteroom, to the world to come, only date from the period of the beginning of Christianity, with little evidence of earlier traditions. The belief in a shady place where nothing much happens and where all is colourless goes back to the biblical period among Jews, and is found in the Biblical Sheol. And, though orthodox Jews do not fear this after-death experience, the uncertainty of it makes them all the more determined to hang on to this life.

Christianity takes a very different view (perhaps I should say views, for, like Judaism, Christianity is not monolithic in its theology). Many Christians believe that this life is a preparation for the world to come. They often experience an intense vision of heaven. There is also hell. Many Christians caring for the dying create a supportive environment that comes from a passionately held faith. Though hospices have medieval origins, the modern hospice movement was founded in Britain by a Christian woman of great vision, Dame Cicely Saunders, O.M. The idea of people dying in pain was totally unacceptable to her. Part of her revulsion was related to her Christian faith – the journey to the afterlife should be a good one, and a good death was much to be desired. For committed Christians looking after the terminally ill, there is much to be gained spiritually from helping to alleviate the earthly pain of the dying, in order to allow them to focus on the end – and on their next life.

In Christianity there is a tradition which argues that suffering ennobles the spirit, that a person of spiritual experience is one who has suffered, emulating Jesus. Judaism, on the other hand, has a marked aversion to suffering, and works hard to get rid of it at all costs. In this crucial area of death, however, most Christians believe in alleviating pain even if it means shortening life, while Jews regard any life-shortening, for whatever reason, as unacceptable, and feel we must simply put up with the pain if its relief is life-threatening.

There is one exception. The maidservant of Rabbi Judah ha-Nasi (the supposed compiler of the Mishnah), decided that his pain was intolerable and had to be stopped. His students were praying for his life to be spared. She dropped a jar she was carrying, causing them, briefly, to stop praying. The Prince slipped away – his suffering was over, and the maidservant was never condemned in Jewish tradition.

In 1994 there was a book in the American bestseller list entitled *How We Die* by Sherwin B. Nuland. It is a passionate call for people's dying moments not to be clinical, not to be at the hospital away from those they love, but near to home or at home and, to some extent under their own control. It is a very well-written book, by a Jewish physician. To someone from Britain it is a recital of the obvious.

More than fifty per cent of deaths in Britain still occur in hospital, but it is a percentage which is falling. The remainder are in familiar surroundings: at home, cared for by family and friends, perhaps with the support of local doctors and nurses or in a nearby hospice or nursing home. When it comes to pain control, no questions are asked, as there are in America, about the danger of addiction. What does it matter, if one is dying anyway? In America, eighty per cent of deaths are in hospital, a percentage which is rising. Although there is an active hospice movement in America, and although the experts have a great knowledge of pain control, the system of health care payment has made it difficult for hospices to be properly funded, and many people die in great pain. It is hardly surprising that there is debate about assisted suicide, and a law requiring institutions in receipt of state funds to ask whether individuals have made an advance directive, demanding a cessation of treatment at some point, or appointed a health care proxy to make end-of-life decisions on their behalf if they are incapable. It is as if America has adopted the Jewish view – do everything you can to save life. This may suggest that Britain is in some ways more institutionally Christian, while America is more deeply evangelised.

Judaism scores well in its attitudes to bereavement. Its rituals mirror what psychologists tell us are the normal stages of grief. The time immediately after a death is involved with rituals surrounding the body, sitting with it, reciting Psalms, then washing the body, and wrapping it in a shroud. The funeral, traditionally a burial, which the community does itself, spades of earth landing on the coffin lid with resounding clangs, is bitter, bringing home the reality of death.

Orthodox Judaism does not allow cremation, but many people who are not synagogue members frequently ask for a cremation to be conducted by the rabbi of a non-orthodox synagogue, sometimes to the irritation of reform and liberal rabbis who feel taken advantage of by people who have never shown any interest in the community during their lifetimes. Nevertheless, Jews who are apparently completely disaffected from the community often choose to have a religious Jewish funeral of some kind.

After the funeral comes the *shiva*, seven days of mourning, with evening prayers in the home every night, with mourners and friends coming to pay their respects, bringing gifts of food (there is always food in the Jewish tradition), encouraging the bereaved to talk about their loss. By the end of seven days the chief mourners are exhausted, delighted to see the back of their callers. Then comes the *shloshim*, the thirty days of lesser mourning but no parties, no celebrations, and daily prayers at the synagogue, which continue into the next stage, the eleven months before the unveiling of the tombstone, when the year of mourning is over and life goes back to normal, as much as it can.

Christianity has lost many of its mourning customs. Though individual Christian communities may be very supportive, and many individuals and families develop excellent ways of coping with grief, there is an underlying assumption that we do not need to talk about death. Anna Quindlen, a columnist on the *New York Times*, wrote on 4 May 1994:

> More than sex, more than faith, even more than its usher death, grief is unspoken, publicly ignored except for those moments at the funeral that are over too quickly.

Judaism and Islam and, to some extent, Sikhism, have ritualised the grieving process, and insisted that the community comes to listen, to hear the outpourings of the broken-hearted. And one must not forget the therapeutic effect of the famed Irish wake . . .

Foolishly, we fail to learn from each other. The Christian concept of the hospice has much to offer us, as has the good death, in terms of fewer interventions, less surgery, less chemotherapy and less misery. Jews could, in my view, come round to alleviating pain, to making sure that loved ones die well, to creating the environment in which the things they want to say can be expressed. I also believe Christians could learn to grieve better. They could learn from the Jewish rituals of mourning that it is possible to structure opportunities to express loss, and fear, and anger, and grief. It is for us Jews to see that in Christian theology there are elements unfamiliar and foreign to us which can lead to a better attitude to death and dying. Christians have the task of looking at Jewish theology, which is so intensely life-affirming that it values the bereaved (having left the dying to get on with it) and that it deliberately creates a structured process of grief.

Many years ago now, in London, the germ of an idea was born – an inter-faith hospice – where Jews, Christians, Muslims and others, would be cared for together. It would not be *non*-denominational. It would be *inter*-denominational. It has now been running for ten years, first as home-care, more recently as an in-patient unit. Though largely serving Jews and Christians, other faiths are represented. Each faith recognises what the others bring.

If we are to do this, we have to throw off the chains of our traditions to some extent. We have to be brave in criticising our own faith and traditions, our own communities. We have also to be generous to the other faiths, traditions and communities, in a way which goes far beyond normal, polite interest. There is always a great danger with interfaith dialogue that it can merely scratch the surface. Real dialogue is uncomfortable, and takes an enormous amount of time. It shows us the gaps in our own faith. It makes us realise how ignorant we are. It sometimes demonstrates how deliberately, in our theological and legal texts, we have downgraded and despised each other. Dialogue can cause pain and discomfiture. It can also bring huge rewards.

If we are serious about looking at how we die and how we support the bereaved, the religious significance of recognising life as God's gift, to be treasured and then handed back, will not be lost on us. 'The Lord gave and the Lord hath taken away. Blessed be the name of the Lord.' If we can do that as well as recognising the value and quality of that life as God's gift, we will treat our friends and family better, and enjoy a richer death ourselves. When we understand that life includes both the good death and support for those who live on, we can join in the Jewish toast to life. Then, and only then, can we say: 'L'Chayyim', 'To life!'

6

'Justice, justice shall you follow':

Social justice in Judaism

I was brought up to believe that anything one can possibly do to alleviate someone else's suffering must be done.

It was not that I came from a particularly socially-aware family, though there was a long tradition of community work, but central to the Jewish tradition is the belief that suffering is to be avoided at all costs. The Christian sense that suffering might ennoble the spirit is foreign to the Judaism I was brought up with. We believe that suffering is neither God's punishment, nor a way of refining the spirit, nor a route to personal redemption. Some Christians point to the Book of Job in the Hebrew bible and believe that Job was made to suffer as a 'test'; but Jews find the Book of Job difficult to understand, to the extent that some Jewish biblical scholars have argued that it is not a Jewish book at all, but a foreign import.

You can find most views in Judaism, if you really try. My colleague and teacher, Rabbi Dr Louis Jacobs, had to refuse the eminent Catholic publishers, Darton, Longman and Todd, when they asked him to write a book about

Jewish theology from an authoritative point of view, because, he said, he could only write a book entitled *A Jewish Theology*, there being so many different, and equally valid, views. There are, however, some central Jewish ideas. Among these is the idea that redemption comes about as a result of human action, and is part of the relationship between the divine and humanity. It comes by action rather than by faith, though the act of repentance is also a spiritual act. That is the main theme of our Day of Atonement, the most solemn day of the Jewish year, when we are required to make our peace with those we have sinned against, and compensate them where possible, before we dare to stand in front of God and seek forgiveness and atonement.

I believe that is absolutely right. I read Auden's 'Musée des Beaux Arts' in my early teens, when I was trying to come to terms with the holocaust, and with the fact that so many people I knew, personally or through their writings, had failed to protest or join a resistance movement. The poem starts: 'About suffering they were never wrong, The Old Masters . . .' In the Brueghel painting, a young man comes tumbling out of the sky but the world doesn't notice. Ordinary life continues unchanged while extraordinary and terrible things are happening.

> About suffering they were never wrong,
> The Old Masters. How well they understood
> Its human position; how it takes place
> While someone else is eating or opening a window, or
> just walking dully along;
> . . .
> They never forgot
> That even the dreadful martyrdom must run its course
> Anyhow in a corner, some untidy spot
> Where the dogs go on with their doggy life and the

torturer's horse
Scratches its innocent behind on a tree . . .

In other ways, the old masters were often wrong: they were unable to convey what suffering was about because they could not depict it pictorially. Thousands of paintings of the passion of Jesus are meant to inspire religious devotion, rather than define suffering. The flagellation, the massacre of the innocents and the martyrdoms of saints are painted with graphic horror to tell stories or create fervour – but how much do they tell us about suffering? Some things cannot be conveyed pictorially.

For me, words do it better, and ideally words from those who have suffered themselves. That way I can begin to understand. During my teenage years, I realised that the only way I could come to terms with the horror which has so affected my family and my people, was by listening to and reading the memories of those who actually suffered. There are those who survived Nazi concentration camps who have no words left. They cannot explain what happened to them, because human expression does not plumb the depths of human suffering. I remember a concentration camp survivor talking about the sense of rising panic as they were loaded on to cattle trucks, sealed so that they could not even see out, and left to travel in appallingly over-crowded conditions for four days without food or drink. Imagine that railway carriage locked overnight, packed with people. No water. Intense heat. Those of us who have been in traffic-jams in a heat-wave should be able to begin to imagine that. But the heat? The stench? The uncontrollable terror? No old master or television picture can depict smell, claustrophobia or fear.

Many of those who have suffered profoundly receive specialist help. The rest of us are not specialists. Our understanding of suffering is very limited, unless we have personally gone through tragic personal loss. If we are even to begin to understand the nature of the terrible things human beings can do to one another, we have to extend our imagination, listen to the experiences of those who have suffered, and be willing to stop and give some comfort.

Auden's poem described Brueghel's painting in which Icarus, trying to fly, is ignored when he falls out of the sky and drowns. One *has* to act and it is those who act, and risk their own well-being to alleviate others' suffering, who are truly praiseworthy, and as near as Judaism gets to the idea of saints.

Judaism is a religion of action. The general view, though by no means wholly and always felt, is that the bulk of human suffering is a result of human action, and that we actively bring the most terrible things upon each other. Hugo Gryn, congregational rabbi and distinguished broadcaster, sometimes tells a story about what happened when a group of rabbis put God on trial at Auschwitz for what He was allowing to happen to the Jews in the concentration camps. God was found guilty, at which point one of the rabbis stood up and said: 'My friends, the time has come for the evening prayer . . .' God was guilty, because He could have intervened, but chose not to. Guilty though He was, He was still due human worship and adoration.

The problem is the nature of divine intervention, and the question of whether God can intervene (of course He can, He's omnipotent, isn't He?), but won't. The usual reply is that He has given us free will. This is the trite answer. The sophisticated answer is also free will, for the nature of divinely-given free will that allows us to do the most dreadful things to one another and then says, if it gets too dreadful I shall intervene, is not free will as we understand it.

There are other sorts of suffering, of disease of body or mind, the 'natural' disasters (as our frozen pipes were described by our insurance company). This is on the whole suffering which is not the 'fault' of humans, although it could be a human failure to prevent diseases, or insufficient human effort in trying to find cures. It is worth pondering what Judaism might have to say about such situations, other than an absolute requirement, with our strong life-affirming tradition, for more resources to be poured into research.

Judaism has a well-known, prophetic punishment for wrong-doing – the certainty that sin will be rewarded by awful events, and that God will not stint in his application of thunderbolts and exile from the land. Indeed, there are those, mostly among the ultra-orthodox, fundamentalist wing of Judaism, who even argue that the holocaust was a punishment from God for lack of adherence to the laws on the part of the Jewish people. I find that view reprehensible. There are also the chastisements of love – the theory that God will chastise especially hard those whom He loves best, one of the interpretations of the suffering servant of Isaiah. For Christians, the suffering servant is the forerunner of Jesus, but for Jews he is the people Israel, and he is suffering because God loves him too much, not too little. Jews also explain suffering with a curious, and uncharacteristic, fatalism – that this is the way of the world, the way things happen. The line, 'Purge me with hyssop' (Psalm 51:7) is an important phrase within Judaism. Perhaps we can learn from suffering.

All explanations of suffering lead to the requirement of human endeavour, be it the effort of a sick person to get better, or of specialists and carers to heal. All laws but three can be broken to save a single human life, underlining the extent to which life is considered by Judaism to be of paramount value.

What this means in terms of life-support machines or transplants is not clear. What are the implications in relation to the allocation of scarce resources? What do QALYs (Quality Adjusted Life Years) have to offer? What should we say about an attitude that requires us to keep alive people who no longer wish to live? We don't have all the answers, but we do know that it is our obligation to take action. The Isaianic prophetic message is to 'open the blind eyes', 'to heal the sick' and 'free the captive from his chains' (Isaiah 42:7 etc). Isaiah also cried out against ritual for its own sake: 'Is this the fast that I have chosen, a day for a man to afflict his soul? Is it just to bow down like a bulrush, and to spread sackcloth and ashes under oneself? Is *this* what you would call a fast, a day acceptable to the Lord? Is it not this kind of fast I have chosen? To loose the bonds of wickedness and undo heavy burdens and let the oppressed go free and break every yoke?' (Isaiah 58:5–6). Religious ritual and rites are to no avail. Faith is of no interest. A sense of justice and compassion is not enough. Redemption requires action. Human suffering requires alleviation. A cure may be possible, but it is not the cure that is important, rather the action taken to help others.

Sometimes, of course, such action is political. The relationship between Judaism and politics is complicated, but there is a clear thrust that the individual must take part in society. Whether that implies a particular stance is a different matter, though there are many Jews who would have said, until relatively recently, that the natural stance of the

Jew was on the left – Labour or Liberal in Britain, Democrat in the United States.

Of course, there have been many distinguished Jewish politicians on the right – including Disraeli (although he was baptised, he was thought of, and thought of himself, as a Jew), Sir Keith Joseph, and Sir Leon Brittan. Voting patterns among Jews suggest that, as with other groups, they move to the right as they become more affluent. There is still a curious relationship with the prophetic tradition, and a feeling that the Jews have to try to put things right in this world, a different role from that of those who would describe themselves as Christian socialists. Judaism is about social justice, certainly, but also about the individual and his or her duties and rights. Christian socialism has a more collective strand, away from the emphasis on the individual.

There are many lectures and seminars on 'Judaism and politics', or 'The natural stance of the Jew in politics is on the Left', or 'Judaism and human rights'. Christian colleagues, on the other hand, often host within their churches a cross-party debate on a variety of issues.

It is no surprise that one finds in Jewish thought comments such as: 'It is as if there are men in a boat, and one man takes an auger and begins to bore a hole underneath his seat. His companions say to him, "What are you doing?" He replies, "What business is it of yours? Am I not boring only under my seat?" They answer, "It is our business, because the water will come in and swamp the boat with us in it".' (Lev. Rabba, IV, 6.) We are all in it together.

There is, of course, a sense of mutual obligation to be found in Christianity as well, but the Church of England is part of an 'establishment' church. Some of their bishops sit as of right in the House of Lords, and those who are not yet bishops may not stand for parliament. They are part of the constitutional fabric of British society. In modern parlance they are official stakeholders in the political process, yet, in one way at least, excluded from it by not being allowed to stand for parliament. They are nevertheless expected, in a curious, unspecified way, to uphold the moral fabric of society. If one is to believe the Press, they are expected to have an essentially conservative view, to maintain the image of England as 'a green and pleasant land'.

The same does not apply to Jews, or non-conformists. Lord Jakobovits does not sit in the House of Lords by virtue of being Chief Rabbi, but because his vision of Britain, his moral stance, seemed deeply sympathetic to Baroness (then Mrs) Thatcher when she was prime minister. In Peregrine Worsthorne's memorable words: 'Judging by the language of the Christian Bishops, Catholic as much as Anglican, this government is bent on doing the Devil's Work. Only the Chief Rabbi, in his pronouncements, makes any attempt to suggest that what she (Mrs Thatcher) is trying to do might be pleasing to God.' (*Sunday Telegraph*, 10 January 1988.)

When I stood for parliament in 1983, for the then SDP, in Tooting, South London, I was hugely amused, and very touched, by the way clergy of other religions reacted. They treated me as one of them, and wanted to support me. There were eight debates in parish churches within and on the edge of the constituency, which the clergy often chaired. While showing no preference, obviously, at the actual debate, they would show their support later on. Some removed their dog-collars and came to campaign on the other side of the constituency, where they would not be recognised. Others passed little notes . . . 'We clergy must stick together . . .' It began to look as if they thought the natural stance of the clergy in politics was in the middle, yet there were difficulties. Should the clergy, including rabbis, preach politics from the pulpit? If the clergy were in the middle, were they alienated from extremes of both right and left? In 1985 the then Archbishop of Canterbury, Dr Robert Runcie, introduced and publicly supported the conclusions of his own commission's working party on the inner city, 'Faith in the City'. There was a national outcry. The press lambasted the report as communist; it displayed a 'bias to the poor'. This was not the stuff of Christianity. This was Marxism.

The Church of England was using the prophetic tradition in criticising both the political and the social attitudes that create human misery. At about the same time, Rabbi Dr Jonathan Sacks, now the Chief Rabbi, published a pamphlet for the Social Affairs Unit, an essentially right-wing think-tank, headed by Dr Digby Anderson, entitled: 'Wealth and Poverty: A Jewish Response'. He pointed out that Judaism regards poverty as an unmitigated evil, that God is the spokesman for the poor by being their champion when they are oppressed, and there is no virtue in embracing poverty, in abandoning worldly goods, or espousing asceticism. The world was made for us by God, and we should enjoy the good things it gives us. There is no Jewish equivalent to the monastic ideal. Salo Baron, author of the vast and authoritative *Social and Religious History of the Jews*, makes it clear that:

There was nothing in that book [the Book of the Pious, a thirteenth century work often cited as a Jewish lay pietistic work with an ascetic streak] which resembled the early Christian and Franciscan ideals of poverty. All that mattered was honesty in dealing with both Jews and Genti-

les and charitableness in dispensing the fruits of one's
labours . . .

Sacks, with others, has classed this as a central plank in
Jewish thought, and believes it is unchallengeable. To fight
to improve conditions for the poor, to regard poverty as
an 'unmitigated evil', does not mean that we have to join
the poor, or to regard God as being biased towards them.
In a 'good' society, the rich take action to assist the poor,
for the sake of the society.

The then Chief Rabbi, now Lord Jakobovits, took a view
that was different from that in 'Faith in the city', a
view which led to something of a furore in the press and
the religious community. He published his response,
entitled 'From Doom to Hope', in which he cited his views
on inner cities, opinions very different from those of many
other Jews – and certainly from mine. Lord Jakobovits'
view is that the proper thing to do is encourage the poor
to stand on their own two feet, to pull themselves up by
their bootstraps and establish their independence. He
didn't question what had brought them into poverty in the
first place. During the mid- to late-eighties, Conservative
ministers quoted with approbation what they took to be a
classic Jewish view. On 19 February, 1986, Kenneth Baker
said, quoting the then Chief Rabbi:

A Jewish religious contribution would lay greater emphasis
on building up self-respect by encouraging ambition and
enterprise . . . let them [parents] encourage ambition and
enterprise in every negro child as Jewish parents encouraged in their children and they will pull down their ghetto
walls as surely as we demolished ours.

Is this a vision for this world? There are any number of
political stances, most of which can be made to accord

with the underlying thrust of religious institutions. The distinction here is between a religious group that regards individuals as part of a community that has little concept of individual salvation, such as Judaism, and another, such as Christianity, where the individual route to salvation is well-marked and, although there are community duties, the sense of the individual's role and own religious path is much greater.

In this officially Christian country, where wealth has grown rapidly, particularly for those aged between twenty-five and forty-five, charitable giving has not kept pace with inflation. Those who made most out of the boom years of the 1980s proportionately gave the least to charity. The obligation in Jewish law is to give ten per cent of one's income. From medieval times, charitable donations enabled the community elders to provide a hand-out of food on a daily basis to the destitute, and dowries for poor girls so that they could get married. The moral obligation of charity is combined with an expectation from the poor in society that they will receive it. Haim Cohn, former Israeli attorney general, makes the excellent point that the duty to give *tsedakah*, the ten per cent of charitable obligation, implies a collateral right on the part of the poor to receive. The meek gratitude associated with some overly sentimentalised Victorian Christian philanthropy is inclined to stick in the Jewish craw. I give simply because I have more than you, and I can afford to. It is chance that I have more than you, and, when I give, it balances better the scales of social justice. It is not something I do out of the incredible generosity of my spirit.

This attitude is combined with an emphasis on particular ways of giving. The great Jewish teacher Maimonides (1135–1204) listed liberating the poor person from ever needing to ask again as the highest of his eight orders of charity (his list starts at giving willingly but not enough, through to giving enough but grudgingly, to giving to an unknown recipient, etc.) Giving ten per cent of income gave one no special moral virtue. For that, one had to give twenty per cent or more, and perform physical acts called 'deeds of lovingkindness', *'gemilut chasadim'*.

Those acts of 'lovingkindness' are the supreme demonstration of charity. The basic ten per cent is merely a form of social taxation, but with the freedom to give it to whom one chooses. It is acts of 'lovingkindness', the willingness to scrub the floor, clean up after an incontinent old lady, mop up the vomit and deal with the stench, which comes nearer to Christian concepts of *caritas*, charity, than the morally upright, accepted command to give *tsedakah*.

All this was enshrined in Jewish law and thought long before the concept of human rights, including those enshrined in the United Nations Covenants on civil and political rights, among which are the rights to food and housing. The supreme dignity of humanity, which is essential for a concept of human rights, is enshrined in early Biblical texts. *Tsedakah* donations are to be made to anyone, not only Jews, for need occurs irrespective of colour, class and community. All races are included, by tracing descent from Adam and Noah. The bulk of the Jewish law was primarily concerned, however, with the specific community of Israelites, covering such areas as slavery, sabbath observance, the rights of those pursued in blood-feuds and establishing fair courts of law.

Thinking about rights and duties and criticising the status quo, though no part of Jewish experience at its outset, has had a profound effect on modern Jewish thought, particularly in the United States. The Declaration of Independence traces rights back to the divine: 'All men are created equal, that they are endowed by their creator with certain unalienable rights, that among these are Life, Liberty, and the pursuit of happiness.' This is, in itself, a peculiar statement, as Judge Pollak observed as quoted by Anthony Lester in *Fundamental Rights: The United Kingdom Isolated*:

> By tracing these rights to the creator and by characterising them as unalienable, the Declaration gave important impetus to the principle – which also had its antecedents in Locke's writings – that some individual rights exist in perpetuity apart from and above the laws periodically prescribed by particular kings and legislatures vested transiently with the power to govern.

These ideas – sympathy for the oppressed, the need to ensure fair trials, the duty of the rich to help the poor and not oppress them, to 'open the blind eyes', 'to free the captive from his chains', and not to celebrate the rituals of religious worship without the accompanying moral and social duties that are far more important – were and are the meat of prophetic thought, the true social vision of biblical thinkers, and the antecedents of the social legislation of the rabbis. That prophetic tradition was picked up as the most important facet of Judaism by the leaders of Liberal Judaism in Britain in 1902. The most scholarly of the founders of British Liberal Judaism was Claude Montefiore, who wrote a mass of essays and books on the subject of prophetic Judaism and the relationship between Judaism and Christianity. It is he who summarised the role of the prophets and saw them as key to the ethical teachings of Judaism, but he also linked this to a perception of what Christianity had to offer and where the two might helpfully work together:

The moral principles which we hold highest are the very

principles which underlie, or are exemplified by, the best Old Testament injunctions, maxims and aspirations ... all the more keen, therefore, is the Old Testament on a good and holy earth, an earthly society of justice and compassion and love. And is not the best temper of our own time determined that, whatever may be in store for men after their deaths, we will seek to make this earth a better dwelling place for them during their lives? The Kingdom of God is to be realised upon earth as well as in Heaven. It is worthwhile, it is right, it is desirable to renovate and transform earth, as well as to expect and to look forward to Heaven. But this renovation or transforming of earth is an Old Testament ideal.

And how is it to be achieved? Should we not, too, say by the two or three virtues of justice, compassion and lovingkindness? Are not these virtues the moving virtues of Old Testament morality? Think how they possessed the Prophets. How they informed the prophetic religion. Justice, mercy, lovingkindness: these are the prophetic ideals. Social justice and social lovingkindness: the prophets set in motion a passion for these excellences, which found expression in the Law, the Psalter and the Wisdom literature ... the best spirits in Israel showed, I think, a genius for social morality, they set going a passion for righteousness ...

(from: *The Old Testament and After*)

A passion for righteousness.... At its best, for me, that is what Judaism has to offer. Montefiore also wrote:

Thus the prophets point forward on the one hand to the Law, which sought by definite enactment and discipline to help on the schooling of the holy nation, living apart and consecrated to God, and on the other to the apostle of Tarsus, who carried the universalistic ideal to its final and practical conclusion.

(The Hibbert Lectures on 'The Origin and Growth of Religion' as illustrated by the ancient Hebrews)

What does this message of justice and compassion and loving kindness mean? It means speaking out, against policies that lead to poverty in big cities, against racial prejudice, against immigration controls operated by colour rather than by need and right. I believe that we Jews should have been there speaking out against the selling-off of public housing, without ensuring that there were homes for those who need them. Some would argue we should be opposed to a dependency culture, yet we support the duty to give the poor, the orphan and the widow, and see in our legal system a collateral right on their part to receive it. Are these *political* issues, or are they more profound, reflecting a malaise about which the prophets had much to say:

> Woe to them that devise iniquity,
> Who design evil upon their beds.
> When morning dawns, they execute it,
> because they have the power.
> They covet fields and they seize them,
> Houses and take them away,
> They defraud men of their homes
> and people of their land.

(Micah 2:1–2)

Isaiah's cry on the same subject:

> He looked for justice,
> But behold violence!
> For equity
> But behold iniquity!
> Woe to those who join house to house
> and add field to field
> till there is no room
> and you must live alone in the midst of the land.

(Isaiah 5:7–8)

The prophets were profoundly and deliberately political. Isaiah was a court prophet, there to disturb the status quo. The difficulty comes when, in a modern democracy, we are clearly associated with one party, one distinct view. This can lead to an uneasy silence and the ability only to campaign on issues where there is little disagreement – for instance, for Jews, on the persecution of Jews in other countries. We have been brave and effective in working for our fellow Jews, we are excellent at defending ourselves when we believe we are under attack, but we fail to campaign publicly for changes to the tax law to encourage greater giving to charity, for instance, a good non-party political issue. We also often fail on the race issue, in which we have a direct and indirect interest, and immigration, despite most of us being of immigrant stock.

Judaism, with its strong *this*-life-affirming thought-pattern, seeing this world, this life, as the stage on which God's plan for humanity and man's route to salvation will be played out, prophetic Judaism with its message of justice and compassion, ought to have a clear view about these matters – a view of society and community that accords to some extent with those of other groups, but which has a unique strength. The difficulty for any community which is in a minority, and particularly the Jewish community in the wake of the holocaust, is to look beyond itself and into the wider communities in which it lives.

Friends and colleagues occasionally say: 'If I had not been Jewish, I think I would have been a Quaker.' The reasons are not hard to find. 'Let us pray for the starving in India. . .' will not be heard in a Quaker meeting, but journeying to India, driving a truck full of medical supplies, is the stuff of Quaker social action.

Reading the Quakers' agenda for their Yearly Meeting adds

to this positive impression. The agenda varies from year to year, but often takes a topic of an apparently political nature. In 1989 they were discussing 'The Secret State', specifically the Official Secrets Act and the Security Service Act. Their worry was about the openness of government, the accountability of earthly powers to those whom they govern. For that reason they have been consistent in their support for a Bill of Rights and a Freedom of Information Act.

It is worth considering why the Religious Society of Friends should take this strong line. They are very few in number, some twenty thousand. They have a history of persecution, which may lead them to understand better the nature of the persecution of others and how it can happen effortlessly, unnoticeably, unless there are entrenched protective measures within a country's constitution. They see no distinction between the proper stuff of politics and the proper stuff of religion. To them, a religious life is not possible if it is not lived alongside the highest moral standards in public and private life. A government which refuses to tell its people why it does what it does in their name, for their benefit, must be up for close examination by Quaker standards. If the government has nothing to hide, how can it justify not telling us what is being done in our name and why? In the view of the Religious Society of Friends, it is the duty of every person to involve himself or herself in the affairs of the state, at least to the extent of objecting to immoral actions. Sitting in the pew, enjoying a good old sing-song of rousing hymns, is not a religious expression as far as they are concerned. Nor are study groups, all too common in my brand of Judaism. We should be out there doing something. If more religious groups had followed the lead of the Quakers in acting on behalf of Jews and gypsies before and during World War Two, hundreds of thousands of people might have been saved.

Jews have a strong moral message, but are less good at expressing it. To recognise these human rights-based traditions in Judaism, one has to look both at the prophets of the Hebrew bible and at the Exodus story. The Exodus story has a universal message as well as its own particular one, especially as interpreted by some modern *haggadot*, the service books used for the Passover service and meal in Jewish homes each year at the *seder*, on the first (and sometimes second) nights of Passover:

> We too give thanks for Israel's liberation; we too remember what it means to be a slave. And so we pray for all who are still fettered, still denied their human rights. Let all God's children sit at His table, drink the wine of deliverance, eat the bread of freedom.
>
> (Union of Liberal and Progressive Synagogues, 1981)

This must be set alongside prophetic injunctions that festivals are valueless if at the same time the poor are oppressed, enslaved or in chains:

> Your countless sacrifices, what are they to me? says the Lord ... The offer of your gifts is useless ... New moons and Sabbath and assemblies I cannot endure. There is blood on your hands ... Cease to do evil and learn to do right. Pursue justice and champion the oppressed, give the orphan his rights and plead the widow's cause.
>
> (Isaiah 1:11–17)

The concept of justice is intertwined with that crucial journey from slavery to freedom. In one sense the journey is taken entirely literally, but it also became spiritualised, symbolic, 'Remember you were slaves in the land of

Egypt', a justification for observing the ten commandments, and particularly the sabbath, when everyone has a right to rest from labour – Jew, non-Jew, slave, free person, man, woman, and animal. Freedom, righteousness and justice, as in the giving of charity, are the mainstays of early Jewish thought. They are also the central tenets in any vision of what this world should be. The roots of the American Declaration may lie precisely in the prophetic, and particularly Isaianic, insistence on the nature of the human mission:

> I the Lord have called thee to righteousness, and have taken hold of thy hand, and have kept thee and set thee for a covenant of the people, for a light to the nations: to open the blind eyes, to bring out the prisoners from the dungeon, and them that sit in darkness out of the prison-house. I am the Lord, that is my name.
>
> (Isaiah 42:6–8)

This is a religious duty, a *mitzvah*, a positive commandment. These are rules to live by. Similarly, the emphasis on fair trials and a proper judicial system first appears in prophetic writings as a general injunction, particularly in Isaiah's description of the ideal ruler in Chapter 11, verse 4: 'He will judge the poor with equity and decide justly for the lowly in the land.' This is further elaborated in Deuteronomy, with the magnificent injunction, based on the equality precepts so emphasised by the eighth century prophets:

> Hear the causes between your brethren, and judge righteously between every man and his brother, and the stranger that is with him. Ye shall not respect persons in judgment but ye shall hear the small as well as the great; ye shall not be afraid of the face of any man.
>
> (Deut: 1:16–17)

Deuteronomy is a setting for the principle of fundamental equality before the law. David Daube suggests that judicial procedure and equality before the law with their roots in the prophets of Israel and their development in biblical and rabbinic law, are the first signs of what we would genuinely understand as rights-based Jewish thinking.

Although it is difficult to ascribe particular rights, as later codified, to prophetic thought, the general principles of fairness and equity, of rights to shelter, food and clothing (as the UN Covenants guarantee so ineffectively), are in fact there: 'Cease to do evil, learn to do well, seek justice, relieve the oppressed, judge the fatherless, and plead the widow's cause.' (Isaiah 1:16–17.) One could argue that there was no distinction between justice and kindness. A.J. Heschel quoted Neibuhr as saying, in terms instantly recognisable to those who know well the wording of 'Faith in the City': 'Justice was not equal justice but a bias in favour of the poor. Justice always leaned towards mercy for the widows and the orphans.'

If one adds to this the view that man is accountable both for his deeds and his destiny, that this world is the main scene of individual human endeavour, and that human life is paramount, one can see how the social vision of Judaism came into being. Within the law-based system, there came a duty to do things for others which resulted in those others having an implied collateral right to receive, be it the gleanings of the harvest or protection from oppression. Stopping favour towards the rich and powerful led to a fair judicial system, to due process, and equality before the law. That was true of Judaism as a whole, but it became the clarion call of early reform Judaism and of the liberal, universalist tradition.

These principles are emphasised for Jews by the journey

from slavery to freedom that the Israelites took from Egypt to the Promised Land, and are repeated each year in the celebration of the Passover. It is the memory of that journey which is adduced time and again in biblical texts to justify the duty of the Israelites to perform acts of charity and social justice for others. 'For you know the heart of the stranger . . . for you were strangers in the land of Egypt . . .' (Deuteronomy 10:19.)

There is a further question, as to what extent it is within the prophetic tradition to campaign for further change. Should we agree with Samuel Horsley, Bishop of St Asaph's in the last century, who said in the House of Lords: 'What have the people of England to do with the laws except obey them?' Should we not also campaign for changes in the British legal system and encourage the use of law for education purposes, with human rights legislation being only a small part of a much larger task that lies ahead of us? Jewish teaching, particularly that of the prophets, makes clear the required action and the basic underlying principles. The very urgency of the tone of the prophets is, to my mind, one of the key factors suggesting that we should aim to change the status quo and act as reformers. Yet we hesitate to put our noses over the parapet, in case we are attacked for holding the wrong political views – or for being Jews. With our tradition of respect for social justice and for fundamental human rights, that will not do. If British Jews look to their fellow Jews in America, they see a plurality of responses to social issues. The European Jewish experience, particularly, should have led us to reform. Although individual Jews have been key figures in politics for generations, the community involvement is weak. With our tradition and our history, we ought, for example, to be at the forefront of campaigning on race issues. This is in its infancy among British Jews, though it

Julius and Anna Schwab, my paternal grandparents,
just before they left Frankfurt for London in 1906.

Anna Schwab – a formidable woman – at the
height of her powers in the 1940s, when she
was working with refugees.

My father and his older brother, Sigmund, in
1918, aged five and seven. They look just
like little English boys being brought up to
be English gentlemen.

My father, Walter, in the First Army, and his brother, Harry, in the Eighth Army, meeting by chance in North Africa in 1943.

My mother, Liesel, looking for all the world like a picture of Aryan beauty, aged about seventeen, c. 1930.

My maternal grandparents, Ludwig and Hermine Rosenthal, in 1914 – shortly after they married and before he joined the German army.

My grandfather Ludwig as a German prisoner of war in France, c. 1916. A loyal and good German.

c. 1918. My great aunt Berta Stern, youngest sister of Ludwig Rosenthal, with my mother on her lap. She died in the holocaust. It is not known how, when or where.

Emma Dornacher, sister of Ludwig Rosenthal, in the 1920s. She is reputed to have jumped off a train en route to a concentration camp in c. 1940, and killed herself. We do not know exactly where or when.

My mother, Liesel Rosenthal, shortly after she came to Britain as a refugee in 1937.

The main gate at Dachau.
The words on the gate mean 'Work makes you free'.
(Erich Hartmann/Magnum)

Wooden barracks used as sleeping quarters at Birkenau.
(Erich Hartmann/Magnum)

My father, Walter Schwab,
holding me as a baby,
c. 1951.

My mother with me on her lap,
c. 1958.

Our wedding in 1973.
Left to right: Professor Albert Neuberger, Lilian Neuberger,
Anthony Neuberger, Julia Neuberger, Liesel Schwab, Walter Schwab. *(Jo Spence)*

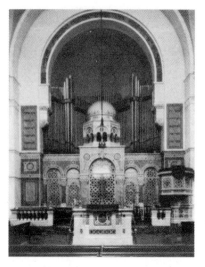

The inside of the West London
Synagogue, where I grew up.
(West London Synagogue)

Standing in front of the ark
at South London Liberal Synagogue,
c. 1987.

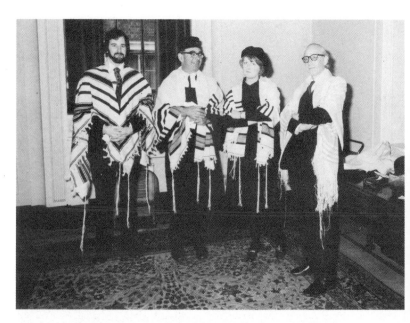

Ordination in 1977. *Left to right:* Rabbi Daniel Smith, Rabbi Lionel Blue,
Rabbi Julia Neuberger, Professor Raphael Loewe. *(Leo Baeck College)*

Photographed for an *Observer* profile, 1986, by Jane Bown.

Relaxing in Ireland, 1993, outside our barn.
(Arny Austin)

My parents, Liesel and Walter Schwab, as they are now – London, late 1980s.

Harriet Neuberger in Heilbronn-am-Neckar, my mother's birthplace, 1994.

My family – Anthony, Harriet and Matthew Neuberger, Autumn 1994. *(The Bishop of Oxford, the Rt Rev Richard Harries)*

is beginning to grow, led by some remarkable people who voice a 'Jewish' concern. It is our responsibility to open the blind eyes and to free the captive from his chains. And that is just the beginning of a process of reaching towards a goal that seems far away:

> The Lord will make in this land
> For all nations
> A feast of rich foods,
> A feast of choice wines,
> Rich foods seasoned with marrow,
> Choice wines fully clarified.
> And in this land He will destroy the shroud
> That covers the faces of all peoples,
> The covering that is spread over all the nations.
> He will destroy death for ever.
> The Lord, my God, will wipe the tears away from all
>   faces
> And will put an end to the reproach of people all over
>   the earth.
> For the Lord has spoken.

(Isaiah 25:6–8)

7

Two Jews, three opinions:

Varieties of being Jewish

There is an old joke about a Jew who was stranded on a desert island, and immediately started building two synagogues. After his rescue he was asked, in some amazement, why he had needed both, when surely there had been more pressing concerns. His reply was that one was the synagogue he went to, the other the synagogue he did not go to.

In Britain, there are several varieties of Jewish observance. The largest group is the United Synagogue, orthodox but not extreme. It has more orthodox synagogues to its 'right' wing (such as the Adath Yisroel, the very orthodox, largely North London grouping) and several other smaller groupings, including the new expanding hassidic groups. Hassidism, a movement which started in Eastern Europe in the eighteenth century, introduced the idea of a master or leader who was the rabbi of a community, whom everyone would follow. Early Hassidism was notable for its joy in Judaism, its lightness of touch, and its extreme spirituality. In more modern times it has become ultra-orthodox and often less than joyful. The biggest hassidic grouping in Britain is Lubavitch, followers of the Lubavitcher rabbi, of the Schneerson family in New York. Lubavitch is making considerable inroads into mainstream orthodoxy, particularly among the young. There is also the conservative Masorti movement, relatively new and growing quite fast; the reform movement, founded in Britain in 1840 with early German origins; and the liberal and progressive movement, founded in Britain in 1902.

There are different groupings in the United States, where the non-orthodox are in the majority. Reform is parallel roughly to left-wing English reform and liberal, and conservative is parallel roughly to right-wing British reform and masorti.

There are also the Reconstructionists, who believe in Judaism as a civilisation rather than a religion, and the Jewish humanists who do not believe in God. To add to all this, there is the divide between Ashkenazi Jews, who originate from Europe (Ashkenaz was the Hebrew for Germany) and Sephardi Jews, who originate from Spain, Portugal and North Africa (Sepharad was the Hebrew for Spain).

When giving lectures about Judaism, I always feel like saying 'Got that?' after this long list.

In Britain the United Synagogue, the old mainstream orthodoxy, is parallel in many ways with the Church of England. It was the United Synagogue which instigated the office of Chief Rabbi, to match the presence of the Archbishop of Canterbury on ceremonial occasions. In the nineteenth century, Chief Rabbi Adler dressed in robes with points at his neck very similar to ecclesiastical garb. Ultra-orthodox critics of the institution of Chief Rabbi, which they say is *chukkat ha-goy* (the custom of the non-

Jewish people among whom Jews live), argue that the office was deliberately set up to match the Archbishop of Canterbury and plays no real role in the Jewish community.

In more recent times there have been some difficulties for Chief Rabbis who have wanted to go along the path of old-style, formal leadership of Anglo-Jewry. Though the old United Synagogue was tolerant, and orthodox rabbis used to step inside the portals of non-orthodox synagogues, in recent years that tolerance has abated. Orthodox rabbis, and particularly Chief Rabbis, have made sweeping comments about doctrine and belief which are utterly atypical of a religion which has always been far more concerned with action than with what its adherents believe. We are good at divisions in the Jewish community in Britain. They started with the breakaway by the first reform synagogue from the arid orthodoxy of the late 1830s. The story is one that reminds us of all the ways in which Jews disagree even now – the old joke of two Jews, three opinions, is clearly no joke at all, but to be taken very seriously.

The main synagogues of the Jewish community were in the East End of London. There was Bevis Marks, on the edge of the City, the oldest synagogue of the new wave of Jews, which has a beam given by Queen Anne, and is a well-established community of Jews of Spanish and Portuguese origin, who went to Holland from Spain and Portugal after their expulsions in 1492 and 1498 respectively. One of the elders of the Dutch Jewish community, Manasseh ben Israel, came and petitioned Cromwell to readmit the Jews, and it is their synagogue that is the oldest and in many ways the finest in Britain. There were also Duke's Place, the big Ashkenazi synagogue for Jews of German and Eastern European origin, and the Hambro, the synagogue for the community of Jews whose origins were in Hamburg. The time came when Jews were gradually settling in the West End of London, and needed a synagogue near their homes, as it was forbidden to drive, or to ask a horse or a coachman to work on the sabbath. At the very suggestion of building a new synagogue in the West End, the *mahamad* – the council – of the Spanish and Portuguese congregation at Bevis Marks threw up its hands in horror. The group who made the suggestion were also demanding such unlikely things as decorum in the services. They were aware of how they were regarded by the outside world, for non-Jewish visitors occasionally attended services, including the celebrated diarist, Samuel Pepys. He recorded what he saw on October 14th 1663 without realising that he had visited the synagogue on Simchat Torah, the festival of the rejoicing of the law, which is celebrated in a manner not far short of carnival in even the most decorous synagogues.

> But Lord! To see the disorder, laughing, sporting and no attention but confusion in all their service, more like brutes than people knowing the true God, would make a man forswear ever seeing them more: and, indeed, I never could have imagined there had been any religion in the world so absurdly performed as this. [I left] with my mind strongly disturbed.

Services were probably not always as anarchic as the one Pepys attended, but there were plenty of Jews who were getting worried about the impression they were making, and who in any case wanted a different style, including prayers and sermons in English. Services used to be entirely in Hebrew (and still are in orthodox synagogues, bar the sermon). There were no sermons except on the Great Sabbath, before Passover, when detailed instructions about the preparations for Passover were given, and on the Sabbath of Repentance which falls between New Year and Yom Kippur. Decorum probably was poor, since it was not thought wrong, and still is not thought unusual in many orthodox synagogues, for people to hold conversations during the service, rather than concentrating on the prayers.

The group of Jews who wanted a new synagogue persisted. There were eighteen families from the Sephardi community of Bevis Marks, and six from the Ashkenazi community. They founded their own synagogue, in Cartwright Gardens, Euston, in 1840, without any help from the religious authorities. They were put under a *cherem* (a ban) for a few years. Families were split, and people who had regularly been in business with each other did not speak. Out of this fracas emerged the West London Synagogue of British Jews. Its first minister, the Reverend Dr D.W. Marks, in 1842 preached his consecration sermon in which he pleaded with the congregation to educate its daughters as well as its sons.

The demands this new reform congregation made of the old congregations in the East End and the City were relatively minor compared with the radicalism of the reform movement which was growing in Germany and America. There one could find the abolition of bar mitzvah, replaced with confirmation for boys and girls older than thirteen. Services were held almost entirely in the vernacular. Some synagogues even had church bells to call the faithful to prayer, and the attitude to traditional Jewish law was that it did not have to be observed unless it was of biblical origin.

The West London entitled itself the West London Synagogue of British Jews, presumably to distinguish themselves from any other kind of Jew, but also to make a point about identity, that Jews were British subjects. It was an important point to make. In Germany, both orthodox and reform-minded Jews had witnessed the emancipation of the Jews, the so-called Enlightenment, when Jews were liberated from the ghettos. The response to the relaxing of anti-Jewish rules and customs was a huge thirst on the part of many Jews for secular knowledge. They were allowed into the universities and the professions. They studied secular law, and medicine, in a wider, non-Jewish way. They became academics within a variety of disciplines. Enlightenment was a headlong rush into new and non-religious knowledge. And while some of it was hugely beneficial – I am myself a child of the Enlightenment – some of it resulted in losing the thing that was precious about Jewish learning, understanding and practice.

The Enlightenment took place at the beginning of the nineteenth century. It varied from city to city in pre-unification Germany, but the mood of change was there, and Jews were being freed of their restrictions. What did it mean to be restricted no longer? Were the Jews now good Germans just like everyone else? Or could they never be good Germans unless they converted to Christianity, as did one of the most famous of them all, the poet Heinrich Heine? Could one be a good German citizen and a Jew? The conclusion was that one could be a German citizen of the Jewish faith, a model which the West London Synagogue imitated. It is ironic that German Jews, so convinced by their newly acquired citizenship and so in thrall to the idea of German-ness as expressed throughout the latter part of the nineteenth century, quickly and tragically found out that their compatriots did not think of them as German at all. I am not in a position to judge whether British people regard Jews as 'properly British' or whether for most non-Jews the first defining feature of a Jew is that he, or she, is a Jew, from which everything else follows.

Reform in Britain, starting as it did in such a typically Anglo-Jewish way – with a row – was strongly influenced by a variety of other factors. There was already a radical reform movement in Germany. The move to educate women and the pressure to change to a more formal, solemn and pious style of worship, however, had its roots in a desire to be more like Anglicans than wanting to change the way the Jewish faith was practised. Nevertheless, the founding families were deeply serious about their commitment, and many of their descendants, Mocattas and Montefiores, are still involved in the affairs of the West London Synagogue to this day. They wanted to make religion more approachable, to keep children in the fold rather than facing them with incomprehensible religious practices, and to become part of the general civic society, all the while maintaining a difference in religious approach that was compared to the difference between Catholics and Protestants.

The move was a successful one, and reform flourished, albeit slowly, in Britain. It also influenced the United Synagogue, where sermons in English were heard, and where a certain new formality was noted, though conversations during services still can be heard today. Services were shorter than they had been in the orthodox synagogue and there were prayers in English. It was not, however, a hugely radical change.

It was much later that strong radicalism hit British Jewry. It came about in 1902, with the Jewish Religious Union, which ultimately grew into liberal Judaism. Its founders were the Hon. Lily Montagu, a woman who would have liked to have been a rabbi but for whom it was not thought possible, and Claude Montefiore, as well as the first minister of the liberal movement, Israel Mattuck. Their vision was different from the moderate aims of the early

reformers. They had been influenced by the reform movement in Germany and America, and were keen to preach
a Judaism comprehensible and accessible to everyone.
Montefiore was a great scholar, particularly of New Testament thought. Montagu was an inspired leader of young
women's clubs, and had been drawn to the new form of
Judaism when she realised shop-girls worked on Saturday
mornings and could not attend the services. She started
services on Saturday afternoons – her main congregation
still holds its services in the afternoon – and encouraged
the young women to sing hymns which were theologically
acceptable, but sounded more like what one might hear in
a church or chapel. Through such means she developed a
simple way of describing the fundamental values of
Judaism.

Liberal Judaism was radical and universalistic. It was
concerned with prophetic Judaism; it saw itself as within
the prophetic tradition, and defined itself by its emphasis
on social work (many of its adherents were particularly
involved in the boys' and girls' club movements of the
poorer Jewish communities of the East End of London),
and meaningful prayer. It also became involved in interfaith dialogue with Christians, and reworked the traditional liturgy to rid itself of the mention of a personal
Messiah and the Temple. Traditional Judaism still prays
for the coming of the Messiah, and asserts in the morning
prayers: 'though He tarry, I wait daily for His coming'.
The Messiah has not yet come for Jews. The Liberal movement did not, and does not, believe in a personal Messiah.
There will be no one hero who will rescue the world.
Instead, the Messianic age (an age of no war, no famine,
peace and plenty) will dawn as the result of human
endeavour, work and energy. The Messianic age will be a

human creation, inspired by God's will and by human belief and trust in His law and will.

Until just before the Second World War, despite occasional rows and difficulties, Anglo-Jewry, an intellectually undemanding community, rubbed along with its three divisions of Jews – orthodox, reform and liberal. There was also the rather more conservative, traditionally Eastern European, orthodox Federation of Synagogues. Little synagogues were set up by immigrants from Russia and Poland who had come to Britain between 1881 and 1905. They had disliked the 'Anglican' style of the United Synagogue, and grouped together to form another orthodox movement, not very different in belief from the United Synagogue, but socially extremely different, with its own style to this day.

The Federation of Synagogues was built on the idea of the old *shtiebl*, the small synagogues, tiny congregations, or *chevras*, of Eastern Europe. These were not the large synagogues of German orthodoxy, or even the grand synagogues of the big cities of Russia and Poland. They were in someone's back room, over a shop, in a room used for some other purpose the rest of the time. People huddled together, prayed with a different kind of fervour, nearer the hassidic style. They were chaotic, and deeply orthodox, and developed customs that would have shocked the United Synagogue with their attention to orthodox detail, and their way of coping with poor physical conditions.

In all divisions of Anglo-Jewry the rabbi plays a critical part. Rabbis are teachers, not priests. We are there to teach our congregations about the great Jewish tradition, the scholarship, the history and the practices. Many of us, whichever section of the community we serve, would argue that we are increasingly influenced, whether it is admitted or not, by the idea of 'ministry' in the Christian church. We are expected to be good pastors, which I certainly found to be an incredibly satisfying part of my life as a congregational rabbi for twelve years. We are expected to visit the sick (though traditionally there was a group in the community which visited the sick, the people who performed the *mitzvah* of *bikkur cholim*). We are expected to sit with the dying, again not something traditionally expected of a rabbi, but where I found profound spirituality. We are often expected to run the religion school, though many of us have no training or experience in teaching the young, and we are expected to visit members of the congregation, making sure that the elderly do not become isolated.

I remember something one winter when the weather was terrible and my congregation were worried about the elderly members being trapped at home, unable to get out because of three-feet of snow. We organised a ring-round of all the members over sixty years old, anyone with a known disability and those who were just a bit frail. It took hours, and was far from the usual responsibility of the traditional rabbi, but I believe that it was much valued by the old and the isolated, as well as being much enjoyed by those who did the telephoning. This sort of action is the duty of any kind of caring community.

I loved my congregation, of which my own family are still members. I do not think that I have ever known such privilege, and such satisfaction, as being allowed to share some people's most intimate moments, and being able, sometimes, to offer help to those in great difficulties. Often I would fail. Sometimes I would be able to do something, or simply bring some kind of support. We rarely cured, but I think at our best we often alleviated distress. One of the most satisfying things was having a group of young people working together in the community, to run social action, visit people, and to take on some of the difficult cases. There was no way one rabbi could visit six hundred members of the congregation. If we were told that things were not going well for someone, one of us – a group of some twenty or so – could usually go and talk, listen, and sometimes help.

The worst thing in any Jewish organisation is the meetings. I still remember the council meetings with horror. They used to go on for hours, and I could affect very little of what was discussed, but as the one full-time employee, I had to be there. I still wake up on the first Wednesday of the month relieved that I do not have go to to that meeting. I am assured the time-wasting and muddle is as bad in most well-meaning organisations, and that it is not a particularly Jewish phenomenon, but when I read the tales of American congregations taking votes on whether to keep their rabbis or fire them, I sometimes wonder! It is a peculiar position to be in, as the direct employee (in non-orthodox congregations) and leader of the congregation. Accountability to the council is obviously proper and essential, but I sometimes think that there are other ways of ensuring it rather than by monthly meetings.

The rabbis of Germany who came to Britain as refugees before the war must have been appalled by our system. They had been state employees, paid for by church tax, which every citizen had to pay. They would not have felt financially accountable to their congregation. Indeed, their arrival caused things to change. There had been a vibrant non-orthodox intellectual community in Germany, and many of its rabbis and members were among the people who managed to escape persecution. They came to Britain and set up further reform communities, and also joined the liberal movement. They injected an intellectual strength into reform Judaism which it had lacked until then, and they revived the thinking behind progressive Judaism. At the same time, a large number of truly orthodox Jews arrived as refugees, and took the broad church of the United Synagogue sharply to the right. It was not a comfortable experience for those who were used to the old style and who had rejoiced in the tolerance of the United Synagogue. These changes – the increased vibrancy of non-orthodoxy and orthodoxy – set the scene for the rows of the 1960s, which continue to this very day.

The British tradition is one of tolerance, with institutions like the Board of Deputies, which is a sort of parliament for Britain's Jews. It has a somewhat eccentric electoral and funding system, but exists with the support of almost all the affiliated parts of the community. The Board deals with the Home Office on issues to do with communal security; it lobbies on educational issues; and it plays a major part in keeping the fabric of Anglo-Jewry together, despite its divisions. Equally tolerant in its way is the old style United Synagogue, with its lay leadership, made up, historically speaking, of members of the so-called Anglo-Jewish cousinhood, the wealthy families who came in the seventeenth and eighteenth centuries and intermarried with each other, and, socially at least, assimilated into the ways of the British upper-classes. There is also a relatively recent extremism, which manifests itself in neo-orthodoxy.

The present Chief Rabbi, Dr Jonathan Sacks, who came to office with a promise of considerable tolerance towards other forms of Jewish expression, criticised the synagogal organisation which calls itself 'Masorti'. In America, Masorti would be equivalent to the conservative move-ment. It is traditional in its practices but not orthodox in its beliefs. Its congregations – and it is now growing quite rapidly – range from holding services which are virtually indistinguishable from orthodox services, conducted by men with no participation by women, to a more egalitarian view of Judaism where services are conducted in traditional style with men and women playing equal roles. Their services are still very similar to orthodox services, though their prayer books have similarities with some reform innovations, notably in the use of the vernacular on a few occasions, and some attempts to equalise the language of prayer according to gender.

Late in 1994, the Masorti movement wanted to set up a new community in Manchester, one of the biggest centres of Jewish population outside London. Several leaders of the Manchester Jewish community were interested in forming the new breakaway community, and some of the lay people involved claimed that a former Chief Rabbi, Dr J.H. Hertz, was in fact a Masorti Jew, and that the present Chief Rabbi himself had recognised weddings conducted in Masorti congregations. Dr Sacks denied both allegations. Certainly, many of those who knew him would say that Chief Rabbi Hertz was 'mixed' in his Jewish views. On the one hand, he was desperately concerned that Jewish children coming as refugees to Britain from Nazi Germany should be brought up in Jewish homes, even when there were not enough Jewish volunteers to take them all, and he was keen to maintain orthodoxy for them. On the other, he certainly did not take an extreme orthodox line.

Early in 1995, Chief Rabbi Sacks wrote an article for the ultra-orthodox periodical, the *Jewish Tribune*, using language in which he would not normally speak. He condemned Masorti outright, and argued that:

> ... an individual who does not believe in 'Torah min ha-shamayim' [the doctrine that the Torah was literally given by God to Moses on Mount Sinai] has cut himself off from

living connection with 'shamayim'. He has severed his links with the faith of his ancestors.

There was an outcry. Many of the correspondents to the *Jewish Chronicle*, the mainstream publication for Anglo-Jewry, which has consistently taken a pro-tolerance line, were opposed to his statement. Chief Rabbi Sacks then retracted part of what he said in an article in the *Jewish Chronicle*, arguing that while he owed his allegiance to Torah-true Judaism, his office would hold out its hand to those less orthodox, and he would be tolerant to those who held different views. His apologia seemed to say that the only form of Judaism to take seriously was Torah-true Judaism, that is to say orthodoxy, but that he thought it worth being polite to those who held different views, particularly if they realised that the Judaism they ought to be involved with was his brand. In my opinion, it was a contradictory piece, in which tolerance was promised but only one version of Judaism recognised, and it did little to assuage the feelings of the Masorti movement.

The question of orthodoxy versus the rest is of course much older than the events of 1995. As far as Masorti is concerned, it started in 1962. Rabbi Dr Louis Jacobs was then the rabbi of the New West End Synagogue (a United synagogue in London). He was by far the most distinguished rabbinical scholar in Anglo-Jewry at the time, and was hotly tipped to become both Principal of Jews' College, the rabbinical training college of orthodoxy, and Chief Rabbi. He was brilliant, educated, knowledgeable, and had published, originally in 1957 and again in 1962, a volume entitled *We have reason to believe* . . . , which argued that the five books of Moses, the Torah, could not possibly have been given, as they stood, by God to Moses on Mount

Sinai because of the internal textual evidence of repetition and differences between two versions of the Ten Commandments, and other textual difficulties. Strongly influenced by scholarship, particularly that which had been put forward in the nineteenth century by distinguished German scholars, he argued that one had to view the Torah through the light of reason, and it simply could not be a single whole, dictated in that fashion by God.

To some members of my family it was as if he had uttered foul obscenities. I remember the conversations in my grandmother's drawing-room at the time. My grandmother was an orthodox Jewess, but was prepared to defend Rabbi Dr Jacobs. By this stage, she was old and ill, and had little energy. As a twelve-year-old, I did not know much about the subject. I knew only that I was on the 'liberal' side – not that it was very liberal – and that it seemed likely to me that one could not assume the whole lot had literally been dictated by God to Moses. Nor did I believe then, any more than I do now, that those who were shouting the loudest believed that it was all literally true either. This was a debate about the use of human reason in religion. Some argued that reason is God's creation and must be used to assess the veracity of things that are passed down as 'gospel'. Others said that we must put human reason on one side and allow ourselves simply to have faith, because to challenge the authority of religious belief itself is to attack the foundations of religious truth. The latter position was upheld loudly by those who termed themselves orthodox; the rest sat open-mouthed at the number of things they were prepared to deny, or to close their eyes to, in order to maintain their position.

Some became convinced that Louis Jacobs was a great sinner, and believed his views were unacceptable. He should be put under a *cherem* (a ban – a form of excommunication). Although he was not put under a *cherem*, his future was – in orthodox eyes – ruined by not being appointed to the Jews' College post, and later, by Chief Rabbi Brodie's refusal to re-appoint him to his position as rabbi of the New West End Synagogue. Dr Jacobs left the congregation, taking with him many of its members who were appalled by the way he had been treated by the establishment. They were certain that asking Jews to believe three impossible things before breakfast was not the way forward for British Jewry!

For many years there was only one Masorti synagogue, the New London, in St John's Wood. During the 1970s and early 1980s, however, the idea of Masorti grew, and several other congregations were established in the London area, gaining ground among the orthodox intelligentsia, and supporting its own rabbis, trained with the reform and liberal rabbis at Leo Baeck College. As mainstream orthodoxy in the shape of the United Synagogue moved to the religious right, the Masorti movement began to look more and more attractive, and its influence spread to the less orthodox as well, so that many of its customs appealed to reform and liberal communities too. Gradually, Masorti began to play a part in the growing tapesty of religious diversity that British Jews were experiencing. Masorti was respectable, intellectually honest, tolerant, mostly egalitarian as far as women were concerned (though not in all the congregations), and studious. People in those communities studied Judaism, and regarded their Jewishness as an important part of their everyday lives.

This was different from the United Synagogue's experience. Though nominally orthodox, it was clear that many of its members were members purely for burial purposes, and rarely set foot in the synagogues. The United Synagogue began to lose members to the ultra-orthodox on the one side and to Masorti, reform and liberal on the other. It became increasingly under siege, and its reaction, or that of its Chief Rabbi and rabbis, was to retreat into a kind of backwoodsmen's approach to Judaism. Though Jonathan Sacks had preached tolerance, shortly after he became Chief Rabbi he refused to let the Jewish Gay Group join the rest of the Jewish community on a communal walkabout in Hyde Park to show the diversity of the community. Although he said he was upset about the position of women in Judaism, he set up an inquiry the conclusions of which, where implemented at all, have been very slow, and failed to encourage women into the synagogues or into women-only prayer groups (against which there is no argument in *halachah*, Jewish law) or additional Jewish education for girls which would allow them to read from the Torah in services or say *kaddish* – the mourner's prayer – for their loved ones when they died. He made it clear that tolerance was on his terms – and the United Synagogue's – and that those to whom tolerance was being extended needed to accept that the United Synagogue was the true inheritor of Judaism, and that anyone who felt differently had severed links with the faith of their ancestors.

It is no surprise that Dr Sacks' statements caused such furores, for it is clear that many members of the United Synagogue do not believe all that they are told to believe. Like many others, they are worried by the lack of a real desire to compromise to enable a 'broad church' to survive. Jonathan Sacks is a distinguished philosopher, a man of intellectual strength and ability, whose Reith lectures for the BBC were universally admired. This makes it all the more alarming that he is prepared to espouse what many would regard an irrational approach to religious thought. The furore, like its predecessors, is typical of all I have ever known of Jewish community politics in Britain. It seems to me that our community often lacks the stature and the vibrancy of the much larger, far better educated in Jewish terms, pluralistic community of the United States of America.

The orthodox believe that the Torah was given by God to Moses on Mount Sinai on one single occasion of revelation. With the Torah came the oral Torah, the two great works of early rabbinic codification and discussion, the Mishnah and the Talmud. These are referred to as the 'oral law', and are seen as having a binding role on the Jewish community. The Mishnah was probably edited by about the year 200 CE by a great teacher and rabbi called Judah ha-Nasi, Judah the Prince. It is a compilation, with a certain amount of codification, of the teachings of earlier generations of rabbis, who had discussed the law and come up with an authoritative position. The Talmud comes in two versions, the most often used and quoted being the Babylonian Talmud, probably finally finished in the editing around the year 500 CE. Its companion, the Jerusalem, or Palestinian, Talmud, is shorter and less often quoted. The two versions exist because there were Jewish communities with academies and rabbinic discussion in both places at the time.

Knowing as we do that the Talmud is later than the Mishnah (it uses passages of teaching from the Mishnah which it then discusses at length), it is odd for orthodox Jews to argue seriously that this is all part of the oral law given by God to Moses on Mount Sinai. Even if one assumed that the five books of Moses were themselves wholly divine, it is hard to imagine that something dating from a much later period was part of that same divine revelation. Nonetheless, the strictly orthodox, who hold to the tenets of orthodox belief without criticising them, would argue that this is so. They also argue that all the commandments, positive and negative, contained in the Torah and the oral law, are binding, and that all Jews must obey them.

These commandments – *mitzvot* – include such things as the dietary laws, quite complicated for non-Jews to understand. First, animals fit to eat must have a cloven hoof and chew the cud. Then, there are the rules about the way the animal is killed, with a single cut through the windpipe and no pre-stunning. The blood is not eaten, so that kosher meat is soaked and salted to remove the blood, and the hind-quarters of the meat with thick veins in them are either cut to remove the blood vessels (porging) or not eaten by those who keep the laws. There are rules about which birds may be eaten, with an exclusion on birds of prey and a requirement that birds are killed as animals are, which precludes game birds unless they are killed in the orthodox manner. Fish have to have fins and scales. Shellfish are ruled out, as are skate and arguably sturgeon. If it were only a question of how the meat or fowl was killed, or which fish were kosher, life would not be particularly complicated. The difficulties arise with the prohibition on mixing meat and milk.

The origins of this custom go back to a verse in Exodus which runs: 'Thou shalt not seethe a kid in its mother's milk' (Exodus 24:19). According to one of the Jewish legal principles, you put a fence around the law to prevent yourself breaking it by accident. So, the reasoning goes, if you have a lump of meat in one hand and a jug of milk in the other and you are not certain of their origins, how can you be sure that the milk into which you are about to put the lump of meat is not the milk which comes from the mother of the animal which was killed for the meat? You cannot be sure, and therefore to prevent breaking God's law by accident, you never mix milk and meat. The argument then runs on. If you have milk and meat in your stomach at the same time, once again you might be inadvertently mixing the meat and milk that come from child and mother. Milk products can be eaten up to an hour before meat ones, since milk is speedily digested. You must leave several hours (it varies from community to community) between eating meat, which is slow in the digestion, and milk products. The pudding at a kosher meat meal cannot have real cream or milk. Specially made ice cream can be *parev*, neither milk nor meat, and chocolate mousses can be made of innumerable eggs and brandy and chocolate, but no cream. It is a relatively rich diet, as I experienced at my grandmother's house. It also tends to be meat-based, unusual in an age when generally less meat is being eaten.

The laws about milk and meat do not apply to fish, so celebratory meals were and are often fish-based. Jewish functions often serve cold salmon (just like many non-Jews, as it is easy party food), but there are other joys such as cold fried fish, which is delicious. There is the traditionally Eastern European gefilte fish, either fried or boiled. Gefilte fish (literally stuffed fish) is in fact minced mixed fish flavoured with carrot and spices and either boiled in fish stock into a form of fish dumpling or fried in deep oil, like fish-cakes. As a child I always found the boiled gefilte fish, on the rare occasions I was given it, rather slimy and disgusting, though gourmet friends compare it with that delicacy made of pike, *quenelles de brochet*, but the fried fish was, and is, delicious, and a great contribution from Judaism to world cuisine.

Cold fried fish is traditional Passover food at least among families which come from Eastern Europe. I never had it as a child at my grandmother's house because we were German Jews, but since I have had my own family and we have been holding our own *seder*, we have chosen cold fried fish, because it is so delicious and traditional. The fish is coated in matzo meal (ground-up matzo), dipped in beaten egg, fried in medium deep oil, left to dry on kitchen paper, and served with lemon, pickled cucumbers and *chrein*, a mixture of beetroot and horseradish. It sounds disgusting, but it has a magic all its own. I only cook it once a year, for Passover. The only way to do it is to start early in the morning, in one's nightdress, cook the fish (a major task if there are twenty or thirty people coming to *seder*) and then wash everything, open all the doors and windows, put the nightdress through the wash, have a bath and wash one's hair ... and often I can *still* smell the fish!

There are other commandments that are difficult to understand, among which are those about ritual purity, laws which the ultra-orthodox tend to observe but which few other Jews hold to in these days. The laws include the requirement for a woman to go to the *mikveh*, the ritual bath, at the end of her period, before she is 'fit' for her husband again, and details about the use of the *mikveh* by women after childbirth, or even for proselytes after conversion – the origin of baptism in Christianity.

The great medieval Jewish philosopher, commentator and doctor of Spain and Egypt, Maimonides, wrote:

> It is plain and manifest that the laws about cleanness and uncleanness are decrees laid down by Scripture and not matters about which human understanding is capable of forming a judgment; for behold they are included among the arbitrary decrees.

'Unclean' does not mean 'dirty' as we would understand it; the translation should convey the specialised sense of being 'impure', and therefore unable to approach the altar. Mary Douglas, in her great work *Purity and Danger*, makes the case that those who are ritually impure may convey danger to others. The woman who has just given birth is ritually impure for seven days plus an additional thirty-three days if she gave birth to a boy, and fourteen days plus sixty-six if a girl. During that time she cannot touch her husband, because she would convey that ritual impurity to him. Blood is a life-force, and in menstruation and after child-birth it is seen to be ebbing away. The same is true with inanimate objects. If a dead rat falls on to a pile of grain which is dry, the grain can be consumed. If the grain was wet, because it had been soaked for some purpose, then the impurity of the animal is conveyed to the grain, which spells danger. The rules are complex in the extreme, but there is a pattern that suggests that bodily fluids and wetness have a major contributory role.

At some stage, becoming ritually impure was considered divine punishment. Here we have the link into later thought, both Jewish and Christian, about the way that, for example, biblical leprosy was seen as divine punishment. That thinking led to leprosy being regarded as shameful. Jesus showed the way by sitting among the lepers. The terrible danger is that modern 'lepers' are treated as metaphorical lepers and are shunned, patronised and blamed. AIDS has come to have an association with this biblical condition. The biblical system was essentially one of ritual purity, with the priest pronouncing the end of defilement. The requirement of the people was that they tried to keep themselves ritually pure. To be impure because of disease was a sadness, even a disaster, but not, in the earliest period, a punishment.

The punishment idea developed, however, and became linked with other punishments, and God's warning to the people not to indulge in 'abominations'. To understand this at all we need to realise the extent to which this is a system of taboos, a system where purity and holiness, impurity and unholiness, unseparateness, were of prime importance. The 'abominations' are such that, if they are indulged in, the land will 'vomit out' the people. In sexual terms, the 'abominations' were the forbidden sexual unions of Leviticus, Chapter 18, forbidding bestiality, male homo-sexuality and incestuous relationships. In other areas of life, obedience to the laws meant not yoking the ox and the ass together, not wearing wool and linen together, not having mixed marriages between Jew and non-Jew, and not mixing milk and meat.

Any disturbance of what is fit leads to trouble. Things, and people, have to be kept in their proper order. Food has to be fit to be sacrificed to God. When humans eat, they are eating what could have been sacrificed to God. Should they eat what is blemished and unfit for sacrifice, it must at least be of a species that is 'proper'. The sense of what is 'proper' and 'fitting' goes very deep, and it is the disturbance of that system – by human beings having 'unnatural' bodily discharges (such as running sores) or dangerous bodily discharges (such as blood) – that engen-ders fear. A system for dealing with fear involves ritualis-ing how these things are treated.

These are just some of the rules which are carefully adhered to in orthodox circles. One has to recognise the incredible joy, within orthodox thinking, of a way of life which requires little in the way of questioning for everyday events. The law is clear about how they are to live their daily lives. Every aspect of life is covered – their food, their sexual life, their learning, their working hours, how they celebrate the sabbath and festivals, how they bring up their children, and so on. Within that somewhat rigid framework there is a comfort, and a happiness, not known to non-orthodox Jews. The intellectual discipline lies in obeying the law, and in debating its finer points – if one is male. Yet orthodoxy encourages the sleep of reason. You do not have to think; the rabbinical tradition is going to tell you what to do. You may not challenge that authority at all, since it is, by virtue of this way of thinking, divine. That is the way it is, and therefore the way you have to live your life.

Non-orthodoxy, of whatever ilk, is different. Though Masorti is traditional, with many of its adherents living as if they were orthodox, the use of reason is encouraged. Matters of belief are open for discussion. The search for spiritual and moral values in the modern age is on the agenda. There is a keenness of intellect, and a desire to know what Judaism has to say about the relief of poverty, about questions of public dignity and public standards, and a search for Jewish meaning in everyday life.

Throughout all the non-orthodox communities there is the assumption that the Torah is not wholly divine, that it was written down at different times and has its difficulties. Non-orthodox Jews accept that the Torah was written down by humans with divine inspiration. The extent to which they believe it to be divinely inspired varies from individual to individual, but they share in common the sense that revelation was not once and for all on Mount Sinai, as described in the Torah itself, but in different ways at different times to different people. The way that one interprets the Torah and uses human knowledge to extract more from it, is the test of how the non-orthodox Jew approaches Judaism. However non-orthodox, Judaism is a text-based religion – a religion of books more than a religion of faith.

Commandments and prohibitions are the stuff of orthodox Judaism, which argues that Judaism is unchanging and that modern scientific knowledge is not relevant. Therefore many of those laws, which seem to a liberal thinker such as I am to be simply man-made creations which look at the world through a vision bound by time and place, seem to them to be God's truth. If they are firmly of the view that they are God's truth, then nothing will shake them. Central to orthodox belief is the system of *halachah*, literally meaning the 'going' or the path on which one should walk. This *halachic* thought is how Judaism works and debates its laws and customs. If one argues that the whole structure is divine, there can be no opting out of any of the laws. If, however, one rejects the structure as not being divine, there is no difficulty in saying that one does not have to obey *all* the laws.

Suppose one is not orthodox. Suppose one is some form of non-orthodox Jew, be it conservative, Masorti, reform or liberal. The relationship with the *halachah* is then more problematic. One is left with a difficult question: to what extent is the whole edifice human, and not divine at all? If one took the most liberal view of all, one might argue that the whole thing was indeed human. Given the relationship we know the rabbis had with the texts of Judaism, they must have *thought* they were divinely inspired even when what they were writing was abundantly and obviously human, and often very male to boot. The copying and re-copying of earlier texts is an important part of the editing process of the Torah and the Hebrew bible. The texts reflect several generations of editors, and those editors doubtless did their work in the name of God and many believed with divine inspiration, too. Modern scholarship can point to all sorts of parallel texts in cognate languages and other Near Eastern cultures, such as the *Epic of Gilgamesh*, with its flood story uncannily similar to the Noah story, or the Babylonian *Epic of Creation*, which has links with the creation story in Genesis. Many ancient scholars would have known different versions of the texts, if the discovery of the Dead Sea scrolls, very early versions of some of the biblical books, such as Isaiah, is significant. Though the variations are minor, they are sufficiently ever-present to pose a problem to those who argue that there was only one version of these books.

Modern scholarship has pointed to several sources for the Torah. A German Lutheran orientalist, Julius Wellhausen (1844–1918), was convinced that he could prove that there were four sources for the Torah texts. He argued for the 'J' source, which uses the tetragrammaton, the four-letter name of God sometimes transliterated by Christian scholars as Yahweh, traditionally uttered only by the High Priest in the Holy of Holies on the Day of Atonement. Though Jews read the four-letter name of God, the tetragrammaton, as simply 'Adonai', meaning 'My Lord', Wellhausen read it as Jahweh, in the German spelling. Then there was the 'E' source, which uses Elohim as the name of God, a curious plural form; the priestly source, 'P', which gives the priesthood pride of place; and the Deuteronomist 'D', the one who came along last, inserted short sections in a variety of places, wrote Deuteronomy and probably wrote or edited Joshua, Judges, Samuel and Kings. The Deuteronomist may have been someone whose chief aim in life was to centralise worship and observance in Jerusalem. Jerusalem was not yet technically in existence at the time that Deuteronomy was supposed to take place, but the writer, when Moses is giving his final majestic sermons to the people in the wilderness, uses the odd phrase 'the place which I will choose for my name to dwell there', in other words Jerusalem, the capital. Few people, however academic or liberal, would hold to Wellhausen's neat divisions nowadays. Relatively few even believe that there were four sources for the texts. Many authorities now argue that it does not matter how many individual sources there were for the Torah, nor which exactly they were, as long as one accepts that there were several. Some people think that the Torah, indeed the Hebrew bible as a whole, is an anthology of holy writings. Some of these holy writings made it into the canon of scripture and others did not. The questions of the apocrypha (the hidden books) and the pseudepigrapha (the false writings) are of considerable interest.

If one takes as liberal a view of the texts as I do, then it is essential to regard them in an historical light. For me, and many other Jews, Christians and non-believers, what is important is that they were written in a spirit of holiness, to evoke religious faith, and to persuade, cajole and sometimes frighten people into taking God – the God who loves, cares and tends his people, but also throws them out of the land if they misbehave – seriously. Whether the texts were dictated by God is irrelevant. I do not believe, myself, that God ever talked to human beings in that way anyway. I am utterly sure that they were written to encourage belief, and to form a national identity and a recognisable people.

When we read the historical books, the books of Judges, Samuel, Kings and the later Chronicles, some of it is dull, numbering the years of the reigns of the kings of Israel and Judah. As far as the authors were concerned, these were the kingdoms which came from David's descendants, and were the true Israel, and their difficulties under threat from their neighbours formed the people the Jews became. The historical books are not holy books, as we would normally understand them, but fascinating records of the wanderings in the wilderness, the wars and the tribulations which bred a people's identity. They have survived largely because they were included in the canon; doubtless equally fascinating texts have disappeared because they were never canonised, treasured and recorded. That is why the Dead Sea scrolls are so important. They are collections of texts, largely messianic and apocalyptic, a sort of wisdom literature. In the Dead Sea scrolls we have a record of some of the texts which were significant to a first century (or perhaps earlier – the dates are much disputed) group of Jews. Even if the texts date from the second century BCE, as many suggest they do, they give us the Isaiah scroll, which is fascinating because it is different from the version we have in the Hebrew bible. Other, hitherto unknown, texts of devotion give a dualistic vision of the world. There are the good guys, the sons of light on the one hand, presumably the community at Qumran which some people think were Essenes, a semi-ascetic group of Jews, ranged against the bad guys, the sons of darkness (possibly the Romans), whom they had to destroy.

For me, the way to study the Hebrew bible is to view it historically, as a record of how the Israelites/Hebrews identified themselves, conceived their shared history with the journey from slavery to Egypt to freedom in the Promised Land – whatever the historicity of that story itself, for it is quite possible that it never really happened – and began to form the religion that we know today as Judaism. It moves through an intense land-based nationalism, some of which is picked up today in the fundamentalist Jews' argument for the whole of biblical Judea and Samaria to be part of the State of Israel, because they were promised to the Jews by God in the Hebrew bible. It is understandable when viewed historically, as tribes were staking out their claims, and people moved from a nomadic lifestyle to a settled agricultural life. Bringing it into political play nowadays, however, is highly questionable, for it requires several leaps of faith to think that God literally gave the land at all, rather than the tribes defeating those who were already there, as the books of Joshua and Judges suggest with their record of bloody battles.

After the taking of the land, the tone begins to change. We are told of the development of the monarchy, and there is a record of disquiet about having a monarchy just like everyone else and losing the centrality of divine authority. Alongside the monarchy is the development of biblical prophecy, for many of us liberal Jews the acme of writing in the Bible, with wonderful, eternal truths in great poetry. The prophets teach us about the exploitation of the poor; the need to look after widows and orphans; and the uselessness of religious ritual unless it is backed up by moral behaviour. In the writings of Amos, Hosea, Isaiah, Jeremiah and Micah we find the unchanging truths those of us with a religious bent are always searching for, set in their historical context. Isaiah, the court prophet with his elegant turn of phrase and his relationship with the king, Jeremiah, who was forced to flee to Egypt as his kingdom collapsed and the Babylonians took the Jews into exile, told the people to settle in that foreign land: 'Seek the peace of the city whither I have caused you to be carried away captive . . .' (Jeremiah 29:7.) He continued in words dear to the heart of any English Jew, that they should build houses and plant gardens and settle down in exile. The prophets speak to us down the ages. Their inspiration, their devotion, can become ours, and through the study of their words and the intensity of their feeling we can find out what it means to be related so closely to the book, to be a text-based people.

Orthodox and non-orthodox alike, we Jews are text-based and law-based rather than belief-based. We have our beliefs, but fundamental to our way of thinking is the fact that we are creatures of law. We believe that all the law is contained in the Torah. There are, theoretically, two hundred and forty-eight positive commandments of the 'You shall do . . .' variety, and three hundred and sixty-five negative commandments or prohibitions. Everything stems from that. There are very few positive commandments for women, other than the commandment to light the sabbath candles, one of the few *mitzvot* for which there is no original Torah verse. It is derived from the idea of enjoying the sabbath – one could not enjoy the sabbath in the dark and therefore lights must be lit beforehand. The blessing goes: 'Blessed are you O Lord our God, king of the universe, who has sanctified us by His commandments and commanded us to light the Sabbath lights.' God Himself did not command us to light sabbath lights – it is one example of stretching of the law to include in it something you want to do anyway.

Jews tend to argue about what the law is, how it should be obeyed, and, in non-orthodox Judaism, whether it should be obeyed at all. It is frequently argued by orthodox Jews that the attitude of the non-orthodox allows them to pick and choose which laws they are going to observe, and to discard any laws they don't like the look of. First, it is important to note that it is not only non-orthodox Jews who pick and choose which laws to observe. There are laws about stoning adulterers to death which few orthodox Jews would countenance these days – and not only because Jews do not usually have judicial control of that kind. In Israel, the legal system is largely based on the British system, dating from the time of the British Mandate in Palestine. It would be possible, theoretically, to extend the area where Jewish laws holds sway at present – personal Jewish status, divorce, marriage and so on – to other issues such as questions of adultery or breaking the sabbath. But there is virtually no pressure to do so. Indeed, I would argue that no orthodox communities would pursue it, any more than they would want to put to death a man caught collecting firewood on the sabbath. It simply is not how we think these days, however orthodox we are. In very orthodox areas of Jersualem, where there are strong feelings about driving on the sabbath, no one attempts to kill the drivers – although they do stone the cars, which is quite intolerant enough. The sabbath is to be kept by 'doing no work'. The debate revolves around what work *is*, and whether driving, and thereby creating a spark in the engine, is work. Obviously, in the days of horse and cart, it was clear-cut – it was wrong to force the horse to work. But inanimate cars? The orthodox rabbis are clear – no driving, no cooking, no use of electricity unless it is on a time-switch. No pressing of a button on the lift, so Jerusalem hotels have a paternoster system which stops at every floor, and is automatically driven. For those of us who are not orthodox, this seems bizarre. The benefits of a day of rest for everyone, when no work is done, is of enormous importance. But what is rest? For those of us who are not orthodox, rest might mean writing letters or reading novels, or taking a trip by car to walk somewhere beautiful. It might mean cooking for fun.

There are further complications in the orthodox attitude to Jewish law – wonderful legal 'fictions', which enable people to get round some of the most inconvenient features of the law. Take, for instance, the recent furious debate in north-west London about the *eruv*. An *eruv* is an enclosed area, effected by a kind of fence or boundary. Calvin Trillin put it for *The New Yorker* (12 December 1994): 'the important thing to know about an *eruv* is that it exists mainly in the minds of people who believe in it'. The *eruv* is a stairway or courtyard or common place shared by families, which meant that that within the area on the sabbath Jews could carry things – pans, or handkerchiefs for instance – or wheel baby-buggies or wheelchairs. If a large chunk of north-west London could be made into an *eruv*, it would be enormously convenient for the very orthodox Jews who live there, for on the sabbath they would be able to carry their handkerchiefs, wheel their children's buggies, and, indeed, use their wheelchairs if they needed them to get to synagogue. In order to put the *eruv* in place, twenty-foot posts would need to be erected where there was not already a natural boundary such as the underground line or the M1 motorway. These posts would need to be linked by some kind of wire or string for the *eruv* to exist. The debate has been fascinating – and distinctly unpleasant.

The fuss started at the annual general meeting of the Hampstead Garden Suburb Trust, for the Hampstead Garden Suburb was to be enclosed entirely within the *eruv*. Its chairman, Lord McGregor of Durris, had written to the planning officers of Barnet Council, objecting strongly. Those in favour had sent out a call for their supporters to attend the AGM and make the case for the *eruv*, to 'demonstrate the commitment of our community to freedom of religious practice and against anti-Semitism whenever it arises and in whatever guise'. When Lord McGregor tried to explain his views at the AGM he was shouted down with cries of 'Shame!', and he resigned on the spot. Hampstead Garden Suburb then became the centre of resistance to the proposed *eruv*, and nobody found it odd, as Calvin Trillin pointed out in his article, 'that so much of the opposition was coming from an area that was to have only eight posts, all of them in a wooded area that wasn't in sight of any houses'. The anti-*eruv* residents suggested that people had lived in harmony in the Suburb for many years by treating religion as a private matter, and that it was divisive for a minority to foist its religious symbols on anyone else. What was not voiced was that the *eruv* might become a self-imposed ghetto, a symbol of the sort of place where Jews lived, and by extension more Jews would then want to live in the Suburb.

Many Jews ranged themselves on the side opposing the *eruv,* on the grounds of its unsightliness, or, as some cynics might argue, because the *eruv* would be conspicuous and they wanted to do the traditional Anglo-Jewish thing of keeping a low profile. They argued that the wires at the top of the poles would be a reminder to survivors of the concentration camps, some of whom do indeed live in the Suburb. The *eruv* would attract anti-semitism; it would increase the numbers of very orthodox Jews and upset the minority mix already *in situ*. This reflects the way that Jews in Britain have dressed just like everybody else, have kept quiet, have not gone out of their way to draw attention to their Jewishness. These Jews are shocked by the neo-orthodoxy of which the *eruv* is an expression. They find it distasteful that Jews are prepared to have a public *menorah* for Chanukah, or go in for too much obvious celebration of Jewish festivals.

I am intrigued by the legal 'fiction'. Plainly, large areas of Hampstead Garden Suburb are not, in any real sense, a shared courtyard or stairway. For the purposes of getting round the law about sabbath observance, however, it counts. This thinking seems extraordinary to us liberals. I don't oppose the *eruv*. If it makes the orthodox Jews in this area happy, makes their lives easier and does not disturb anyone else (which is debatable in this particular case) I don't object. But the fact that they believe that the *eruv* somehow gets round God's law, that God will *believe* that this is a shared courtyard, seems nonsensical.

Orthodox Jews, on the other hand, would say that the capacity of the non-orthodox to pick and choose is equally daft. Why, they might say, if we do not acknowledge the law as divine, are we bothering with it at all? Our explanation lies in the sense that those who wrote the law regarded themselves as divinely inspired, that some of the time they probably were, and that they were expressing the laws and customs of our ancestors; that the explanation and clarification and emendation of law is a process that went on over the ages, very often with the sense that divine will was being carried out.

That is only a part of it. The other element so critical within this, and so important for those of us who are non-orthodox, is the concept of the enlightened conscience. As there is no absolutely hard-and-fast rule for telling which bit of the text is divinely inspired and which not, the requirement is that one must understand it all – which demands a great deal of knowledge, on which many Jews of all shades of opinion fall down lamentably. Having understood it, one must make an honest decision about actions in the light of one's conscience. The decision should not be simply that which is easiest. It is easier to drive on the sabbath than not to. It does not necessarily mean it is right. I have thought about it and have decided, for myself, that if we were still using pack-animals it would not be right to make these beasts work on the sabbath, for they too are entitled to a day off. Since we use the motor car, the commandment not to work on the sabbath cannot reasonably be expected to include not using the car, particularly if driving makes it easier for us to get to synagogue or to enjoy the day of rest.

There are other examples. Many non-orthodox Jews do not keep all the dietary laws, or keep them at home but not out, or keep only those which are biblical. If one takes the view that this section of Torah is divinely inspired, then it seems to me that one must keep the dietary laws, at home and in restaurants, though the extent to which one would go to make sure the plates had never been used for non-kosher food may be more limited than the ultra-orthodox would wish. If, however, one feels that the laws within the Torah about forbidden birds, animals and fish are about what is 'fit' and what is 'unfit', that they predate the religion, and that dietary laws are there to make it difficult for Jews to eat with non-Jews, I would argue that there is no moral element here, and that it is reasonable not to observe these laws. Indeed, one could take it further and say that if one wanted to introduce a moral element into dietary questions within Judaism, it might be more sensible to opt for a vegetarian alternative, which would also keep one in line with Jewish dietary laws. I have never believed the hygiene argument so often adduced – that the reason pig was forbidden was that it was such a health risk, since pork becomes so easily infected in hot climates. All meat becomes easily infected in the heat. The pseudo-scientific argument will not do, and one has to take refuge in the argument about what animals were thought, in the most ancient of times, to be 'proper' animals, fit to sacrifice to God and therefore fit to eat. Does that have any relevance to modern Jews? For me, it does not. For others, defining themselves as Jewish by keeping the dietary laws is very important.

This all has something to do with how we are brought up as Jewish children. I was not brought up observing the dietary laws, though one lot of cousins and my paternal grandmother observed them strictly. Not observing those laws did not make me feel any less Jewish, but I can imagine that had I lived in a more isolated Jewish community, less aware of Jewishness all around me, keeping the dietary laws might have been a way of labelling myself. For me, it has never been necessary, something which has been a source of real concern to fellow Jews who find it extraordinary that a rabbi should admit to not keeping the dietary laws.

I believe it is hypocritical to lie. The fact that dietary laws are in the text is not, for me, a good argument. For orthodox Jews, it is the key argument, but for non-orthodox Jews it is much more complex, to do with labelling ourselves as Jews, being regarded as 'authentic' Jews, doing what people expect Jews to do. I think that the most important thing is to be honest about these things, and in all honesty, I cannot believe that the dietary laws were handed down by God to Moses, or even written down by men out of divine inspiration. I think they are a relic of a primitive way of looking at animals, to do with sacrificial cult. The dietary laws about mixing meat and milk seem to me even more extraordinary in modern life.

What does being Jewish mean, if we do not use our consciences? We have to study Jewish law for all its instructions about how to treat our fellow human beings, but to extrapolate from that what we should do in the modern age, for often the law is time-bound. A good example might be the instruction in the Jerusalem Talmud (Dem. IV, para 6): 'In a city where there are both Jews and non-Jews we are told to feed the poor of both, visit the sick of both, bury the dead of both and comfort the mourners of both "for the sake of peace".' The instruction is obvious – except that the boundaries that are now drawn are not only between Jew and non-Jew but between Jews of different sorts of observance. When is a Jew not a Jew? What does having Jewish status mean?

The traditional, orthodox view is that a person is a Jew if

she or he has a Jewish mother. Orthodox synagogues ask you to prove you have a Jewish mother, if you wish to marry under their auspices. In biblical times the inheritance of status almost certainly went through the father. Foreign women were brought into the community, though the prophets often railed against it, and Solomon almost certainly made a large number of diplomatic alliances. Their children were Israelites (or Hebrews). If you look through the Hebrew Bible, and particularly the Torah, there are pages and pages of what we often refer to as 'the begatteries'. So-and-so begat so-and-so who begat so-and-so. These are, of course, tribal lineages. At some point – perhaps to do with persecution, or maybe a practical view about proof of parentage – things were changed to ascribe Jewish status through the mother.

Some authorities have taken a dim view of such a practical approach to affirming Jewish status, but it has to be seen in the context of communities which were often persecuted and dispersed, where rape was by no means unknown, and where children needed to be protected and have their status assured, whoever their fathers were.

In Britain today, Jewish status through the mother is accepted by all movements in Judaism except the liberal and progressive, where the same rules apply as those governing American reform, that status goes through the mother or the father, and is fully acquired via a Jewish education. This leads to certain complications. First, proof of Jewish status is sometimes anything but easy in the post-Holocaust period in Europe. There are many people, whom Stefan Zweig, the great Austrian-Jewish author, might have described as demi-semi-Jews, people who had one Jewish parent but no Jewish upbringing, or a Jewish grandparent, but for whom the knowledge of being Jewish was lost or deliberately suppressed. Those whom

Hitler regarded as Jews are not always regarded as Jews by the Jewish community. People died because they were Jews in Hitler's terms but were not allowed to live as Jews within the practising Jewish community – without conversion.

Some would accuse us of racism of our own, because of our excluding attitude to Jewish status. My own view is that, as an accusation, that is unfair and inaccurate. I do think that the whole area needs looking at again, for it is extraordinary to me that we make conversion to Judaism very difficult, and have such narrow definitions of who is a Jew. That is further complicated by the State of Israel where, under the Law of Return, all Jews from any part of the world, as long as they are regarded as Jewish by any Jewish authority, may go and live in Israel, but if, once they get there, they are not seen as Jewish under traditional, *halachic*, Jewish law, then they are not classed as Jews for marriage purposes! Add to that the fact that the most liberal of the groupings within Judaism – the liberal and progressive in Britain and the reform in America – actually make it harder to be classed as a Jew if one had a Jewish mother but no Jewish upbringing, and one begins to tear out one's hair.

People have argued – some in a spirit of anti-semitism – that it is because we regard ourselves as the chosen people that we want to make it difficult, indeed near impossible, for anyone to join us. That is untrue, and a misrepresentation of the concept of the chosen people, which is more about being chosen by God to carry out a purpose than being special in any other way. What is true is that in ancient times it was remarkably easy to become Jewish. The Book of Ruth, in the Hebrew bible, is about a woman who decides to leave her country and her ways and customs to join her mother-in-law Naomi on the trek back home to Israel, saying: 'Thy people shall be my people, and thy God my God. Where thou diest, I will die, and there will I be buried ... nothing but death shall part thee and me' (Ruth 1:16–17). This is the non-Jew throwing in her lot with the Jewish people. Judaism was, in its origins, probably a proselytising religion. The proselytising of the early Christians may have been based on Jewish traditions. The Idumeans (Edomites) were alleged to have been converted to Judaism by force, and there are numerous examples of early conversions, where people had to say they wished to be Jewish, go through the ritual bath and, if they were male, be circumcised, no small matter if one was an adult.

Modern Jewish authorities require very considerable learning from their would-be converts. Even the most liberal authorities in Britain require well over a year of study, the writing of essays, an interview with a rabbinic board, and some learning of Hebrew. More orthodox authorities require much more, including, for an orthodox conversion in Britain (which technically cannot be for marriage reasons alone), living with an orthodox family for a period of time, experiencing an utterly orthodox Jewish life. For most people this is an intolerable demand, which is why the majority of conversions take place under reform or liberal auspices. Even there it would be possible to argue that less could be required of those who convert to Judaism, since what they are doing is associating themselves with the community by their very willingness to become Jewish. They could be asked to know the basics of the faith, and something of Jewish history and values, but it might not need to be necessary for them to study for upwards of a year to become Jewish. That is a debatable point, as clearly there are many people who have converted to Judaism who have found the study, which they often do with their partner, very rewarding. Through studying jointly, the relationship can become much enriched. It is equally clear, however, that the study and the requirements are sufficient to put off some hopeful, sincere, would-be converts, who might have made very good members of our communities had we not been so demanding.

I think we do ourselves damage by not being more open to people who want to convert, provided they have good motives. We could be much more relaxed in the demands we make on them. Is it, in this day and age, necessary to ask adult males to go through circumcision, as if it were some kind of tribal rite? Circumcision is a tribal rite. I find it extraordinary that non-orthodox Judaism does not question the necessity of circumcising baby boys. There are hygienic arguments for it, and some scientists argue that women who are the sexual partners of circumcised men are less likely to contract cervical cancer (a slightly tendentious claim because of other factors such as class, social mores and environmental factors). The point, though, is that circumcision done eight days after a birth is usually not for health reasons, but because the child is a Jew. Should we be encouraging unnecessary surgery of any kind, especially on babies? I am ambivalent about this. I have no wish to forbid others to do it, but I have found that the strength of feeling is such that not to have one's baby boy circumcised is tantamount to saying he is not Jewish – a ludicrous state of affairs. The answer for those of us who challenge this is simply to have it done, if Jewish fathers insist, quietly, with no religious ceremony, acknowledging we are giving in to an atavistic instinct.

When it comes to adults, I am more concerned. We are still fewer than we were before the holocaust. Our numbers have not yet grown beyond those in 1939. Though some would say, as Gerald Jacobs did in the *Jewish Chronicle* (10 February 1995), that it is a miracle that we have numbers as high as that, given the temptations to disappear into the wider community after the holocaust, I believe that we should make it easier for non-Jewish spouses and non-Jewish friends who want to join us, let alone those who regard themselves as Jewish for whatever reason but whom the community does not accept as Jewish because they do not fit the rules.

Within liberal Judaism we have a system by which people who have regarded themselves as Jewish, but do not quite fit the normal definitions of Jewish status according to the liberal practice, can in some circumstances affirm their Jewish status rather than going through conversion. Though better, I do not think it is good enough. The only really honourable thing would be to include in our community all who, in one way or another, identify themselves as Jewish. To exclude people who want to be part of the community – because they had the 'wrong' Jewish parent or no Jewish upbringing – seems to me to be short-sighted, narrowly exclusivist and unkind.

Mixed marriages bring further complications. The official line from all sides of the Jewish community is that intermarriage is unacceptable. Different brands of Judaism, having made that statement one way and another, then tackle it differently when it occurs, as it assuredly does and will. Traditional orthodoxy still tries to ignore mixed marriages, although the demographic studies of the Jewish communities of Europe and America suggest they are simply no longer ignorable. It is thought that just under half of all young American Jews marry out, and the assumption is that in France and Britain it is not very different. (In Britain, it looks as if only one in three people who could get married in a synagogue do so. Figures are unclear.) The desire to ignore intermarriage leads to some appalling examples of how a family can be entirely dysfunctional. When a child marries 'out', in some cases the parents sit *shiva* (go through the mourning process) as if their son or daughter were dead. Then they have no further future contact, often until one of the parents is dead, whereupon the other may try to mend the bridges. Such a rigid reaction is, thankfully, increasingly unusual. Many Jewish parents express sadness or rage. With much weeping, they forego the prospect of a 'proper' Jewish wedding, and, unwillingly, they accept the situation, realising that it means that the family is no longer a 'proper' Jewish family. Daughters who marry out are not taken so seriously, because their children, according to Jewish law, will be Jewish anyway. When a son marries out of the faith, the children are not going to be Jewish in the traditional Jewish view, and it causes even greater misery. Orthodox Judaism, conservative Judaism, and reform Judaism in Europe take that view. Judaism in America and liberal and progressive Judaism in Britain do not face the same prospect, as the child can be Jewish with a Jewish upbringing. Provided discussions are held in advance about what religion the children will be and in what community they will grow up, the Jewish line can be maintained.

There are already signs of great divisions within the community as a result of these different views on Jewish status. The liberal, progressive and American Reform view is more logical. It gives the parents within the mixed marriage the capacity to make some proper decisions about the upbringing of their children, and to work out what religion they want their children to be. The traditional view is still more powerful. Even amongst non-orthodox Jews, it carries considerable weight by virtue of its traditionality. It is only in very recent years that British reform Judaism has taken the issue of intermarriage seriously, to the extent that there are conferences run for intermarried couples by the reform movement.

Jewish authorities world-wide are going to have to face this issue. Living in an open society, as we do, by choice, our children are going to meet, and fall in love with, people who are not Jewish. This is a penalty of living in the open society. But it also has great advantages, anti-semitism has diminished as a result, too. There is no longer shame attached, in the outside communities, to marrying a Jew or Jewess. We are no longer exotic. We are normal members of society who happen to be Jewish. We send our children to schools where they meet non-Jews, we allow them to go to parties where they meet non-Jews, they go to university and meet non-Jews. Indeed, it is remarkable that many of them marry other Jews. This has to do with the nature of the Jewish family, and the ties that invisibly bind our young to our communities.

There are many people within our Jewish communities who argue that the only way to prevent intermarriage is to keep our young people within Jewish day schools, and to send them to Jewish colleges or to universities with a large number of Jewish students. That is no longer living in the open society, which has brought so much that is good for Jews. It is living in a self-imposed ghetto. It is actually denying to our children the things that many of us had, purely so that they marry other Jews. While ensuring the continuity of the Jewish people is of paramount importance, to do it by imposing a ghetto upon ourselves is a nonsense. It can only be done because we make it attractive enough, desirable enough and important enough for our young people to want it themselves.

We should be more accepting of intermarriage, and should encourage those who have intermarried not to lose their ties with the Jewish community. We should urge them to bring up their children as Jewish, irrespective of which parent is Jewish. That means all community organisations have to extend a hand of friendship to non-Jews, so that those who do not choose to convert to Judaism nevertheless feel that they can participate in the community, and that they are loved and admired for what they do in bringing up their children as Jews when they are not Jewish themselves. That requires a realisation that Judaism is in no sense superior to other faiths, and an understanding that many people of other faiths, whilst respecting Judaism, do not wish to be part of it, but are perfectly happy, generously, one might add, to have their children grow up Jewish.

Conversion is an option exercised by some people when they marry Jews. Sometimes it is a condition of the marriage, insisted upon by either the would-be spouse or his/her parents. That insistence can be problematic. It is legitimate to ask why anyone should be asked to change their religion in an open society because of whom they are about to marry. I have always found it remarkable that so many people convert to Judaism out of love for their partner or respect for their future parents-in-law. A conversion which is a condition of the marriage can cause considerable problems later on. When the marriage is in difficulties, as most marriages are at some point in their existence, the accusation of being forced to convert to 'your rotten Judaism' is frequently thrown at the Jewish-born partner in the relationship. For that reason, it seems more sensible, and more in keeping with living in an open society, to suggest to couples that they should not make the marriage conditional on one partner converting, since that is a poor basis for a relationship that should last for life, but that they should marry and then the non-Jewish spouse can convert later, if he or she decides he or she wants to, or can participate without ever converting. This way precludes the big Jewish wedding, since that can only take place where both partners are Jewish. The ceremony could always be celebrated later, while a register office wedding can suffice in the short term.

We have a situation in Britain where rabbis cannot officiate at a marriage between a Jew and a non-Jew, which is plainly absurd especially as it is carried to the lengths that we cannot even officiate at a blessing. While Jewish marriage and, say, Christian marriage are different (Jewish marriage being about a contract and Christian marriage mirroring the union between Jesus and the Church), it should be perfectly possible to have a civil marriage and then a joint religious service asking God's blessing upon the union, irrespective of whether both are Jews. Yet, in this country, only a very few rabbis will officiate at such a service of blessing, and even then it can only be held in private. I think this sends the wrong message to the wider community and also discourages Jews who have fallen in love with non-Jews and want to marry them, from any communal activity. If we were truly worried about Jewish continuity, rather than Jewish status according to orthodox tenets, we would be much more open and encouraging towards people in mixed marriages, and welcome their children and grandchildren, should they wish to associate with our community at all.

Many of those we might accept as Jewish will not be regarded as such by the orthodox communities. My own view is that that should not matter, and that we should stop worrying too much about what orthodox Jews think about these matters. We should move to a more inclusivist position, while making it clear to those who choose to join us that they will probably not be accepted as Jewish by orthodox authorities. I suspect many of them will not mind, and will be happy to be associated with us. This means we must take a pro-active line on encouraging into Judaism people who have a sincere interest. It also means being quite clear with the orthodox that we are making no attempt to conform to their requirements of conversion. It will certainly lead to further complications in the already difficult relationship between orthodox and non-orthodox Jews. Perhaps that cannot be helped, and a braver line from the non-orthodox would help us make more sense of this business of being Jewish in the post-holocaust twentieth century.

8

Identity crisis?

British and Jewish

I feel intensely British. Some would say I often behave as if I am more British than the British, more English than the English. I feel it, at least in part, because of my refugee origins, because of my sense of deep gratitude to this country for the welcome it gave my mother and so many of my relatives. Alongside my Britishness, my pride in this country and my love for it, however, I am aware that many refugees have not been let in and that anti-semitism is growing again, albeit slowly, a creeping menace.

This is not a country where anti-semitism was never known. Indeed, it was in England that the 'blood libel' was first heard, the libel that Jews use the blood of a Christian child to make unleavened bread for Passover. A child called William of Norwich was supposedly used so in 1144. Other English children were later alleged to have been forcibly circumcised. Such smears in medieval England were part of the typical attitude to Jews, who were possessions of and protected by the king, but often became victims of his greed and need for money. In 1290, under Edward I, the Jews were expelled – a very sorry story.

Jews were almost certainly in England before 1066. They probably came in the Roman period, were expelled around the beginning of the eleventh century, and reappeared with William the Conqueror. There were early Jewish settlements in Oxford, London, Lincoln, York, Bury St Edmunds and Norwich. Jews flourished reasonably well under William I, and, particularly well under William Rufus (William II) who was no great friend of the church, and under Henry I. They would have received royal protection – for a consideration – and been allowed to continue their trade.

This must be set against a background of attitudes to usury. The Christian church did not allow the lending of money by a Christian to a Christian at interest. (Nor did Jews allow it to fellow Jews. Exod. 22:248) This is based on the passage in Psalm 15 'who putteth not out his money to usury ...' Therefore, Jews – for a variety of reasons including the prohibition upon them from owning land – became the 'usurers' to the Christians of Europe. After the Fourth Lateran Council of 1215, Jews had to wear special badges (yellow circles), and were increasingly restricted in their ability to do anything but lend money at interest. They were also getting threats from other groups, notably the Lombards, who were beginning to enter the 'banking' business themselves.

Life for Jews in medieval England gradually became impossible. Riots against Jews were commonplace, as was the cry of Christ-killer. Peter the Hermit, preaching to the rabble in France before the First Crusade, argued that there was little point going to the east to destroy the infidel when there were plenty of infidels all along the Rhine in France and Germany to kill first. Jews in the cities along the Rhine were massacred in the twelfth century. Richard I, Coeur de Lion, so beloved of the British as hero of the Crusades, was a fanatical Jew-hater. When he came to the throne, he sent out an edict forbidding any Jew from entering the Palace of Westminster during the coronation. Several wealthy and influential Jews took it upon themselves to approach the king with great gifts. They went only as far as the gates of the palace, when the mob wounded some and killed others, while still others were dragged forward into the forbidden area and beaten to death. A few Jews were immediately baptised to save their lives. Violence started in other places, notably in York. There was looting and killing. The Jews took refuge in York Castle, but then suspected that the governor was plotting against them. While he was away, they closed the gates against him, which was taken as an insult to the king's authority. 'Destroy the enemies of Christ! Destroy the enemies of Christ!' went the cry. The Jews fought and offered money for their lives – in vain. They all decided to commit suicide in Clifford's Tower, led by their rabbi, who argued that it was better to kill themselves than to be tortured. The suicide is remembered by Jews to this day.

There were, of course, men of great wealth and influence in the Anglo-Jewish community, notably Aaron of Lincoln and Elijah of London. Though England was not one of the great centres of Jewish learning in the western world, it was a creditable outpost of the Rhineland communities, subject, in the wake of the Crusades, to the same attacks. Jews in medieval England were often used in the conflicts between kings and the church – some kings saw them as an asset, while the church saw them as Christ-killers, usurers and murderers of Christian children.

We do not know why Edward I expelled the Jews,

although it certainly has something to do with the gradual tightening of the attitudes of the church after the Fourth Lateran Council, which made it more difficult to appear a good Christian monarch and to defend the Jews.

Shakespeare's *Merchant of Venice* portrays Jews as Shylock, who wants his 'pound of flesh', is money-grubbing, and whose daughter is 'redeemed' by the love of a Christian. I have only seen it on stage once, and I never want to go again. Even acted sensitively, and by a Jew, Shylock nevertheless reeks of anti-semitism.

John Gross's study of Shylock is revealing in the suggestions that he makes that Shakespeare was influenced by the death by hanging, drawing and quartering of the Queen's physician, Rodrigo Lopez, a Jew. He quotes Stephen Dedalus, in James Joyce's *Ulysses*, arguing that:

> All events brought grist to his mill. Shylock chimes with the jewbaiting that followed the hanging and quartering of the queen's leech Lopez, his jew's heart being plucked forth whilst the sheeny was yet alive . . .

John Gross draws comparisons with an anonymous Middle English poem entitled 'Cursor Mundi', probably written by a priest from Northumbria, in which a Christian craftsman working for 'Queen Eline' (St Helena, the mother of the emperor Constantine) borrows money from a Jew and finds herself unable to pay it back. When the Jew goes to court to claim his 'pound of flesh' in the usual way, he is foiled. He curses the judges, and the queen orders that his goods should be confiscated and his tongue cut out; but then relents after he promises to show her where the True Cross is buried – 'where your Lord's rood-tree lies'. Gross points out that the poet was setting up a link between the pound of flesh and the crucifixion, and that he was writing against the background of the expulsion of the Jews under Edward I in 1290. Thus: 'Shakespeare can hardly have been aware of it, but *The Merchant of Venice* picks up a thread that goes back across three centuries to the last days of medieval English Jewry.'

An even cruder depiction of the Jew comes from Marlowe's *The Jew of Malta*, which also has a reference which does not occur in Shakespeare, but which was of paramount importance. Barabas regales his servant Ithamore with details of his criminal career:

> As for myself, I walk abroad a-nights
> And kill sick people groaning under the walls:
> Sometimes I go about and poison wells . . .

The accusation made of the Jews that they poisoned the wells was a popular fantasy in much of Europe at the time of the Black Death. The physician, Rodrigo Lopez, was supposed to have tried to poison Elizabeth I. Hitler referred to the Jews as poisoners of the world, and Stalin went to his grave convinced he might be murdered by a team of Jewish doctors. The myth continued until the 1950s in Russia. And anti-semitism there makes it all too likely it will begin again.

Throughout Elizabethan literature one can find references to Jews which are highly unfavourable and highly charged – written at a time when there were few Jews in the country, and many of these writers would never have met a Jew. Jews did, in fact, play a part in wider national and international events over that period. A recent book by David Katz suggests that Lopez may in fact have been guilty of treason as then interpreted. There was communication between Jews within the Spanish-dominated world and those in England, even though Jews had been expelled from Spain in 1492 and from England in 1290. Jews were not technically allowed to live in England at all in Elizabeth I's reign, but there was nevertheless a significant community.

There had also been a Jewish community in England in the days of Elizabeth's father, Henry VIII. Jewish arguments about levirate marriage (where a brother of a dead man is required to marry his deceased brother's widow, if he died childless, to carry on the man's name through her) were used during the debate over Henry's first divorce. In fact, the arguments did not hold, partly because the scholars who went off to consult the Jewish scholars of Italy had not realised that there were two main groups of customs among the Jews: one for the Ashkenazim, the Jews of northern Europe, and one for the Sephardim, the Jews of Spain, Italy and North Africa. The views of each group often conflicted with the other – thus failing to give a single opinion to be used as evidence. Henry VIII also had at his court up to nineteen Jewish musicians, who possibly pretended, as did so many, to be Christians, although it was well known that they were Jews. Rabbinical arguments may not have helped Henry in the end, nor stopped him from establishing his own church, but Jewish arguments were undoubtedly thought significant in the debate.

Under Cromwell, in 1656, the Jews returned to England. This was a result of factors more complicated than kindness towards a troubled community, or economic good sense because of Jewish trade connections. There was a strongly held belief among some people that the millennium was around the corner, the Messiah was at hand, and that the Jews – seeing the Protestant faith in practice without all that Catholic overlay – would be bound to convert and thus bring the Second Coming nearer. Others would have none of this – it was unbelievable that the Jews would even think of converting, so devilish were they in their religious practices.

> And you should, if you please, refuse
> Till the conversion of the Jews

When I first read Marvell's poem 'To His Coy Mistress', I found this to be a mildly anti-semitic remark, the implication being that the Jews will never convert. Recent research shows that this was the stuff of genuine debate. The Jews were allowed back into England because it was hoped that they *would* convert.

This evidence needs to be seen in conjunction with the Renaissance interest in Jewish mysticism and biblical Hebrew. Indeed, Hebrew was a subject of intense study, leading to splendid translations of the Bible into English directly from the Hebrew rather than from the Greek Septuagint or the Latin Vulgate. The Jews may not have been welcome, but the Hebrew language was becoming an essential part of the cultured person's study, be it the young Elizabeth I, the young Edward VI, or the boys of Westminster School. The King James' Bible, a monument of beautiful prose, is a lasting tribute to this obsession.

Until the beginning of the nineteenth century, Jews were still mostly in small communities which kept themselves to themselves. They were involved in trade, particularly as naval agents at the sea ports and as bullion and other forms of city traders in the City of London. It was during the last century that the discussion began about the removal of Jewish disabilities, so that Jews could attend universities. (The foundation of University College,

London, was largely for the benefit of Jews and non-conformists who were barred from Oxford and Cambridge because of the requirement to pass a theological examination and be recognised as a good Anglican.) Many Jews were already active and thought utterly respectable within the City of London. The Rothschilds were beginning to make their mark, as was David Salomons. The traditional view among Anglo-Jewish historians has been that Britain was a relatively tolerant society and that the nineteenth century, with its optimism and its belief in trade, created a positive atmosphere; but one scholar, David Feldman, argues differently. Examination of *Hansard*, the *Jewish Chronicle* and other texts has thrown up far more anti-semitism than the old view of liberal, tolerant England suggested. We read of the attempt to retain 'the Christian character of the nation', or of the danger that admitting the Jews would open the way to the 'Hindoo', the 'Parsee', and the 'votary of Boodh', and of Charles Ewan Law's vision of a 'Christian England – here we have a Christian constitution – here we all profess ourselves at least to be Christians'. When Lionel de Rothschild was elected as an M.P. for the City of London in 1847 and tried to take his seat swearing on an Old Testament, the House went into uproar. Central to the political debate was the 'vision of the nation', a vision of a hierarchical, Christian country.

Supporters of the removal of the disabilities from the Jews had some concept of the rights of human beings, and were determined to trim some of the church's powers. Society was changing, but not fast enough. When the Earl of Aberdeen, then prime minister, changed sides to support the Jewish cause in 1853, he acknowledged a remnant of prejudice. He faced opponents though, such as Henry Drummond, conservative and evangelical, who castigated this new-found liberalism:

But what was liberalism? The antagonist and opponent of religion . . . Liberalism was just egotism, it led every man to seek his own interest and of no other person . . . the French revolution was the triumph of liberalism.

Israel Finestein, recently retired as president of the Board of Deputies of British Jews, wrote that '. . . what was called the Jewish question was essentially a Christian or at least a Gentile question. Namely, in what circumstances was society prepared to accommodate the Jews into full citizenship. . .'. Nineteenth century Jews, a different generation living in another world, hoped for complete Jewish emancipation while they feared that it would never come. They hoped for the right to hold public office, from which Jews had been specifically excluded when non-conformists and Catholics gained the right in the 1820s. If they were denied reform, they believed virulent anti-semitism, of which there were plenty of examples on the continent and in Russia, was just around the corner.

The Jews relied heavily on non-Jews such as Macaulay and Lord John Russell to campaign on their behalf. While believing in Jewish emancipation, however, these men thought Jews were not wholly loyal to Britain. Macaulay wrote in his famous essay 'On Jewish Disabilities' based on his 1830 speech in the House of Commons:

It has always been the trick of bigotry to govern as if a section of the state was the whole and to censure the other sections of the state for their want of patriotic spirit. If the Jews have not felt towards England like children, it is because she has treated them like step-children.

The issue of identity is, I believe, still important for Jews and other minorities. The majority often seems to feel impatient when minorities express doubts about how fully they belong. Macaulay's response illustrates that the same ambivalence towards minorities existed in the nineteenth century. Certainly, the evidence we gathered for the Runnymede Trust's Commission on anti-semitism, published in 1994 under the title *A Very Light Sleeper*, suggests that ambivalence remains. Reports of financial scandals in the media often contain anti-semitic overtones, and criticisms of the government of Israel frequently appear (but are not necessarily) to be expressions of anti-semitism.

In 1993 a British National Party candidate was elected in a local bye-election in Tower Hamlets, London. Some thought it a flash in the pan, but the opinion polls of the time suggested otherwise; in one poll, a staggering thirty-six per cent of those polled pronounced themselves in favour of 'the forcible repatriation of immigrants'. Racially motivated violence is on the increase. An Asian student was killed in south-east London in 1993. The nature of the anti-semitic material in Britain is becoming more offensive. The old canard about Jews having sex with young girls three years and a day old and upwards has been revived, and the possible *eruv* in North London has brought out a terrific amount of anti-semitism.

The Runnymede Commission distinguished between three kinds of anti-semitism, since the categories are often muddled. There is anti-Judaism, the hostility to the beliefs and practices of the Jewish religion; there is anti-semitic racism, which is hostility to Jews based on the incorrect assumption that they constitute a separate race; and there is anti-Zionism, hostility towards the expression of Jewish national identity which finds its focus in the State of Israel.

The problem is that the distinctions only work to some extent. While it might be true to say that those who criticise or oppose Zionism are not those who see Jews as genetically 'different', often the three kinds of discourse do overlap and intertwine, and it is difficult to disentangle them. For instance, a Chanukah card sent anonymously to many members of the British Jewish community in 1992, including me, used the language of the gas chamber and was illustrated by a robin sitting on top of a tin of Zyklon-B gas, entitled 'Giftgaz'. That is probably 'racial' anti-semitism, but it might also, given the abusive messages sent with it, be partly to do with anti-Zionism. It is also linked with the industry of holocaust denial, which has reached greater proportions than I have ever known in the last two years.

Holocaust denial has become so extreme that scholars are now working on it as a serious subject, notably Deborah Lipstadt at Emory University in America. Lipstadt caused her friends some consternation when she decided to devote her research to the denial of the holocaust. She was thought to be giving anti-semites too much credibility; they were in no way worthy of academic study. They seemed to believe that one should surely leave the deniers to their absurdity and venom, treat them as fringe campaigners of a peculiarly vicious kind, and, above all, not take them seriously. I believe that holocaust denial is truly dangerous, and an issue today, just as extreme anti-semitism can be, and therefore one which should be studied, so it can be countered effectively.

In 1993 a letter was sent out from a fictitious organisation, calling itself the Anglo-Catholic Fellowship, with a fictitious address in north London. It warned people of the risk to children from the hassidic Jews and opposed a possible ultra-orthodox hassidic housing project in Shenley in Hertfordshire. Among other calumnies it contained the sentence:

Whilst I am confident that most of the hassidim are entirely respectable people there is, in my opinion, a real risk of increased sexual offences in this area, and all teachers and parents are respectfully reminded of their duty to protect children from these vile and blasphemous practices.

Nothing changes.

Anti-Zionism is the most difficult component of the three 'types' of anti-semitism to analyse, partly because it seems to me that some of the criticism of the State of Israel is legitimate, and might just as well be uttered by Jews. Much of it, however, is not legitimate. It is complicated by the fact that Israel is the only Jewish state, which rose out of the ashes of the holocaust, giving it a special significance for many Jews quite apart from its status as the Jewish state. Though many Jews will criticise the State of Israel, none would go so far, I imagine, as to agree with the sort of anti-Zionist propaganda being sent out from anti-semitic organisations in Britain and America during the early 1990s. They argued that:

Judaism is the mother of all religions and the source of our code of morality, Zionism is a philosophy purely of self-aggrandisement, a vicious, egocentric, nationalistic movement far worse than either apartheid or Nazism. It is in fact nothing less than a well-organised and quite insidious international criminal conspiracy which is responsible for the oppression, torture and murder of the Palestinian people and the expropriation of their land.

Its tone makes it clear that this is anti-semitic against Jews as well as anti-Zionist. Despite hopes that the peace accord between the PLO and Israel might lead to a cessation of such missives, there is evidence that they continue and that extremely negative feelings against the State of Israel still exist in some quarters. That negativity is combined with outright anti-semitism, and with disgraceful descriptions of Jews. Foremost amongst the organisations involved in such publications is an extremist Muslim organisation, Hizb ut-Tahrir, which also attacks Pakistan and the PLO, supported the Hamas killing of a 'Jewish soldier' and argued in 1992 that 'the Jews are belligerent enemies and we are in a state of war with them'. One can also find similar comments in Arab state-run newspapers as well as, for instance in Kuwait's *Sawt al-Kuwait*, in which Mahmoud Shamman wrote in the wake of the electoral defeat of President Bush in 1992:

> The Jews have unleashed their dogs to tear at the flesh of the President who refused to be putty in their hands. They vowed to make him a solitary figure, isolated in the White House ... Here are the Jews of Hollywood mocking the President daily on their television screens. And whenever the economy improves, the analysts among Wall Street's usurers inform the American nation that it is in ruins ... in the new American age, the Jews have taken over the media and the economy, looting the public, gagging them, leading them to certain doom.

The imagery of Jews as usurers, the old medieval accusation, is all too apparent.

The serious increase in anti-semitism in Britain is demonstrated by the Board of Deputies, which has experienced an eighty-five per cent increase in reports of anti-semitic incidents. Some of that can be put down to greater awareness of the need to report, but nevertheless the increase is staggering. It certainly accords with what many of my Jewish friends and I are experiencing, and mirrors what is happening to other minority groups. The atmosphere in which I grew up was supportive and largely free of this kind of attack. This is different.

In some cases, the increase in anti-semitism actually makes people more inclined to stand up and be counted. It encourages others to keep their heads down, in the hope it will go away. If Jews are faint-hearted, it is because those of us who are in some sense leaders of the community, we, with our failure of confidence, have failed them. This is a historical problem which goes back to before the last war. In those days, the Anglo-Jewish community, insofar as it shared attitudes at all, believed in liberal democracy and that things would improve for humanity. Those who had lived in Britain for more than the previous fifty years had seen emancipation of the Jews grow alongside the removal of disadvantages for Catholics and non-conformists. The roots of emancipation were in early nineteenth century European liberal thought, which had helped free the Jews from the ghettoes and allowed them into German universities, and encouraged poets such as Heine to write lyrically about emancipation and freedom. In an extract from an 1897 sermon by Claude Montefiore, leader of the liberal Jewish movement, in the then Chief Rabbi Dr Hertz's volume *A Book of Jewish Thoughts*, we read: 'Ten bad Jews may help to damn us; ten good Jews may help to save us; which minyan [quorum required for a full service] will you join?' By the actions of a few bad eggs, the whole community is condemned.

The politics of fear before the last world war encouraged a view that any outspoken statements or tough actions by the Jews could lead to anti-semitism. The Anglo-Jewish community was inclined to keep a low profile and to display almost obsequious gratitude when non-Jews showed concern, offered help or expressed their shared outrage at events in Nazi Germany. Jews would warn each other to be sure to be seen to be putting a lot into the war effort, and not to become involved in the black market once rationing began. The danger of anti-semitism was genuine, and rested on the experience of the Mosley-led Fascist marches of the late 1930s. The Anglo-Jewish community also genuinely believed that Jews could influence the prevalence of anti-semitism by their behaviour, and shared the view that anti-semitism was as much their own fault as that of others.

The theory that 'bad' Jews somehow taint other Jews hasn't died out. During the first Guinness trial the press revelled in the 'Jewish' origins of 'dishonest' people, suggesting that greed was a Jewish characteristic. In the 1950s and early 1960s, the term 'Rachmanism' was coined to describe the extortionistic activities of wicked landlords, especially in the London districts of North Kensington and Notting Hill. Yet not all the bad landlords were Jews.

These days, we are inclined to say that lumping all Jews together and characterising them on the basis of a few is a form of anti-semitism. Attitudes have changed since the war. Jews in Britain now believe that anti-semitism is the fault of others, and not themselves. They get angry when it is suggested that a Jewish wrong-doer has brought disrepute on Jews as a whole or has behaved 'typically'. Jews have grown in confidence. They are proud to be in the outer world. They share their culture with non-Jews. They even share their jokes. The success of Vanessa Feltz playing herself as the Jewish mother in her television chat show, mocked for her size and her flash qualities, is a case in point. Maureen Lipman starred as Beattie, the easily identifiable Jewish-mother-to-beat-all-Jewish-mothers in the British Telecom advertisements. Ruby Wax, Stephen Fry and Alexei Sayle are all people who have made no secret of the fact they are Jewish, joke about it and even trade upon it.

There is also a growing number of 'media rabbis', of whom the best known is probably Rabbi Lionel Blue, much loved for his frequent 'Thought for the day', and his uncanny way of telling a personal story so that it gives the listener an insight into his or her own life. We know about Lionel's mother and aunt, now both sadly dead, wonderful women who supported him in all he did. We know about Lionel's cooking – he writes cookery books, after all – and some of us have experienced his cooking at its best, and worst, including the treacle tart which gave us lockjaw for the rest of the evening, so we could not speak. We know about his doubts and his moments of joy, and we have gained an astonishing intimacy with a man who is in some ways a very private person.

Rabbi Hugo Gryn has also become loved by the nation, in a very different way. Hugo is an old friend and the rabbi who officiated at our wedding. He features on *The Moral Maze* on radio, and, like Lionel, puts across his points by telling us stories. His anecdotes tend to be far less personal in context, but are equally personal in the telling. Hugo is a survivor of the concentration camps – he can describe at first hand what happened to him, which has given him an authority and a message for the nation. Often, though, he simply talks like a traditional rabbi, telling an old rabbinic story to good effect, to illustrate a point. The present Chief Rabbi is also an accomplished broadcaster, as are Rabbis Jonathan Romain, Alexandra Wright and Jonathan Magonet. The BBC and other media companies look for Jews to fill 'religious' slots as if somehow we touch the hearts and minds of the nation – often of people who are not in any sense religious – more than the traditional Anglican vicar. Yet some of the best broadcasters I know are Anglicans. It is very odd, but suddenly it is hip to be Jewish. In the words of Matthew Kalman, the editor of *New Moon*, we are 'stepping out of the kosher closet'.

With all the stepping out, the growing confidence, the changes in thinking so that we do not believe that we have to keep our heads down, we have still done poorly at encouraging our children to be part of the community. Synagogue membership is falling. Intermarriage rates are up. Increasingly, Jews are identifying themselves as Jews but not joining any Jewish organisation, failing to find any kind of relevance to their lives within the standard communal organisations. There is such richness in the Jewish tradition – emotional, intellectual and historical – that it depresses me to know that people who want to show the world that they are Jewish, who want to stand up and be counted, know almost nothing about Judaism.

There are some young Jews who would say that, although marrying a non-Jew is no disaster, it might have been different had they lived a 'proper' life, been able to ask questions, participate in Jewish activities, and meet other young Jews. It is true to say that many Jewish parents of my generation and slightly older have been disaffected by Judaism as a result of the incredibly tiresome Jewish education to which they were subjected. They were taught for bar mitzvah (and sometimes bat mitzvah) as if it did not matter, as if it were a tribal rite one had to get through but not anything with meaning. They learned their portion of the Torah by rote and went unwillingly to religion school, where people told them things they did not understand, and certainly could not believe. As a result, their children suffered from what the parents thought was the 'relief' of not having to go through all that. No religion school, often no bar or bat mitzvah, no sense of what it might mean to be Jewish. All these children were told was that they were Jewish; their identity was emphasised strongly to them without any signs of it to hang on to. They probably had no Passover celebration, or, if they did, it would be without much religious content. Perhaps the grandfather, who wanted to do it properly, would be encouraged to hurry up, so they could get on with the food. They enjoyed Christmas rather than Chanukah; they had no Jewish New Year, but might have been taken sheepishly to a synagogue for a couple of hours on Yom Kippur, though their parents would half-mock the real religious feeling present there. These young people, now in their twenties and thirties, have been deprived of their heritage. It leaves them feeling they do not know who they are, or why they should be Jewish at all. Marrying in or out of their community has no significance to people who have no sense of what that community might be. We have to think again about messages to young Jews.

The effort we put into trying to improve Jewish education and funding alternative Jewish magazines like *New Moon*, the hip alternative to the *Jewish Chronicle*, is still not enough to explain why we have not done a better job of explaining to our children why it should *matter* to be Jewish and to remain so, and ultimately to have Jewish children. Are we Europeans too influenced by the lack of confidence of the older generation, in which, for this purpose I include myself? Has our confidence been so shaken by the holocaust that we find it hard to make sense of any Jewish future? Has our thinking become somewhat unimaginative?

Much of the intellectual input into Anglo-Jewry just before and during the war came from the refugees from Nazi

Germany. Many of them were part of that German Jewish enlightenment, the merging of Jewish and non-Jewish intellectual traditions into the scientific study of Judaism (*Wissenschaft des Judentums*). Jews in Britain despised this, for many of them hailed from the Pale of Settlement, from the Eastern European traditions that the German Jewish intellectuals despised, particularly for their mystical, hassidic style. The intellectual rigour of the German Jews had not stopped Hitler's advances. After the holocaust those from the Eastern European traditions argued that the German Jewish intellectuals' experiment had failed – that it was not possible for Jews to involve themselves with modern intellectual developments and remain as authentic Jews. That debate, one way or another, still continues. The Anglo-Jewish community is decidedly unintellectual in its Judaism, and the professions in Britain are filled with bright, clever, well-educated young Jews, whose knowledge of Judaism and understanding of the holocaust tradition and dilemma, is pitifully small. There is again a marked distinction between our community and the community in America, where the academic study of Judaism is a major part of many universities' offered courses, and where some intellectual understanding of Judaism is a requirement. We have divorced the two: Judaism is what you do on High Holy Days; it is not an integral part of the way you think.

The answers to this problem lie partly in improved Jewish education. They also lie in opening up the nature of holocaust debate, across the community spectrum, including orthodox and non-orthodox, religious and non-religious, Zionist and non-Zionist. For a brief period, the Institute of Jewish Affairs ran a 'Younger Generation Group'. We were all above thirty and some of us were pushing fifty, but that is young in the parlance of the leadership of Britain's Jewish community. Its membership spanned the whole gamut of Jewish identification, and the discussions, with Chatham House rules applying where nothing could be attributed to any individual, were fascinating. Those discussions need to start again. Those debates – about being Jewish, the nature of Jewish identity, the encouragement of the young to find something in their Jewishness – must continue.

The modern Jewish family will not be able to convince its young to remain within the fold without a great deal of external help. Many of our young don't feel anything for Judaism. There has to be the vibrancy one feels in the United States of America about Jews and Judaism, or a passion, such as that among many young Israelis about their Jewish identity.

There is a younger generation of Jews who are not religious but are happy to demonstrate themselves to be cultural Jews. They are involved in Jewish theatre or writing, in Jewish film or comedy. The cultural side of Jewish life has changed dramatically over the last few years, and is a sign of optimism for the future. Part of that 'Jewish awareness' is probably something to do with the sense of being part of a minority. It is no coincidence that other minorities are experiencing the same phenomenon, and that the return to ethnic nationalism has some kind of effect even in quiet old Britain, where people are labelling themselves more by their identity as Jewish, Irish, Italian, Bangladeshi, Muslim, Sikh, Hindu or Catholic. In Britain this is difficult to deal with, because of the underlying, unstated, sense of Britishness to which we are all expected to conform.

It is in this environment that Jews live in Britain. It is this scenario which has seen a change from the Jewish life of my childhood, where most self-confessed Jews were members of a synagogue or a recognisable Jewish organisation, to a community where Jews are more assertive, more 'fashionable', but where their identity has become more confused. That ambivalence was well illustrated by the row over the *eruv*, which was debated for north London. Only very orthodox Jews would be affected by this, but the discussion of whether an *eruv* was necessary at all in north-west London is a new one in Britain, unlike in America, where *eruvin* are commonplace in many cities. The nature of the opposition to the *eruv*, from non-Jews and Jews alike, makes for interesting reflection. In the past, the orthodox would not have wanted to make the fuss necessary to have planning permission to go ahead with the *eruv*. They do not like Jews being in the newspapers unless it is to report something good. They are uncomfortable with public Jews unless they think they are good representatives. They are nervous if too many Jews are seen as successful. While many of them were upset by John Stokes's tone, when he referred to his desire to see a red-blooded Englishman in the job after Leon Brittan's resignation as a minister over the Westland affair, they may have privately have had some sympathy with the alleged remarks of the former prime minister Sir Harold Macmillan at his club, where he is reported to have said: 'I see that there are now more Etonians than Estonians in the cabinet.' They would probably not have disagreed with Lord Soper, the distinguished Methodist minister, when he described the would-be *eruv* as 'a piece of impertinence', because they may have thought so, too. This business has illustrated a change between the old-style view of being Jewish and British – accepting their status as that of a guest – and a new-style view which is far more up-front, if less religious. In the United States of America everyone is a citizen; no one is a guest. Britain is now nearer that way of thinking.

Traditionally in Britain, all Jews belonged to a synagogue. Even if they never went there, membership gave a sense of belonging. Even if religion itself meant nothing, as it did for many Jews of Eastern European origin who had grown up in the Jewish socialist movement, or had become Jewish atheists in the post-war years, they would still join a synagogue for burial reasons.

New immigrants tend to define themselves by how they marry their young and bury their people, and by their birth and maturation ceremonies. Thus Jews marked themselves, and still do, by male circumcision, by bar and bat mitzvah, by the Jewish wedding, and by the Jewish funeral and its accompanying *shiva*. As the immigrants become more established, however, and if religious feeling itself wanes, then those life-cycle events become less important. The desire to have circumcision becomes less, bar and bat mitzvah becomes less common because Jewish observance of any kind has diminished, and many Jews marry non-Jews, thereby foregoing the traditional Jewish wedding. The last meaningful ritual to go is the final one – the funeral. Even disaffected Jews want a Jewish funeral.

As we define ourselves by our life-cycle events, so we define ourselves more and more as both British and Jewish. Two overlapping identities in a country where more than one identity has been thought of as confusing, where feelings against minorities are running higher than ever, and where, suddenly, in some areas, it has become fashionable to be Jewish. Confusion reigns for many Jews, but optimism lies in the fact that it is easier to express ourselves as Jews in Britain than it used to be culturally, religiously and socially.

I have no doubt that I am British, but my sense of being

British is governed by a feeling that other British people do not regard me as wholly British. Many non-Jews regard me as 'Jewish' and themselves as 'English'. Black, brown, Jewish – however *we* may feel, there is still a strong sense among a large number of people that we are not properly British, because we are not part of the white Protestant culture. We have to work against these almost unconscious prejudices before Britain becomes riven with ethnic and tribal tensions.

9

Jews, Christians and Muslims:

Interfaith relationships

In recent years, relationships between Jews and other faiths have become more formalised. The Council of Christians and Jews was set up during the Second World War, as news of what was going on in the Nazi death camps began to reach Britain. Previously, there had been the London Society of Jews and Christians, a group that continues to run lectures on a regular basis. Its origins were in the friendship between the Dean of St Paul's and the Senior Minister of the Liberal Jewish Synagogue before the Second World War. It had been an effective channel of communication for ideas between the two men and their congregations, but had not striven to reach the national stage.

The Council for Christians and Jews (CCJ) is different. It has groups around the country, and while it can be rather unchallenging, it facilitates true dialogue. It allows those who are interested to study and discuss the hard issues, such as the nature of Jewish irritation with Christian attempts to proselytise. It is not uncommon to spend time, as a rabbi or rabbinic student, with the noblest and best of Christians who want to study Judaism, as they see it, the religion of Jesus, and want us to study Christianity, as they describe it, as the proper fulfilment of the Old Testament. I well remember a weekend of enormous pleasure at the Community of the Resurrection at Mirfield, near Leeds. I was a student; it was an interfaith weekend. After a Friday evening and Saturday celebrating the Jewish sabbath, we had a Christian Sunday, with prayers starting on the Saturday night with the most spiritual rendition of Compline. The two organisers asked us Jews whether we had been moved, and indeed we had. I think their assumption was that this would have swayed our belief towards theirs. We had to point out that after the experience of the Jewish sabbath, they did not seem to be inspired to abandon the New Testament for the Old and to follow the same religion as Jesus.

Centuries of Christian anti-semitism and Jewish rudeness about Christians are the overlay on top of these points of view. Yet interfaith dialogue requires asking the really hard questions, and allowing theological space for the other. At the end of the 1980s a small interfaith group gathered together by Rabbi Tony Bayfield, the Manor House Group, found a level of trust and mutual commitment. Tony Bayfield had chosen avowed liberals for the group. No one was in the business of trying to convert anyone else. The conclusions of his group will remain with me for ever. Two of the more humorous – but nevertheless significant – conclusions were that Jews interrupt much more and are far less courteous than Christians in debate, and that Christians are better walkers (no surprise: Jews are largely urban dwellers with little experience of country pursuits). Such was the good-humoured competitiveness that the Jewish walkers were soon objects of great amusement to their colleagues who could not keep up!

It was one of the best interfaith groups of which I had ever been part. We came up with a product – a book of essays which tried to analyse where we were in our relationship – *Dialogue with a Difference: The Manor House Group Experience*. When we launched the book, the assembled gathering argued that we sounded as if we were about to go into mourning for the end of a grouping of people with whom we had become close friends, as indeed we had.

I am also involved in an interfaith group in Jordan. The link between Jews and Muslims is all too clear, since their legal systems are very similar, and both religions are based on a legal system more than on a system of faith. At any Jewish, Christian and Muslim gathering, the Jews and the Muslims, having pushed their political difficulties out of the way, find themselves allied against the Christians, whom they consider to hold strange views about sex and the body.

It is particularly important that the Jewish and Christian communities work with Muslims in interfaith dialogue (or is it trialogue?) at a time when Muslims are having a tough time in Britain and other western countries. During the Gulf War, there were disturbing accounts of how, in some parts of London, Muslim children, mostly of Pakistani or Bangladeshi origin, were being beaten up by white, 'Christian' children. Since the Gulf War, British Muslims, who are mostly, but not all, brown-skinned, have undoubtedly been victimised. Since the Rushdie affair, Islam has been held up to ridicule and disapproval. More cases than ever of 'Islamic court' punishments have been reported in the newspapers, such as the undoubtedly appalling and disturbing flogging of a fourteen-year-old girl rape *victim*.

None of this is news of which the Muslim communities can be proud, nor would most of them go along with such things. Islam is held up as monolithic, and the things that a few Muslims do are used to justify attacking the religion.

In Spain in the middle ages, Islam was the most civilised of the three 'religions of the Book', and living under Islamic rule was a joy for Jews in comparison with their experience of the Inquisition of Christian, northern Spain. It is dangerous and untrue to argue that 'we' – in this case Jews and Christians – are any more 'civilised' than Muslims. Neither Judaism nor Christianity can claim an unblemished record, and the desire to prove superiority is itself a sign of weakness. It is hard to discuss these issues. Multicultural education has become problematic in modern Britain, though for many Jews, like me, it was a feature in the curriculum much to be welcomed. Some people regard 'multi-cultural' as almost a form of abuse, to be spat out like 'liberal' by those who hate that expression. Where but in the classroom can we discuss these issues with young people who will shape our society? Will we allow such issues, such worries, to be discussed only at home within the single culture family? What suffering do we bring upon ourselves as a nation if we allow this triumphalism to flourish – west over east, liberal Christian (and Jewish, too, for these purposes) values over fundamentalist Muslim ones? What possible redemption from that nightmare scenario of racial tension and violence can there be if we do not take rapid action?

Redemption will lie in strong interfaith action – in building together institutions, hospitals, schools, colleges and other multi-purpose buildings. I am a patron of the North London Hospice, the first interfaith hospice in Britain, and it has been a joy to see how many local clergy of all denominations are involved. This builds contacts between people who would never otherwise have met, and gradually erodes prejudice. We Jews still need to do more, having had the experience ourselves of being treated with hostility. In learning to tolerate differences, we may have an answer. In learning to recognise suffering in all sorts of others, we may also find our way to a kind of redemption.

I find myself increasingly optimistic that people will be prepared to discuss these issues openly, that major institutions will start to worry about these matters; that concern about race/ethnicity and religion will no longer be considered freakish. I believe it will come through dialogue and understanding. For hope to be translated into something effective there are two requirements – the first is absolute honesty; the second is joint action. When there have been enough words, we must all act together to rebuild shattered lives. That is the road to redemption for us all.

The sort of example I would like to see is Jews and Christians helping Muslims in their campaign for voluntary aided status for their schools, government funding for schools run by religious organisations. This is a complicated issue, for I would prefer, as many people would, a situation where there were no voluntarily aided religious schools, where the state pays most of the costs of a school whatever religious group runs it. Britain has lots of Church of England schools, plenty of Roman Catholic schools, and a few Jewish schools, which all receive state money. Thus far, Muslims have not been granted voluntarily aided status for any of their schools – this seems desperately unfair and smacks of prejudice.

We have sectarian education in Britain. Once we accept, as we essentially already have, that education in our state schools must be broadly Christian, we are saying that those who cannot describe any part of their identity as 'broadly Christian' do not fit. Any straight accusation of religious intolerance has always been deflected by the voluntarily aided sector. When Jewish immigration became a serious issue in the late nineteenth and early twentieth century, serious questions about Jewish schools were raised. The numbers of Jews coming into this country, their special dietary requirements and their desire to practise their religion required action. The Jews' Free School was set up in two places, one now sadly disappeared in south London. Today, the immigrants are Hindus and Muslims, but there are no voluntary aided Muslim schools. This is not for want of trying on the part of the Muslim population. The numbers of Muslims in Britain is something between one and two million, with a rising birthrate and clear patterns of settlement that would make Muslim schools easy to fill and easy to run. There are just some 300,000 Jews in Britain, but there are voluntary aided Jewish schools. What is the problem?

A comparison with the United States of America is useful in this debate. Religion is a private matter in America, unlike in England, where the church is established and the Queen is Defender of the Faith. In Britain, acts of worship take place daily, or at least regularly, in our schools. In America, you might see an act of allegiance to the flag, but unless you were in a parochial school, not supported by the state, you would not find an act of worship. The historical reasons are well known. The foundation of the early States as havens from religious persecution led to a firm decision to keep church and state separate. Not that it always works. On a Sunday you cannot buy alcohol in Massachussetts; in liberal Texas alcohol is only sold between noon and five; and there is no jazz to be heard on the streets of Austin. Dissatisfaction with public schools in many inner-city areas has even led to a movement to fund church schools. Although religious influences have bitten deep into the life of the country, and America is one of the most profoundly evangelised countries in the western world (with varying estimates of regular church attendance ranging from fifty per cent to eighty per cent of the population, compared with our pathetic two to three per cent), within education and the public provision of goods and services, religion and state are unconnected.

America takes pride in immigration. When the Ellis Island and Statue of Liberty Committee were trying to raise the money for the museum of immigration at Ellis Island, they could count on many Americans of immigrant stock wanting to help. They hit on a brilliant marketing ploy. Everyone who sent $100 or more for the museum had his or her name engraved into the wall surrounding the museum grounds – the money flowed unceasingly. If we tried a similar exercise here, there are countless people who would wish to deny they are of immigrant stock. There are far more who might not necessarily know that they had foreign blood in them at all. Yet the number of people in England who can genuinely say that they can trace their ancestry back to the Norman conquest – an immigration of sorts – or the Saxon period – of which the same can be said – is precious few. Britain is a land of immigrants: we are a nation made up of Saxons, Normans, Danes, Jutes, Huguenots and Dutch traders, Lombards and Germans, Jews and Irish, Chinese, Africans, West Indians, Pakistanis, Bangladeshis and Indians. We are no less a country of immigration than America, but our attitude has been entirely different. Where diversity has been cele-brated in America, it has been discouraged here. Where everyone wears a dual identity with pride in the States – African-American, Irish-American, Italian-American, Jewish-American – the British have always felt happier with the idea of a cultural unity. We see diversity as a sign of weakness, and believe that education is the key to making children of immigrant parents into true little Brits.

From a personal perspective, I suspect that is why Jewish life in Britain is so much less interesting and stimulating than it is in America. If you wish to be actively involved in Judaism here, you are seen as making a statement about your identity, and not being a true, fully-fledged, committed Brit – you are saying that some other identity takes precedence, or is equally important. You are excluding yourself from part of the cultural and political whole, with the result that those who want to play on the centre of the British stage, culturally or politically, tend to play a relatively small part in the life of their religious/cultural community, thus leaving religious and ethnic affairs to those who are possibly disaffected from the main political process in Britain.

I have simplified the argument, but it is important. I am not suggesting that no one who is interested in making a life on the wider British stage can also be involved in Jewish life. That is patently untrue. I am suggesting that involvement in Jewish life is hard to combine with mainstream political and cultural activity on a grand scale, making the Jewish scene duller, less intellectual and less political than it might otherwise be. In America, practising Jews are commonplace, they play their full part in public life, and have a satisfying religious and cultural life, running successfully in tandem.

An argument often adduced in the polite dining-rooms of the chattering classes is that Muslims are a relatively new population in Britain. The significant Muslim population dates back to the 1950s and early 1960s – more than thirty years ago. The same liberals argue that women, who have been entering the medical and legal professions in numbers roughly equal with men for over thirty years, do not have equality of opportunity. Should Muslims in this country argue that they have not reached equality with other groups in the population? Is it not legitimate for Muslims to protest that part of that inequality rests on religious intolerance, one facet of racial intolerance? They could protest, and often do. So-called intellectual opinion has it that what is wrong with Islam is that it is fundamentalist, that it discriminates against women, that the killing of animals in their prescribed way is barbaric and that Muslims are violent. I believe the Press fans these prejudices. It is true that Muslims believe in an unchanging law; some of them believe in an innate superiority of Islam over all other faiths. It is equally true, however, that there are fundamentalist Christians in abundance throughout the world. Christians who believe abortion is wrong try, often using violence, to force others to follow their guidelines. There are fundamentalists in every religious group. There is the religious and political fundamentalism of Sikhs and Hindus, of the Israeli Gush Emunim and other Jewish groups in Israel and America. There is growing tension world-wide between what is religious and what is political because, for so many fundamentalists, the two are indistinguishable, and political policies are God's will.

Muslims are attacked more than most for their fundamentalist views. The whole world knows about the Rushdie affair. In a sense I think the reaction among white liberals to the Ayatollah's ban on Salman Rushdie's book *Satanic Verses* and the death threat to Rushdie himself was a failure to understand the nature of Islam and a deep revulsion – particularly among journalists – to censorship. The liberal left was caught up in knots. The Ayatollah was acting with the bigotry of a fundamentalist, and was impinging on the freedoms of the rest of the world, but to speak out against the death threat and in support of freedom to publish also suggested some intolerance against the religion of Islam. Liberal after liberal condemned the *fatwa*, in my view rightly so. Fewer advocated the abolition in this country of the blasphemy legislation, which protects only Christianity – absurd in a multi-cultural society – or to support new legislation making it a criminal offence to cause offence to any religious grouping, which would recognise the equal status of other religions. Those who most vociferously condemned the death threat and accused Islam of fundamentalism did nothing to overturn the vastly outdated legislation. It shows an acceptance that Christianity is the religion of our country.

In the west, where religion and ethnicity are seen as two very different things, the idea that your religious grouping is a cultural definition is very foreign. The idea that belief is less important than action, and that one is judged by one's actions and observance of religious law, is alien to those who hold that salvation comes through faith – especially if one is British and that faith is a Christian one. Indeed, one of the reasons why tolerance might be difficult for some Christians, is that they have failed to see what it is they are being asked to be tolerant of. It is not of a different faith *per se*, though that is a profound part of it. It is of cultural definitions, cultural allegiances that are expressed by religious ritual. It is of a sense of peoplehood. Judaism, Islam, Sikhism, Hinduism, particularly in their various diasporas, are defined by a mixture of allegiances – to a people and to a set of religious and cultural practices. Although many have strong religious beliefs as well, faith comes second for the majority. Self-definition as part of a minority group, clearly identified by its own practices, is the most important factor. Questions about being absorbed into the mass, assimilating, losing cultural and religious identity, are what most concern these groups. There is a fear of intermarriage, loss of religious identity of children, loss of the values that keep these communities together. This can be both enriching and suffocating for the next generation.

We need to look at how religious groups can be tolerant of others, comfortable within themselves, and permissive towards their own members as well as supplying a strong foundation in religious and cultural traditions.

First, there needs to be a change of heart about the predominantly Christian thrust of education legislation. After all, the majority of the Christian population does not go to church, and there are significant number of non-Christian minorities in Britain. Recognition of that would allow a sense of acceptance to percolate through the Jewish, Muslim, Sikh and Hindu communities. Secondly, there is a need for those communities themselves to be more forthcoming in talking to each other and in talking to Christian groups. Knowledge and understanding are sadly lacking. Medical staff, for example, who are wholly well-disposed to providing care and are sensitive to different religious and cultural needs, are hampered by a lack of willingness on the part of minority religious groups to come and speak to them about their special requirements. Thirdly, there is a need for the language of tolerance, heard in almost all religious groupings, to be put into practice. That means Christians giving up space in the House of Lords for the religious leaders of other faiths – on principle. That means the Church of England campaigning hard for multi-cultural religious education in schools, and realising that heavy religious indoctrination is not the role of the schools. It means having multi-faith institutions for care, such as the North London Hospice. Instead, the nearest to this is usually non-denominational rather than recognising many faiths. Religious figures of all persuasions must have the right to enter hospitals and hospices to give comfort to patients, as they do if they are regarded as chaplains. It means education in multi-culturalism. It means those religious groups which proselytise must come to realise that this very activity can be offensive. There needs to be a theological change of heart, recognising as equal, but different, the faiths of other people, and no longer trying to convert them to one's own faith on the grounds that it promises salvation, has better rules, or is the 'true' way.

It is hard for some Christians not to evangelise. There was, however, a brave attempt to regard Jews as people not to be proselytised at the last Lambeth conference in 1988. The Bishop of Oxford, speaking on the subject of interfaith dialogue between Jews, Christians and Muslims, tried to persuade his colleagues to stop regarding Judaism as the forerunner of Christianity:

> There are other Christians in the Anglican communion today who believe that our whole relationship with Judaism needs to be radically rethought, particularly in the light of the Holocaust, and they feel, until Christian lives can bear a truer witness, a divine obligation to affirm Jews in the worship and sense of the God and Father of Jesus. This document . . . calls us all to look at this matter more deeply with thought and prayer in the light of scripture and the facts of history . . . This document . . . does offer a very workable basis for dialogue, and . . . if we approach dialogue in the spirit of understanding and affirmation and sharing as illustrated in the document, our relationship with both Jews and Muslims will get off to a much better footing than it ever has in the past . . .

He was applauded for saying this, but what was truly brave was the desire to banish the theory of Judaism as a superseded, outdated religion, a religion of people who 'ought' to have seen the light and become Christians. The document itself, entitled 'The Truth Shall Make you Free', in which the Bishop of Oxford had played a major part, stated:

> In relation to Judaism, this means, first of all, recognising that Judaism is still a living religion to be respected in its own right. The Judaism of today is not that of any one of the sects of first-century Palestine, and certainly not that of the plain text of the Hebrew Scriptures. Its definitive works, such as the Mishnah and the Talmud, as well as its current liturgy, were produced by the post-Pharisee rabbis in the same period, the first to fifth centuries, in which the fathers of the Church were defining the meaning of Christianity. Great care should be taken not to misrepresent Judaism by imputing to it, e.g., the literal implementation of 'an eye for an eye', which was repudiated by the rabbis, or the denial of life after death. This is also true of the long-standing stereotype of Judaism as a religion of works, completely ignoring the deep Jewish sense of the grace of God. Judaism is a living and still developing religion, which has shown spiritual and intellectual vitality throughout the medieval and modern periods despite its history of being maligned and persecuted. . . .

In his speech at the Lambeth Conference, the Bishop of Oxford continued by saying:

> It is hardly surprising, given the historical views of Judaism amongst Christians, that Jews were targets of huge attempts to convert them, not ended yet, even in the Anglican communion. But it is encouraging to see a change of heart, not for everybody but for a significant tranche of the Anglican church, towards a different view, that takes away

the desire, indeed the theological necessity, of proselytising amongst the Jews.

What was remarkable about that particular debate was that the Bishop of Oxford, and other like-minded Anglicans, sought to change their own religion's view of Jews and Muslims, and to try to view the three religions of the book as having something of significance to say to each other, without any one of the three taking a dominant position.

It is irrelevant how often one religion has tried to convert the members of another faith. What needs to be taken on board today is whether other religions have equality with one's own or not. If the answer is yes, then proselytising ceases as of right. If the answer is no, then the limit of tolerance has been reached, and we have to face the truth that the religion is not tolerant. It is in conversion activity, in statements that one form of salvation is the best, to the exclusion of others, and in the quest for religious dominance of education and the provision of goods and services, that one has to draw the line. The Prince of Wales' desire to be Defender of Faith, as opposed to being Defender of *the* Faith (interviews with Jonathan Dimbleby, 1994) was impressive. For the heir to the throne to assert that he does not consider Christianity as paramount (but perhaps first among equals), was an enormously optimistic sign.

As we move nearer the year 2000, are we becoming less tolerant, more triumphalist, less accepting, more condematory? In the midst of political turmoil, is religion playing a major part in defining where people's allegiances lie? Almost all religious organisations preach non-discrimination, but you would find few blacks in your standard Church of England country church. Equally, many Jews have great difficulty welcoming Muslims to their services, and often regard all Muslims as anti-Israeli and many as anti-semites. Many Muslims regard Jews as Zionist oppressors, even after the peace accord between Israel and the PLO and the historic signing of an agreement between Israel and Jordan. The churches, mosques and synagogues contribute to the divisions within society.

Race and religion cannot be discussed in isolation from one another. Most religions have some sort of saying that runs along the lines of a quotation from a late *midrash* (rabbinic commentary) from Seder Eliyyahu Rabba, dating from approximately the tenth century:

> It matters not whether a person be Jew or Gentile, male or female, free person or slave – it is according to their deeds that the Holy Spirit rests up a person.

The willingness to analyse that and act on it, to use the thinking of religion to battle against racism, is far from developed.

From my Jewish background I have a strong sense of what it means to be part of a minority, and feel compelled to campaign on behalf of other minorities. Seeing Britain at its most racist in 1968 with retroactive legislation preventing the East African Asians, carrying British passports which they had opted for rather than Indian ones when Kenya and Uganda became independent states, from coming to Britain because there were too many of them, has made me sensitised to racism in all its forms – be it blatant prejudice on the basis of colour, anti-religious feeling about non-Christian religions, or a sense that Britain is for the British.

I believe that it is possible, indeed likely, that Jews, Christians and Muslims will discuss, debate and argue with each other – in a positive fashion – in Britain. But I also believe that it will be necessary for the more liberal among us – of all those faiths – to resist the desire, when things get tough, to retreat into a separatist corner. Increasingly, we will have to argue for joint endeavours, multi-faith, not non-denominational, religious education to inform, not indoctrinate. It will not be an easy decade, but better relationships are undoubtedly possible.

10

'I believe with perfect faith . . .':

How does it all fit together?

The period of my childhood produced another significant role model in the Jewish world besides my grandmother – Golda Meir. Prime minister of Israel, archetypal Jewish mother and pioneer, forceful orator and also a kibbutznik, Golda Meir was held up to me and my generation as an example of what Jewish womanhood could do.

She was not religious. Her Judaism, like that of many of her contemporaries from Eastern European Jewry, was defined by her Zionism and her socialism. She was born in Kiev in extreme poverty, and her family emigrated to America in 1906, by which time, the doors were closed in Britain by the 1905 Aliens Act, which was aimed at keeping out any more Jewish refugees from Eastern Europe. She joined Po'alei Zion, the workers of Zion, in 1915, aged seventeen, and quickly rose to be a leader in the movement as a result of her ability as a captivating speaker in both Yiddish and English. She and her husband emigrated to Palestine in 1921, and settled on a kibbutz. She became an experienced political operator, alternating between mainstream policies and the women's movement in Zionism (there were always women's organisations in the main Zionist parties). From 1949 she was in the Knesset, the Israeli parliament, and she became successively minister of labour, foreign minister and prime minister of Israel. In some ways, she was the darling of the world, because she explained Israel's moral position with such good effect to world leaders. In other ways, she portrayed herself as the nice gentle Jewish grandmother, a demeanour which belied her sharp intellect and her formidable strategic sense while cleverly creating a 'front' which made her totally acceptable, not only in Israel itself but also in the wider world, where she was in her years as foreign minister loved and adulated.

My feelings about Golda Meir are, in a way, a reflection of my feelings about Israel. For a short time in my late-teens I was a member of Habonim, a socialist Zionist youth movement. It was one way of expressing my Jewish identity. I was proud of the Jewish state, defenceless little Israel as it then seemed. My father had been involved in Habonim in the 1930s, so there seemed to be a family logic. I was not, however, a committed socialist Zionist. I have always had difficulty with the idea that Jews should settle in Israel – unless they want to, or, perhaps even more importantly, they need to escape persecution and gain religious freedom. I still believe that it is possible to live in the Diaspora. The effect of the holocaust on many of my Jewish contemporaries has been never to trust non-Jews – one could be safe only in the Jewish state. But the Jewish state does not have room for all of us. Neither do I, nor many of my contemporaries, *feel* Israeli. And yet, and yet . . . when I am in Israel I feel a curious bond. I am infuriated by the lack of courtesy, the almost deliberate pleasure some Israelis take from their bluntness to the point of rudeness, but I love the fact that Jews of all sorts of backgrounds live there together. I love the fact that here are Bokharan Jews with their wonderful clothes, the very orthodox hassidic Jews, Jews from the Yemen and from North Africa, Russian Jews who have changed the common language of Israel with new phrases, German Jews who came to Israel as refugees, and so on . . .

I first went to Israel in 1963, with my mother. The purpose was to visit a large number of elderly relatives who, it was feared, might not survive until I was likely to go to Israel on my own as a student. It was a fantastic trip in many ways, though I am filled with embarrassment when I remember my grandmother's cousin, Hermann Ellern, who was an interesting and usually fair-minded man, talking to a small Arab boy. His tone was undoubtedly intensely patronising. The child was 'a good Arab boy', patted on the head by an elderly German-Jewish Israeli citizen of considerable wealth. I can still feel the tingling up my spine at the implications.

The smells of Tel-Aviv, the flowers and the sparkling sea alongside jerry-built houses, and the early-morning clatter remain in my mind. So do the sounds of Jerusalem, though it was four years before the old city of Jerusalem became accessible, after the Six Day War in 1967. The street-markets and the lush fields of the irrigated Galilee stay with me.

On my first trip I heard more German than Hebrew, and spoke far more German than Hebrew, something that has never been true since. My parents' fears were right, and most of those elderly cousins and great-aunts and uncles died in the next few years. When I visited Israel for the third time in 1976, not one of them was still alive. The cousins I did see were either Israeli-born or had been brought up there, a different Hebrew- and English-speaking breed, tougher politically in some ways, but more amenable to the political concerns of a rabbinic student cousin.

Until 1967, I was entirely happy with the love of Israel, *chibbat Zion*. Israel was a country of Jews, it had been founded in the wake of the holocaust, it was plucky little Israel, it was exciting, it was right that it was there – which I still believe absolutely – and it was constantly under attack from its Arab neighbours. The Six Day War, and, more importantly, the Yom Kippur War of 1973, when Israel displayed amazing military superiority to her neighbours, made me feel differently. It was not that I was not proud of Israel – it is an odd phenomenon to be proud of the military prowess of a country which is not one's own – but that I was worried about the consequences of those wars, particularly the effect of Israel becoming an occupying power when it did not return the territories it had gained as a result of the wars.

In much more recent times we have seen the aftermath. I have, at times, been extremely critical of Israeli action – notably in 1982 when Christian Phalange troops went into the Palestinian refugee camps of Sabra and Chatila and massacred many people, allowed by the Israelis. Israel was not directly responsible – as many anti-Israel commentators alleged at the time – but the Israeli authorities were indirectly responsible, and they ought to have accepted that their policies had allowed the killing to happen. I was ashamed of what had happened, and despaired at the reaction of the then prime minister, Menachem Begin, who claimed that allegations of Israeli responsibility amounted to a blood libel. To Israel's credit, there was a judicial inquiry, the Kahan commission, which found that the Israeli authorities in Lebanon had behaved badly in their policies. Israel took her share of the blame. I was proud then, and I have been proud since, of the way that she has gone into peace negotiations. Alongside brave people from Egypt, the PLO, Jordan and others in the Arab world, she has begun to see a new future as part of a Near and Middle East consortium of states looking for economic renewal.

I have not always been proud of Israel when her prime ministers have said they wanted to break the bones of children protesting in the occupied territories, or when universities have been closed, or homes razed to the ground. That is not to say Israel behaves worse than many other states – plainly she does not – but I expect better of a *Jewish* state. There's the rub. Like many Jews, I have mixed feelings about a Jewish state which does not always express Jewish values; where the only form of Judaism recognised by the state is orthodoxy; and where the religious parties, though numerically tiny, hold so much power. I have mixed feelings about a state where women are alleged to be equal, but where in the army women express outrage at the way they are sometimes treated. I have mixed feelings about a state where the political cry to many of the Diaspora Jews has been: 'Do not criticise us from the outside. Come and live here. You have no right to criticise us otherwise.' That attitude might be legitimate, if they did not want our financial and moral support as well – from the outside.

And yet, and yet . . . I love Jerusalem, and I love the Dead Sea. I love the smells of the Galilee, and I love seeing the desert bloom. Israel needs the support of Jews in the Diaspora – and of non-Jews as well. It undoubtedly has a right to exist. What is admirable, as I write this now in early 1995, is that we are beginning to see a way through, beginning, albeit painfully and slowly, to see a way forward for peace in the Middle East, founded on new alliances, and a new doctrine of economic cooperation. I will support Israel – and criticise her when I feel it is necessary – and support any peace moves that come, because for Israel, and for Jews outside Israel, peace in the Middle East is essential.

What of my allegiance to Israel? I am often asked which takes precedence – my Jewishness or my Englishness. It reminds me of the old youth group question: 'If Britain went to war against Israel, which side would you be on?' I reply that it would depend on circumstances, but that it is so unlikely as to be the sort of issue not worth bothering about, for there is no question of what I am.

I am English. British, too. By nationality, by subject status, by citizenship. I am Jewish by religion, and by a sense of peoplehood that draws me together with my fellow-Jews in other corners of the world, often in anything but harmony. I am a woman, a feminist. My identity is largely in Britain, as a Jewess, but it covers being Jewish in Israel, where my views, rather than my religion or my people, make me remarkable. It also covers being Jewish in Jordan, which has been largely 'Juden-rein' until very recently, but where I have received extraordinary hospitality and trust. It covers being Jewish in Northern Ireland, where it is a positive advantage to be neither Protestant nor Catholic, and in the south of Ireland, where acceptance is taken for granted, and the Jewish community has, with the exception of one pogrom in the 1920s, a history of peaceful acceptance. My identity is complicated by my feelings of being German-Jewish, whilst uncomfortable in Germany, as a result of that extraordinary German-Jewish symbiosis cut horribly short by the holocaust. Thus I am a European, because my identity and my culture transcend the purely British. The overlaps give me a great deal to draw on.

An overwhelming complacency marks out the Anglo-Jewish establishment, who hate to face tricky questions about identity and belief and what one needs to be a Jew. These are the people who are prepared to contemplate, with little agonising, the thought of a Jewish community in Britain reduced in size but 'somehow better'. They say: 'What we're going to get is quality versus quantity.' Although the present Chief Rabbi, Dr Jonathan Sacks, is deeply concerned about us having Jewish grandchildren, not all Jews share his anxieties. Furthermore, having Jewish grandchildren is, in my view, of little value unless one feels that Judaism itself and the Jewish community have something to give beyond self-perpetuation.

In 1989, the then President of the Board of Deputies, Dr Lionel Kopelowitz, said: 'I don't see that we have a great deal to fear provided we keep ourselves educated and knowledgeable on the matters which concern Jews.' What are these matters? What are we as Jews in Britain, with a falling synagogue membership but the signs of a splendid Jewish cultural revival? The *Jewish Chronicle* is becoming a more literary paper, while the new alternative paper, *New Moon*, provides a witty look at Anglo-Jewry, encourages cultural activities and even has a lonely hearts column for those who find themselves single. Above all, Jews love the domestic life, settling-down and comfort. The slogan of 'Jewish family values' has much to do with liking the comfort and certainty of family against a sometimes hostile outside world.

What about our beliefs? So much of being Jewish is cultural and attitudinal. Most of us cannot say where our beliefs came from. The issue of belief is crucial, yet few of us think it through. I did not become a rabbi through a passionately held belief in Jewish theology; I did not intend to become a rabbi when I went up to Cambridge to read Assyriology. I ended up reading Hebrew as well as Assyriology, but only because Hebrew, as far as I was concerned, was a soft option. I wanted to go on a dig in Iraq in the summer of 1970, but there had been public hangings of Jews in Baghdad and Basra in 1968 and 1969, and shortly afterwards, the British were refused entry to dig in Turkey for a few years, because the Turkish authorities believed a British archaeologist had stolen finds off a site. Being British and Jewish was not a good combination for a would-be Near Eastern archaeologist. So I turned to Hebrew.

I believed I was working towards an academic career in Jewish studies. One of my teachers, Rabbi Dr Nicholas de Lange, reader in Rabbinics, was convinced that I should not aim for a straight academic career and suggested that I became a rabbi. At that stage I had just ended a relationship with a young man who was half-Jewish and whose attitude to religion had been one of blank incomprehension. I was not very religious, also female, and not sure that being a rabbi was sufficiently academically rigorous for me. I allowed myself to be persuaded to give it a go. I went to London one day a week in my fourth year at Cambridge to study at the Leo Baeck College, Bible with Nelly Littmann and Talmud with Rabbi Dr Louis Jacobs, an experience which convinced me that rabbinic studies could be as academically challenging as anything I was likely to find elsewhere. I was hooked.

My time at Leo Baeck College was marred by my first encounter with prejudice. Several of my colleagues were firmly opposed to women rabbis, although Jackie Tabick had been ordained in 1975. I was coming up for ordination, and I was clearly a tough character. I experienced more deliberate attempts to make me feel uncomfortable than at any other stage of my life. Some – though not many – of those attempts were from people who were teaching us. Most were from fellow students, some of whom flatly deny the charge these days. There was no doubt. A woman's place, in their view, was not in the pulpit. Women were supposed to be at home, being 'nice *little* Jewish wives'. The attitude was infuriating and demeaning – and only served to strengthen my resolve. It also warned me that my career would not be quite such plain-sailing as I had anticipated.

I should have known. In my very early student years I had been a student rabbi at one congregation which had only been able to cope with me by treating me as an honorary man. Although they had mixed seating for services, as in reform and liberal congregations, when they went on after the service, for a social gathering, the men trooped to one end of the communal hall and the women to the other. My place was with the men. After the sabbath morning service, the wives went home to prepare lunch, and the boys went to the pub near the synagogue. The publican became used to this, and would jokingly announce us with: 'Here comes the Exodus again.' I was taken with the boys to the pub, but my husband, on the rare occasions when he came too, was taken home with the women. At the Leo Baeck College the administrative staff and honorary officers were hugely supportive. When one congregation said it did not want a woman to come and take their High Holy Day services, the response was that if they did not take me they would not get anyone.

I still have terrible memories of the final examination, when I blanked out completely in the oral test, something that never happened to me before, or since. When asked who was Zunz, an important nineteenth century Jewish thinker, philosopher and historian and one of the founders of the scientific study of Judaism (*Wissenchaft des Judentums*) in Germany, I could only remember that there were several wards in London hospitals named after a woman entitled Annie Zunz, hardly useful for a rabbinic exam. I was more nervous about that exam than I have been about anything. I am no longer impatient with exam nerves in anyone else, having been through it!

After that horror, ordination was a very moving experience. We had a private ceremony in the room of prayer at West London Synagogue, a tiny place with great spiritual presence where evening services are held. I remember being handed the scroll in the traditional way – with the right to teach being handed from one generation to another. I was ordained by Rabbi John Rayner, and since then I have ordained several other, younger colleagues. Later, we had a big service of graduation, at which my colleague in that year, Rabbi Danny Smith, and I, were each handed our ordination certificates. I can still recall my pleasure in finding that Danny's had a pink ribbon on it, and mine a blue. The Leo Baeck College office, fair-minded to the last, had wanted to make a point about gender-equality. It caused a great laugh at the time, but I knew they were telling me something else – that they were supporting me and my female colleagues, encouraging us to be equal. I have never forgotten the generosity of Joan Feldman, Susan Lewin, Bertram Jacobs, (a great man, now sadly no longer with us), and the college officials who wanted women to succeed.

I was no pastor when I began. I thought I might be able to add to Jewish continuity, by teaching the next generation – in my view one of the main duties of a rabbi. I still teach Bible at Leo Baeck College, and would hate to give that up. To teach young, and not so young, students about the manifold ways in which one can study the Hebrew Bible is a source of great pleasure, and to be able to enthuse them, even a little, gives immense satisfaction. That is what being a rabbi is about – teaching and encouraging – if we consider that we have something special to contribute. I do.

Where is the religious belief in that? No Christian would wish to become an ordained priest with a vocation to study and teach but no faith; yet I am not unusual among Jews. We do not, on the whole, think in terms of belief. Gillian Rose, the philosopher, quotes the academic Julius Carlebach: 'An orthodox Jew doesn't have to worry about whether he believes in God or not. As long as he observes the law.' Quite so. If you observe the law whose very existence is predicated on the existence of God as giver of that law, whether you actually believe in God is irrelevant. If you cannot bring yourself to follow that premise, you become prey to worries about whether or not you believe in God and whether these things are 'true' or not.

This kind of argument colours the way Jews think. We spend a lot less time struggling with our belief in God than many other people, perhaps because the view has been for so long that it does not matter, as long as we continue to *behave* as if we believe. Personally, as a non-orthodox Jew, I find much of this relatively easy. I do in fact believe in God. I have what some people have described as a rather peasant-like, uncritical belief. That is not to suggest that I believe in a God who resembles an old man with a long beard sitting on a cloud up in the sky. Far from it. I have no representation of the divine form in my mind at all. What I have, and what I think many of my orthodox friends and acquaintances envy me for, is a deep certainty of something other and beyond, some being who has a plan, a sense of order in the universe, and is the 'creator' of it all. Whether that is what the new physicists are looking for in their search for patterns in the universe, or what scientists are finding in their study of ever smaller and smaller organisms with their complexity and elegance, is irrelevant to me. I do not think we can argue the existence of God from scientific evidence, nor indeed from any other kind of evidence. One either believes or not.

My belief leads me to think that there is more than a human energy behind the passion for righteousness I feel so strongly; behind the informed conscience which some have argued is the voice of the divine within us. I feel the need to give thanks – the traditional Jewish attitude to prayer, since Jews do not on the whole believe in petition-ary prayer, asking God for things when in trouble. I feel the need for a form of spiritual refreshment from time to time, whether it be in a service, in the countryside, or in looking out of the window from our Irish house, gazing at the sea and admiring its power.

I think, in the Jewish world, we have underplayed the role of agnosticism. I suspect that a huge tranche of modern Jewry is actually agnostic. These people do not believe in God, but they do not *not* believe in God, either. They often just don't know. The holocaust destroyed the faith of many. If God exists, how could He allow it? Others have been affected by twentieth century scepticism. Agnosticism is much more common among Jews today than atheism. To be agnostic is to practise Judaism in some way, to gain something from arguing for Jewish survival and encourag-ing lively, open, new thinking. Part of the battle to ensure the value of Jewish survival rests on the ability to instil a spiritual sense. This is to do with allowing quiet into one's life, and we are a noisy lot. It is to do with realising that study, which we value so highly, will not alone breed spirituality. It is partly because we have been poor at expressing that sense of the spiritual that many Jews have taken refuge in psychoanalysis, which offers a different way of looking at the world – often human-centred, but recognising other yearnings and longings most of us crave.

The contemplative, the sense of other and beyond, can be important even if one cannot believe in a deity. In its many different forms, Judaism does have something of the spiritual to offer – reforming zeal about the state of society. Unlike Christianity, Judaism tends to be community-based, and is focused on this world, rather than concerned about what happens to us after our deaths.

For that reason, Judaism failed to develop much of a conventual or monastic tradition – though the Essenes may well have been an exception – and thereby denied some of its followers an expression of their spiritual longings. Medieval Christianity created a religious role even for women. Christian thinking had created a dichotomy. Women could either be sexual beings, bear children, be vain and wear attractive clothes, be dirty (with menstrual blood) and live an earthly inferior life (inferior to the life of men as well as to the religious life) as chattel of some other, usually male, person; or they could enter the spiritual life, be married to the church, spend their days in study, domestic duties, prayer and contemplation in an order consisting only of women, earn respect and satisfy their spiritual longings, if not the physical ones. These women were also likely to be educated and could sometimes wield very considerable power. For Christian women the choice was between the earthly life or the spiritual – an either/or situation. At least these women had the chance to do something religious. In Judaism, women had no such opportunity, and – in orthodoxy at least – must still accept their lot as lower beings. There are few role models of spiritual women for young Jewish women to follow – a hassidic woman leader, Hannah Rachel Werbermacher, the Maid of Ludomir, was an exception.

Christian men, of course, could also choose a monastic life. Judaism has no such opportunity for people of either gender. We have ignored this spiritual dimension. We have our parallels, in the thought of the early hassidic masters. There was a rich spiritual tradition in the hassidic Jewish world, which also supported a folk religion and pietistic tradition, but much of that has been lost, partly as a result of the holocaust, partly as a result of the stultification of some of that thinking in the nineteenth century. Those hassidic Jews behaved as if they were convinced of their belief in God. The stories about them demonstrate an unrestrained joy and a deep spiritual longing. Today, however, the spontaneity, the vigorous faith and the spirituality have largely disappeared, leaving modern Jews with a gaping hole which we find it hard to fill without some other way of expressing that sense of searching for the divine.

I acquired some sense of that spirituality when working as a pastoral rabbi with the terminally ill and the bereaved. I worked largely with fellow-Jews, and I often derived from them a sense of calm and resolution that made me understand a little of what it is like to get nearer one's maker. By no means were all of them believers. Many acquired a spiritual sense in their last months or even weeks. Some would deny that they had acquired any spirituality, but they had certainly learned about calm. Others carried on fighting, certain in their desire to stay around, to do more, to get on with life in this world.

Learning from the dying and the bereaved, I began to think about how we should combine our theological ideas and our practice in a way we are rarely encouraged to do in Judaism. I became more interested in how I could shrug off the dilemma of which laws I obeyed and which I did not, given that we do not need to justify our practices to anyone else. Of course, it was all-important to label myself a Jew. Some have chosen to label themselves by what they eat – keeping kosher because it shows they are Jews, even if they do not believe it is literally a divine command. I have chosen to label myself by what I speak about; by how my family observes the sabbath; by keeping festivals; and by associating myself with fellow Jews. It is a different way of marrying it all together. All of us will have different ways, unless we are so orthodox that we believe there are no questions to be asked at all. It is important for me to keep the passion for social justice in my mind and heart, and the wondrous, strange spirituality of working with the dying has been the key to a deeper understanding of the divine, and what it means to be Jewish. Others have found their spiritual sense elsewhere – some in Buddhism, or in the varieties of Hinduism they have experienced on Indian trips. Others have found it through the study of the monastic tradition in Christianity. We don't, of course, all have to become nuns and monks, but it is useful to understand the nature of retreat. It is a challenge to those of us who are religious to begin to think of ways of rediscovering Jewish spirituality.

We must work together to offer something to those who are rediscovering their Jewish roots, wanting Jewish books (more books of Jewish interest are published in Britain now than I would have believed possible ten years ago), Jewish plays, Jewish films and Jewish music. There is a renaissance of Jewish culture, which has raised an impressive amount of interest. One hears old-fashioned Jews tut-tutting under their breath as they describe this re-discovered Jewish culture as synthetic, a faulty re-invention of the romantic idea of the *shtetl* without recognising that the *shtetl* was dirty, dangerous and very, very poor. These disapproving Jews moan about the ubiquity of the bagel as the symbol of Jewish food, and worry about the depiction of Judaism by Barbra Streisand and her romanticism.

They deny at their peril the flowering of interest in plays about Jewish themes, whether about biblical characters, as in Peter Shaffer's *Yonadab*, the story of Tamar, daughter of King David, or about the holocaust. There are dramatisations of the diary of Anne Frank. The 'Anne Frank in the World' exhibition goes around schools and universities, and teaches people about the dangers of anti-semitism and other forms of racism. Today, we enjoy stand-up Jewish comics, Jewish novels and Jewish art.

The fact is that many young Jews are defining themselves as Jewish by *interest*, rather than by traditional association with synagogues or old-fashioned Jewish organisations. That is where the new Jewish community lies, and where the young Jewish community has something to give to those of us who are older. They have a new enthusiasm, a new certainty, an ability to stand up and feel proud of being Jewish. They seem to have lost the embarrassment. They do not wish to keep their heads down, and are happy to define themselves as Jewish without ever going near a synagogue. All that they do, however, is done in the shadow of the holocaust. Though no longer embarrassed, they are all too aware of what happened. I, too, have lived my Jewish life, all my life, in the shadow of the holocaust. I have worked in the field of race, of human rights, of social justice, precisely because of my family's experience. Mine is a very personal task, to do with being of German-Jewry, and not wanting that legacy to be forgotten. My generation is still coloured by the events of the holocaust, and cannot fail to be. Many of us are tongue-tied and confused. It is my generation's children who find it easy to talk to their grandparents, who lived through it, about these things. My generation's children are beginning to look at the Jewish world in Britain with greater confidence, and have a new-found pride in being up-front about their Jewishness. Among the tasks they face are using the Jewish experience to talk about racism and where it can take you; looking at the nature of intolerance and ethnic awareness; bonding with other groups, to talk about the horrors and dangers of 'ethnic cleansing'; and preaching the message of Judaism. We Jews must stamp out injustice, believe in the rule of law and be prepared to campaign to change the law where it is wrong. We must realise that it is a human duty to campaign for those who are victims of injustice and that turning away is unacceptable. Aiming to open blind eyes and release captives from prison is part of what it is to be Jewish. Among our other tasks is the duty of civic involvement, of using the citizenship that Jews now have. The ghetto is gone. Jews no longer have to fear losing their identity in the outer world. We don't have to compromise or hide. We can be involved on the world stage. There is now a bridge between active Jewish involvement and active world-wide involvement: young Jews can participate and play their part without conflict.

We also have a duty to those who are not Jewish. Now that we are accepted in society, play our role in a world setting, are beyond the ghetto and no longer define ourselves by which synagogue we belong to, we will be able to identify more clearly our responsibility for those who are not part of our community. This is very much about the politics of duty, the idea that one is defined by *mitzvot*, religious commandments or duties. The idea of duty, as reinterpreted to mean obligation to others in society, is an important concept for Jews to develop. Jews have a way of thinking which is *this*-life based, and a legal system which is specific about how we should practise various noble ideals – meaning that we should be able to contribute much more intensively to the debate about how society should best work. We regard charity as social justice, for instance, rather than worrying about the dependency culture. We come from a legal system which believes the poor have a right to receive, just as the rich have a duty to give. We believe that communities have an obligation to help their own, as well as a duty to other communities for the sake of peace. We can begin to define what it means to live in a genuinely multi-cultural society, we can use our differences in a positive way to encourage debate about how we should govern ourselves, and how the values we should hold dear as a society can actually flourish. That debate might, for Jews, be about the value of education, for we are, above all, a learned people, with a strong emphasis on studying. Our contribution would not fit neatly into any political party's agenda, for it cuts across all of them. But it could encourage us to challenge notions about the 'nobility' of poverty, which we regard as something to be alleviated. We might say something about the nature of families. It would also encourage us to look deeper into our prophetic tradition – the prophets cried out about corruption in their society, just as we should in ours.

The next generation of Jews could, therefore, have an important role to play in society in this country. They will choose which battles to fight. What is important is that Jews, while living in symbiosis with British and European cultures, see themselves as rooted in Judaism. We must continue to recognise that being Jewish involves being part of several groups and ways of thinking, and that the richness of the tradition is in coming to terms with all of them.

Whether the young generation of British Jews will be able to carry the old Anglo-Jewish institutions with them, whether they will be able to transform the Anglo-Jewish community into something more like the American-Jewish community, with its pride and its diversity, its energy and its vitality, remains to be seen.

That is the task. The holocaust is in the past. We have survived. Jews and Judaism have something special to bring to the whole world, a contribution they can – and should – make.

Epilogue

I have been writing against a background of a fragile peace in Northern Ireland, where I have many friends, and where I am Chancellor of the University of Ulster.

Ireland has meant a great deal to me. I am not Irish by blood, yet when I am welcomed 'home', it feels like home. In Ireland I have made many close friends, north and south of the border. I have learned how people cope with extreme situations. I have recognised in the Irish a desire to remember – often too much and too long – very like Jews. I have seen how they take religion seriously, but are prepared to battle against the churches when they are too demanding and ask the impossible of their adherents. I have seen how Irish women have reacted against the religious institutions that have tried to limit their power and progress. In many ways, what I have seen in Ireland, and occasionally been allowed to share, has reflected parts of the Jewish experience.

I have also seen the burgeoning of a relationship between the Irish and Jewish communities of the Boston area in America. A Jewess, Professor Adele Dalsimer, head of Irish studies at Boston College, a Jesuit institution, has contributed to this development. She, with others, produced an Irish-Jewish *haggadah* for Passover – for there are similar experiences of exile and return, longing and historical awareness. I saw in Boston how American Jews and Irish-Americans can combine their identities. It is a model we would do well to emulate in Europe. Americans are proud of their multiple identities. I want to be proud of my multiple identities – as a British Jewess with Irish links, as a European female who is politically liberal – none of which seems to me to be contradictory.

It is also a reflection on my upbringing, and the cultural world I experienced as a child. As I was bringing this epilogue to a conclusion, my father saw an uncorrected dust-jacket for this book. He was both angry and saddened by it. 'It is wrong,' he said. 'We are *not* a German-Jewish family. We are a British family, of German origins.' He told me a story which illustrated why he felt so strongly. When he was in the army during the war, in about 1941, in Aldershot, before he went to France, he was called in to see his commanding officer. The officer told him that he had received instructions that my father was to be posted to home service, because of his dual nationality. My father was born in Britain, of parents who had come from Germany. He considers himself as profoundly British. But he did not shout and scream. He merely replied: 'That is fine, provided the same happens to everyone else who could possibly be argued to be of dual nationality . . .' 'What do you mean?' asked the commanding officer. 'I mean that others who could be argued to be of German origin should also be on home service, such as Lord Mountbatten . . .' The commanding officer must have reported this conversation back to the War Office. No more was heard, and my father served in France, Italy and North Africa. His sense of being British outweighs mine, perhaps. Not that I am not patriotic. I am. I have a stronger sense of being European than he does. Of course, having a mother who was a refugee gives me a stronger sense of being of refugee origins. For my father, this book is an attempt to explain how I feel about my identity, which he and my mother did so much to shape.

This is also a letter to my children, Harriet and Matthew. So much of what I think the Jewish community in Britain could be like will be in the hands of their generation. It has changed. We British Jews are more confident. We are less concerned about how we seem to the outside world. These developments in cultural Judaism, Jewish interests, and Jewish excitement in areas other than synagogue organisations is new to us. We have only seen it before in America. If we can bring this off in Britain, the Jewish community has a future. If not, it will die, not so much because of a reduction in numbers but because of an atrophy of the mind and heart. We will still look after our elderly, of course, but we will lack vibrancy and excitement and a sense of the future.

For me, the future of Jewish life in this country must be about vitality, life, buzz, and involvement in the wider world. That means new ways of expressing ourselves as Jews, culturally, religiously, politically, even gastronomically. It means taking on the great inspiration of Jewish social service, Jewish attitudes to the welfare of others, and combining that with a religious tolerance and openness.

In Judaism, in Jewish life, we must let a thousand flowers bloom. We should do it with the excitement of realising that we have flowers, that we have survived. We have a future – as Jews, as citizens of our own countries, as lovers of Israel, religious or not, in God's name.

Epilogue

And here ends the sermon for the next generation.

Julia Neuberger,
London, Cambridge, Mass., and West Cork,
1994–1995

Bibliography

Abrahams, I. and Levy, S.: Macaulay 'On Jewish Disabilities',
  Jewish Historical Society of England, Edinburgh, 1909
Alderman, Geoffrey: *Modern British Jewry*, Oxford University
  Press, Oxford, 1992
Alvarez, A.: *Day of Atonement*, Random House, New York, 1991
The Anglican Consultative Council: *The Truth Shall make You
  Free – the Lambeth Conference, London, 1988*
Armstrong, Karen: *The Gospel According to Woman*, Elm Tree
  Books, London, 1986
Baron, Salo W.: *A Social and Religious History of the Jews*, JPS,
  Philadelphia, 1958
Bayfield, A. and Braybrooke, M. (eds): *Dialogue with a Difference:
  The Manor House Group Experience*, London, 1992
Bean, Philip and Melville, Joy: *Lost Children of the Empire – the
  Untold Story of Britain's Child Migrants*, Unwin Hyman,
  London, 1989
Blue, Lionel: *Tales of Body and Soul*, Hodder and Stoughton,
  London, 1994
Bolchover, Richard: *British Jewry and the Holocaust*, Cambridge
  University Press, Cambridge, 1993
Boswell, John: *The Kindness of Strangers*, Penguin,
  Harmondsworth, 1989
Bower, Tom: *Paperclip Conspiracy*, Michael Joseph, London, 1987
Bower, Tom: *Blind Eye to Murder*, Paladin, London, 1983
Bresheeth, Haim, Hood, Stuart and Jansz, Litza: *The Holocaust
  for Beginners*, Icon Books, London, 1994

Brook, Stephen: *The Club: The Jews of Modern Britain*, Constable, London, 1989

Brown, Peter: *Augustine of Hippo – a biography*, Faber and Faber, London, 1967

Brown, Peter: *The Body and Society – Men, Women, and Sexual Renunciation in Early Christianity*, Faber and Faber, London, 1989

Buber, Martin: *On Zionism – the history of an idea*, T and T Clark, Edinburgh, 1985

Burleigh, Michael: *Death and Deliverance – Euthanasia in Germany 1900–1945*, Cambridge University Press, Cambridge, 1994

Burrin, Philippe, introd. by Friedlaender, Saul: *Hitler and the Jews: the Genesis of the Holocaust*, Edward Arnold, London, 1993

Cesarani, David (ed): *The Making of Modern Anglo-Jewry*, Blackwell, Oxford, 1990

Cheyette, Bryan: *Constructions of 'the Jew' in English Literature and Society*, Cambridge University Press, Cambridge, 1993

Cohn, Haim: *Human Rights in Jewish Law*, Ktav, New York, 1984

Daube, David: 'He that cometh', 1966, St. Paul's Lecture, London Diocesan Council for Christian Jewish Understanding, St. Botolph's Vestry, Aldgate, 1966

Davenport-Hines, Richard: *Sex, Death and Punishment – Attitudes to Sex and Sexuality in Britain since the Renaissance*, Collins, London, 1990

Davidman, Lynn and Tenenbaum, Shelly (eds): *Feminist Perspectives on Jewish Studies*, Yale University Press, Yale, 1995

Douglas, Mary: *Purity and Danger*, Routledge, London, 1966

Dwork, Deborah: *Children with a star – Jewish Youth in Nazi Europe*, Yale University Press, London and New Haven, 1993

Dworkin, Ronald: *Life's Dominion*, HarperCollins, London, 1993

Faith in the City: The Report of the Archbishop of Canterbury's Commission in Urban Priority Areas, Church House Publishing, London, 1985

Feldman, David: *Englishmen and Jews: Social Relations and*

Political Culture 1840–1914, Yale University Press, New Haven and London, 1994

Feldman, David, M.: *Birth Control in Jewish law*, New York University Press, New York and London, 1968

Finestein, Israel: *Jewish Society in Victorian England*, Vallentine Mitchell, London, 1993

Gershon, Karen: *Collected Poems*, Macmillan, London, 1990

Gershon, Karen: *We came as children*, Macmillan, London, 1989

Gilbert, Martin: *Auschwitz and the Allies – the politics of rescue – could the Jews have been saved?* Hamlyn, London, 1983

Gilbert, Martin: *The Dent Atlas of the Holocaust – the complete history*, Dent, London, 1993

Gilman, Sander L.: *Jews in Today's German Culture*, Indiana University Press, Bloomington, Indiana, 1995

Glatzer, Nahum N. (ed.): *The Dynamics of Emancipation – the Jew in the Modern Age*, Beacon Press, Boston, USA, 1965

Glueckel of Hameln: *The Life of Glueckel of Hameln*, 1646–1724, translated by Beth Zion Abrahams, East and West Library, London, 1962

Goldberg, David J. and Rayner, John D.: *The Jewish people – their history and their religion*, Viking, Harmondsworth, 1987

Greenberg, Simon: *A Jewish Philosophy and Pattern of Life*, Jewish Theological Seminary of America, New York, 1981

Gross, John: *Shylock – Four Hundred Years in the Life of a Legend*, Chatto and Windus, London, 1992

Hertz, H.J.: *A Book of Jewish Thoughts*, Oxford University Press, London, 1917

Heschel, Susannah (ed. and introd.): *On being a Jewish feminist – a reader*, Schocken Books, New York, 1983

Hilberg, Raul: *Perpetrators, Victims and Bystanders – the Jewish catastrophe – 1933–1945*, Lime Tree, London, 1993

Holmes, Colin: *A Tolerant Country?* Faber and Faber, London, 1991

Ignatieff, Michael: *Blood and Belonging*, BBC, Chatto and Windus, London, 1993

Jacobs, Gerald: *Sacred Games*, Hamish Hamilton, London, 1995

Jacobs, Louis (ed. and introd.): *The Jewish Mystics*, Kyle Cathie, London, 1990

Jacobs, Louis: *A Jewish Theology*, Darton Longman and Todd, London, 1973

Kahn, Annette: *Why my father died: A daughter confronts her family's past at the trial of Klaus Barbie*, Summit Books (Simon and Schuster), New York, 1992

Katz, David S.: *The Jews in the History of England – 1485–1850*, Oxford University Press, Oxford, 1994

Kenneally, Thomas: *Schindler's Ark*, Hodder and Stoughton, London, 1982

Kessler, Edward: *An English Jew*, Vallentine Mitchell, London, 1989

ed. Kogan, Eugen, Langbein, Hermann and Rueckerl, Adalbert with editorial notes and foreword by Choumoff, Pierre Serge: *Nazi mass Murder – a documentary history of the use of poison gas*, Yale University Press, New Haven and London, 1993

Kushner, Tony: *the Holocaust and the Liberal Imagination – A Social and Cultural History*, Blackwell, Oxford, 1994

Lamm, Maurice: *The Jewish Way in Death and Mourning*, Jonathan David, New York, 1969

Langbein, Hermann: *Against all Hope: Resistance in the Nazi concentration camps 1938–1945*, Constable, London, 1994

Lappin, Elena (ed.): *Jewish Voices, German Words – Growing up Jewish in Postwar Germany and Austria – An anthology*, translated by Krishna Winston, Catbird Press, North Haven, Ct. USA, 1994

Leeson, Edward: *The New Golden Treasury of English Verse*, Macmillan, London, 1980

Lehrer, Tom: *Too Many Songs by Tom Lehrer with not enough drawings by Ronald Searle*, Methuen, London, 1981

Lester, Anthony: 'Fundamental Rights: The United Kingdom Isolated?' in: *Public Law*, Spring 1984, Sweet and Maxwell, London

Levi, Primo: *If this is a man*, Collier (Macmillan), New York, 1961

Levi, Primo and Regge, Tullio: *Conversations*, Tauris, London, 1989

Levy, Alan: *The Wiesenthal File*, Constable, London, 1993

Lifton, Betty Jean: *The King of Children*, Pan, London, 1989

Lipstadt, Deborah: *Denying the Holocaust – The Growing Assault on Truth and Memory*, Penguin, Harmondsworth, 1995

London, Louise: 'Jewish Refugees, Anglo-Jewry and British Government Policy 1930–1940', in: Cesarani, David (ed.): *op. cit.*

Maccoby, Hyam: *Revolution in Judaea – Jesus and the Jewish resistance*, Ocean Books, London, 1973

Maidenbaum, Aryeh and Martin, Stephen A.: *Lingering Shadows: Jungians, Freudians and Anti-Semitism*, Shambhala, Boston and London, 1991

Maimonides: *Mishneh Torah, Book of Cleanness*, ed. M.D. Rabinowitz, Mossad Harav Kook, Jerusalem, 1961

Marks, D.W.: 'Introductory Discourse delivered at the consecration of the West London Synagogue of British Jews', January 27th 1842, from: *Sermons preached on various occasions*, Groombridge and Sons, London, 1851.

Marrus, Michael R.: *The Holocaust in History*, Weidenfeld and Nicolson, London, 1988

Marrus, Michael and Paxton, Robert O.: *Vichy France and the Jews*, Basic Books, New York, 1981

Mendes-Flohr, Paul R. and Reinharz, Jehuda: *The Jew in the Modern World – a documentary history*, Oxford, New York, 1980

Montefiore, C.G.: 'The Old Testament and its Ethical Teaching', in: *Papers for Jewish People*, London, 1917

Montefiore, C.G.: The Hibbert Lectures on 'The Origin and Growth of Religion as illustrated by the Ancient Hebrews', Williams and Norgate, London, 1892

Neuberger, J. (ed.): *The things that matter – an anthology of women's spiritual poetry*, Kyle Cathie, London, 1992

Neusner, J.: *The Idea of Purity in Ancient Judaism*, E. J. Brill, Leiden, 1973

Niebuhr, R.: *Pious and Secular America*, Kelley, USA, 1966

Oz, Amos: *In the Land of Israel*, Harcourt, Brace and Jovanovich, New York, 1983

Philo of Alexandria: Complete works, Loeb edition, with translation by F.H. Colson, Harvard University Press, Cambridge, Mass.

Picciotto, James: *Sketches of Anglo-Jewish History*, ed. Israel Finestein, Soncino Press, London, 1956

Rapoport-Albert, A. and Zipperstein, S.J.: *Jewish History – essays in honour of Chimen Abramsky*, Halban/Weidenfeld and Nicolson, London, 1988

Riemer, Jack (ed.): *Jewish Reflections on Death*, Schocken Books, New York, 1974

Rose, Gillian: *Love's Work*, Chatto and Windus, London, 1995

Rose, Paul Lawrence: *Wagner, Race and revolution*, Faber and Faber, London, 1992

Runnymede Trust: *A Very Light Sleeper*, London, 1994

Samuel, Wilfrid S.: 'The First London Synagogue of the Resettlement', in *Transactions of the Jewish Historical Society of England 1921–3*, London, 1924

Scarf, Mimi: *Battered Jewish Wives, Case Studies in response to rage*, Edwin Mellen Press, Lewiston, New York, 1988

Schachne, Lucie: *Education towards Spiritual resistance – the Jewish Landschulheim Herrlingen 1933–1939*, dipa verlag, Frankfurt-am-Main, 1988

Scholem, Gershom: *Walter Benjamin – the story of a friendship*, Jewish Publication Society of America, Philadelphia, 1981

Sereny, Gitta: *Into that Darkness*, André Deutsch, London, 1974

Shakespeare, William: *The Merchant of Venice*

Shepherd, Naomi: *A Price Below Rubies – Jewish Women as Rebels and Radicals*, Weidenfeld and Nicolson, London, 1993

Sherman, A.J.: *Island Refuge – Britain and Refugees from the Third Reich 1933–1939*, Cass, London, 1994

Shorter, Edward: *A History of Women's Bodies*, Penguin, London, 1984

Silbermann, Neil Asher: *The Hidden Scrolls – Christianity, Judaism, and the war for the Dead Sea Scrolls*, Heinemann, London, 1995

Simpson, John (ed.): *The Oxford Book of Exile*, Oxford University Press, Oxford and New York, 1995

Spiegelman, Art: *Maus II*, Pantheon Books, New York, 1991

Stille, Alexander: *Benevolence and betrayal – Five Italian Jewish Families under Fascism*, Summit Books, New York, 1990

Supple, Carrie: *From Prejudice to Genocide: Learning about the Holocaust*, Trentham Books, 1991

Supple, Carrie: *Voices of the Holocaust*, for the British Library, 1992

Trachtenberg, Joshua: *The Devil and the Jews*, Yale University Press, New Haven, Ct., 1943

Trillin, Calvin: 'Drawing the Line', *New Yorker*, December 12 1994, New York

Turner, Barry: *And the Policeman smiled: Ten Thousand Children Escape from Nazi Europe*, Bloomsbury, London, 1990

Usborne, Cornelie: *The Politics of the Body in Weimar Germany*, Macmillan, London, 1992

Vital, David: *The Origins of Zionism*, Oxford University Press, Oxford, 1975

Warner, Marina: *Alone of all her sex – the Myth and Cult of the Virgin Mary*, Quartet, London, 1978

Wasserstein, Bernard: *Britain and the Jews of Europe 1939–1945*, Oxford University Press, New York and Oxford/Institute of Jewish Affairs, London, 1988

Webster, Paul: *Petain's Crime*, Macmillan, London, 1990

Wegner, Judith Romney: *Chattel or Person? The status of women in the Mishnah*, Oxford University Press, New York and Oxford, 1988

Wiesel, Elie: *Night, Dawn, the Accident*, Robson Books, London, 1974

Wiesel, Elie: *Twilight*, Viking, London, 1988

Williamson, Gordon: *The SS: Hitler's Instruments of Terror – the full story from street fighters to the Waffen-SS*, Sidgwick and Jackson, London, 1994

Wistrich, Robert: *Anti-semitism – The Longest Hatred*, Thames TV and Methuen, London, 1991

Wouk, Herman: *This is my God*, Souvenir Press, London, 1992

Yahil, Leni: *The Rescue of Danish Jewry – test of a Democracy*, Jewish Publication Society of America, Philadelphia, 1969

Young, James E.: *The texture of memory: Holocaust memorials and meaning*, Yale University Press, New Haven and London, 1993

Index

Also available . . .

KAREN ARMSTRONG

A History of God

The idea of a single divine being – God, Yahweh, Allah – has existed for over 4,000 years. But the history of God is also the history of human struggle. While Judaism, Islam and Christianity proclaim the goodness of God, organised religion has too often been the catalyst for violence and ineradicable prejudice.

In this fascinating, extensive and highly original account of the evolution of belief, Karen Armstrong examines Western society's unerring fidelity to this idea of One God and the many conflicting convictions it engenders. A controversial, extraordinary story of worship and war, *A History of God* confronts the most fundamental fact – or fiction – of our lives.

'A splendidly readable book . . . the stage is set for the question: has God a future?"
Sister Wendy Beckett, *Sunday Times*

'Armstrong shows a reverent curiosity and a generosity of spirit, refreshing the understanding of what one knows and providing a clear introduction to the unfamiliar'
Rt Rev Robert Runcie, *Telegraph*

'A fascinating way of approaching the subject'
Rabbi Julia Neuberger

'This is the most fascinating and learned survey of the biggest wild goose chase in history – the quest for God. Karen Armstrong is a genius'
A. N. Wilson

OTHER TITLES OF INTEREST

☐ A History of God	Karen Armstrong	£9.99
☐ Fingerprints of the Gods	Graham Hancock	£7.99
☐ The Orion Mystery	Bauval and Gilbert	£7.99
☐ The Sign and the Seal	Graham Hancock	£8.99
☐ Keeper of Genesis	Bauval and Hancock	£6.99

ALL ARROW BOOKS ARE AVAILABLE THROUGH MAIL ORDER OR FROM YOUR LOCAL BOOKSHOP AND NEWSAGENT.

PLEASE SEND CHEQUE/EUROCHEQUE/POSTAL ORDER (STERLING ONLY) ACCESS, VISA, MASTERCARD, DINERS CARD, SWITCH OR AMEX.

☐☐☐☐☐☐☐☐☐☐☐☐☐☐☐☐

EXPIRY DATE.................. SIGNATURE ....

PLEASE ALLOW 75 PENCE PER BOOK FOR POST AND PACKING U.K.

OVERSEAS CUSTOMERS PLEASE ALLOW £1.00 PER COPY FOR POST AND PACKING.

ALL ORDERS TO:

ARROW BOOKS, BOOK BY POST, TBS LIMITED, THE BOOK SERVICE, COLCHESTER ROAD, FRATING GREEN, COLCHESTER, ESSEX CO7 TDW.

NAME..

ADDRESS...

....

Please allow 28 days for delivery. Please tick box if you do not wish to receive any additional information ☐

Prices and availability subject to change without notice.